Grimshaw's exploration of the role of vision within modern anthro-

ONE WEEK LOAN

KT-574-513

The Ethnographer's Eye

Ways of seeing in anthropology

Anna Grimshaw

CAMBRIDGE
UNIVERSITY PRESS

PUBLISHED BY THE PRESS SYNDICATE OF THE UNIVERSITY OF CAMBRIDGE
The Pitt Building, Trumpington Street, Cambridge, United Kingdom

CAMBRIDGE UNIVERSITY PRESS
The Edinburgh Building, Cambridge CB2 2RU, UK
40 West 20th Street, New York, NY 10011–4211, USA
477 Williamstown Road, Port Melbourne, VIC 3207, Australia
Ruiz de Alarcón 13, 28014 Madrid, Spain
Dock House, The Waterfront, Cape Town 8001, South Africa

http://www.cambridge.org

First published 2001
Reprinted 2002

Printed in the United Kingdom at the University Press, Cambridge

Typeset in Plantin 10/12pt   System 3b2   [CE]

A catalogue record for this book is available from the British Library

Library of Congress Cataloguing in Publication data

Grimshaw, Anna.
The ethnographer's eye: ways of seeing in anthropology / Anna Grimshaw.
    p.   cm.
Includes bibliographical references and index.
ISBN 0 521 77310 5 – ISBN 0 521 77475 6 (pb)
1. Visual anthropology.   I. Title.
GN347.G75 2001   301'078–dc21   00–045556

ISBN 0 521 77310 5 hardback
ISBN 0 521 77475 6 paperback

for my students

Contents

Preface

The Ethnographer's Eye explores the role of vision within twentieth-century anthropology. The book engages with contemporary debates concerning ocularcentrism; that is, it raises questions about the relationship between vision and knowledge in western discourse. My approach is built around the notion of *ways of seeing*. By this I mean the ways that we use vision to refer to how we see and know the world as anthropologists. I will suggest that the modern discipline contains contrasting ways of seeing. Their investigation throws into sharp relief assumptions about the status of anthropological knowledge, technique and form at the heart of contemporary work.

The book grows out of my experiences as a teacher and ethnographer. Its origins lie in the unusual position I occupy as a 'visual' anthropologist at the margins of a discipline dominated by words. Following my appointment to the Granada Centre for Visual Anthropology at the University of Manchester in 1991, I began to explore the contours of the field in which I was now located. Specifically, I wanted to find a way of anchoring my teaching in a coherent anthropological perspective as a counterweight to what Faye Ginsburg calls the 'unruliness' of visual anthropology.[1] The subdiscipline seemed to exist only in the form of occasional conferences, as *ad hoc* collections of papers and, perhaps most frustratingly, as a body of films which seemed almost impossible to obtain.

From the outset, my investigation of vision was not confined to theoretical or historical questions within modern anthropology. Its operation as a method or fieldwork technique was also critical to my enquiry. I had myself started to experiment ethnographically with the use of a video camera. Here, too, I began to be aware of problems. There were plenty of accounts written by film-makers of their ethnographic work; but there was little in the way of a reflexive engagement with the *anthropological* assumptions built into the particular techniques and technologies used.

My own practice and training of students was predicated upon a certain way of seeing the world through the camera lens. Such an approach was adapted from the training I had received as a documentary film-maker. At its centre was the cultivation of something known as an *observational* stance. It was founded upon respect – respect for one's subjects and for the world in which they lived. It was a filmic orientation toward social life that was widely assumed to resonate with anthropological sensibilities. Although like many other ethnographic film-makers I instinctively gravitated toward such an approach, I had no real grasp of the origins of the observational school within cinema, the basis of its harmonisation with an anthropological perspective – or, indeed, what was the nature of this anthropological perspective.[2] The more I cultivated an observational approach toward ethnographic exploration, the more I worried about presuppositions inherent to the techniques that I (and my students) were using to engage with the world. For, as the poet Seamus Heaney once observed, 'technique involves not only a poet's way with words, his management of metre, rhythm and verbal texture; it involves also a definition of his stance towards life, a definition of his own reality.'[3]

The questions at the centre of this book emerged from the interplay between research and teaching, ethnographic engagement and critical reflection, such that each activity became inseparable from the other. At the same time, the location I inhabited within academic anthropology, one mediated by visual techniques and technologies, offered a different perspective on my original training as an ethnographer. How did my earlier anthropological education shape my use of a camera? The question was given focus through consideration of my fieldwork experiences as a doctoral student working in the Himalayas at the end of the 1970s. For me, fieldwork had been an overwhelmingly visual experience. This visual intensity was something I subsequently sought to express in the writing of my experimental ethnography, *Servants of the Buddha*. But what kinds of knowledge or understanding were contained in my 'seeing' the world?

The work I carried out as an ethnographer and the particular role I accorded to vision was founded upon a certain interpretation of the anthropological task. It had been importantly shaped by the teachers I had encountered at Cambridge, especially Edmund Leach; but, equally, I recognised that my own personal sensibilities were reflected in the kind of anthropology I pursued. Increasingly I was aware that my use of vision as an ethnographic technique, a strategy for exploring the world, embodied not just certain ideas but also *beliefs* about reality, the nature of subjectivity and the status of anthropological knowledge.[4]

I began to use the phrase 'ways of seeing' as a means for evoking the different and yet interconnected ways that vision functioned within ethnographic research. Gradually it emerged as the organising motif of the book as a whole. For, in seeking to clarify and extend my understanding of issues concerning vision as a teacher and ethnographer, I recognised that the questions which mattered were not about visual anthropology's legitimacy or coherence as a distinctive field; rather they were about the nature of anthropological visuality in a broader sense – anthropology's different ways of seeing. An investigation of vision offered new insights into the discipline's emergence and consolidation as a modern project, exposing assumptions about the nature of anthropological enquiry whether image-based technologies are used or not.

The Ethnographer's Eye comprises two parts. Its aesthetic is self-consciously cinematic. The first part is organised around the principle of *montage*, in which my thesis moves by leaps and bounds. The latter is animated by the notion of the *mise-en-scène*, whereby an argument emerges through a slow process of accretion. My interest in using cinematic principles as the basis for the textual presentation of ideas arises from the desire to forge a creative connection between form and content. *The Ethnographer's Eye* remains a literary work and it is confined by that form; but I ask the reader to make a leap of the imagination and, above all, to engage in the book with a cinematic sensibility.

Acknowledgements

I have incurred many debts in the course of writing this book. It was begun five years ago at a time of intellectual collaboration with Keith Hart. The development of my ideas were importantly shaped by our Cambridge-based work. I am grateful to Keith Hart for his contribution to the different stages of this project.

Much of the book was drafted in Manchester. Here I owe a particular debt of gratitude to Mark Harris and Colin Murray who were consistently generous as readers, critics and friends. Pete Wade made many valuable suggestions; and I benefited greatly from discussions with doctoral students, Amanda Ravetz and Cristina Grasseni. I would like to thank my cinema companions, too, for their indulgence and encouragement – Inga Burrows, Fiona Devine, Bill Dove, Louise Gooddy, Marie Howes, Jo Lewis and Karen Sykes. The staff of the Portico Library in Manchester helped nurture this book; and Elizabeth Jackson has been of immense assistance in its completion. Gordon Connell performed valuable services as an editor, offering criticism and support in generous measures.

Herb Di Gioia, my teacher at the National Film and Television School during 1991–92, has been an important inspiration in the writing of this book. My approach to understanding cinema has also been immeasurably enhanced by my friendship and collaboration with Roger Crittenden. Judith Okely, Jakob Høgel and Nikos Papastergiadis have engaged enthusiastically with my ideas; and I appreciate Jessica Kuper's patience and commitment to the project through the slow stages of its evolution.

The final stages of the book were undertaken in New York. I would like to acknowledge my intellectual debt to Faye Ginsburg for her pioneering work in the field. She has also been a warm friend and colleague. I appreciate the help of Fred Myers in facilitating my research. Don Kulick and Adele Oltman offered much affectionate support. David Polonoff revived my flagging spirits and made the task of completion much more enjoyable. Finally, the C.L.R. James Institute was a very special place in which to live and work during my sabbatical leave. Particular thanks are owed to Jim Murray who, as my friend and collaborator over many years, persuades me that writing matters.

Anna Grimshaw
Manchester, November 1999

Introduction

Visual anthropology

There is a tribe, known as the ethnographic film-makers, who believe they are invisible. They enter a room where a feast is being celebrated, or the sick cured, or the dead mourned, and, though weighted down with odd machines, entangled with wires, imagine they are unnoticed – or, at most, merely glanced at, quickly ignored, later forgotten.

Outsiders know little of them, for their homes are hidden in the partially uncharted rainforests of the Documentary. Like other Documentarians, they survive by hunting and gathering information. Unlike others of their filmic group, most prefer to consume it raw.

Their culture is unique in that wisdom among them is not passed down from generation to generation; they must discover for themselves what their ancestors knew. They have little communication with the rest of the forest, and are slow to adapt to technical innovations. Their handicrafts are rarely traded, and are used almost exclusively among themselves. Produced in great quantities, the excess must be stored in large archives.[1]

Eliot Weinberger's humorous stereotype gives expression to an image which I suspect is widespread in academic anthropology – that ethnographic film-makers are weighed down by technical encumbrances; that they produce large quantities of boring footage which show strange people doing strange things, usually at a distance; that they are theoretically and methodologically naive. In his depiction of the field, Weinberger also lends weight to the conventional view that ethnographic film-making lies at the heart of what is known as 'visual anthropology'. This project emerged as a distinctive subdiscipline within academic anthropology during the 1970s. Its appearance was part of the profession's postwar academic expansion, which resulted in the consolidation of the discipline at the same time as it fragmented into numerous different areas of specialist interest.[2]

The publication of *Principles of Visual Anthropology* was an important moment in the consolidation of visual anthropology as a distinctive field with its own intellectual concerns and techniques. Writing in the Foreword to his edited collection, Paul Hockings expressed the hope that it would 'serve to put visual anthropology into its proper place as a legitimate subdiscipline of anthropology'.[3] Some twenty years after its publication, Marcus Banks and Howard Morphy, editors of *Rethinking Visual Anthropology*, attempt to take stock of this rapidly expanding field – asking, for example, what constitutes the subdiscipline; what questions does it address; what directions might it be developing in, and so on. Certainly they seek to challenge the narrow focus of the earlier Hockings volume which foregrounded film, and to a lesser degree photography, as constitutive of the field as a whole. By contrast, Banks and Morphy define their area of enquiry as one concerned with what they call 'the anthropology of visual systems or, more broadly, visible cultural forms'.[4] Hence they have in mind a much broader range of intellectual interests and they endeavour to bring into active connection areas of research which are closely linked and yet have hitherto been kept separate – for example, the anthropology of art, material culture, museum ethnography, aesthetics and multi-media.

Practitioners of visual anthropology, like their colleagues working within other subdisciplines which emerged in the same period of academic expansion, have often expressed a sense of being excluded from what they perceive to be the mainstream tradition. They hover precariously at the edge of a discipline of words. Ever since Margaret Mead harangued the profession in apocalyptic terms, she has been followed by countless others who have pointed out the neglect or disparagement of visual anthropology by most academic anthropologists.[5] Despite a growing confidence in the field, and a new openness within the discipline to experimentation in ethnographic method and form, the feeling of marginality has been difficult to shake off.

Frequently, as a teacher, I hear students expressing frustration with the conservatism of academic anthropology. Attracted initially by what they perceive to be one of the distinctive qualities of the subject, its people-centredness, students all too often experience the discipline as a series of dry, academic texts in which human presence is rarely glimpsed. The stubborn persistence of a particular literary form, indeed its reification in the current climate of academic auditing, seems increasingly archaic.[6] It offers little by way of an understanding of the contemporary world in which visual media play such a central role. Often impatient working from within the confines of an abstract specialist language, younger anthropologists respond enthusiastically to opportunities for experimentation with visual techniques and technologies. Their use becomes an important means for humanising the discipline, engaging people concretely, for example, within films as subjects and collaborators or as audiences for anthropological work.[7]

Images by their very nature establish a different relationship between the ethnographer and the world she or he explores. Moreover, image-based technologies mediate different kinds of relationships between ethnographers, subjects and audiences than those associated with the production of literary texts. For instance, students quickly discover that working with a video camera makes them visible, publicly accountable and dependent upon forging new kinds of ethnographic collaborations. Pursuing such an approach offers interesting challenges to students who are committed to operating in society, rather than in the academy, as anthropologists. At the same time as they explore new ways of collective working, students also discover that visual technologies offer scope for individual self-expression, something perceived to be virtually impossible within the conventional academic text. Ironically, it is the very marginality of visual anthropology with respect to the mainstream text-based tradition which opens up an important space for experimentation. Here students try out a range of forms in an effort to give anthropological expression to their identity and interests.[8]

Anthropology's 'iconophobia'

The perception by visual anthropologists of operating within the cracks of a text-based discipline is, I believe, particularly acute among those trained in the tradition of the classical British school. This was the context in which I myself was formed as an anthropologist. Hence I experienced first-hand the curious paradox that other commentators have noted – the centrality of vision to the kind of ethnographic field-work developed by Malinowski and his contemporaries, and yet the disappearance of explicit acknowledgement concerning the role of visual techniques and technologies, indeed vision itself, in the new fieldwork-based monograph.[9]

Modern anthropology, as I was taught it, was not about making films, interrogating photographs, or experimenting with images and words. It was about writing texts. But even this activity was not, until recently, specifically addressed. Writing was assumed to be straightforward, a largely mechanical exercise by which the emotional messiness of field-work experience was translated into the neat categories of an academic argument. Different styles of writing, or the use of particular narrative conventions to shape and interpret materials through the process of writing itself, remained unacknowledged problems in much twentieth-century anthropological discourse.[10]

My investigation into the role played by vision within modern anthro-pology began, then, with an acknowledgement of the paradox at the heart of my own identity as an ethnographer. Vision was central to how I worked; but I had never critically reflected upon the assumptions which underlay its use as a fieldwork strategy or the kinds of knowledge it yielded. Once I began to explore the origins and particular preoccupa-tions of visual anthropology as a specialist subdiscipline emerging in the 1960s and 1970s, I found myself addressing questions concerning the models of fieldwork (extensive/intensive) and the different intellectual contexts associated with anthropology's evolution as a modern project.[11] Like others trained as Malinowskian ethnographers, I had accepted the conventional grounds by which visual anthropology was dismissed or reduced to the margins of the mainstream discipline. For instance, as ethnographic film-making or photography, visual anthro-pology was (and frequently still is) understood to be about the acquisi-tion of technical skills; and, as such, it was assumed not to be informed by ideas or theory.

Recent interest in questions of technique and embodiment is evidence of an important shift in anthropological thinking; but it has not, as yet, been properly extended into a reflexive enquiry into ethnographic technique itself.[12] Visual anthropologists are still considered to be unusually interested in such questions. They are stereotyped as people hopelessly tangled up in wires and boringly concerned with the workings of different kinds of recording equipment.

I discovered that I had also absorbed from my teachers, trained as they were in the classic structural-functionalism of the British school, a profound scepticism of visual anthropology as about photography, art or material culture. These were the tangible links to a Victorian past from which the modern ethnographers were so anxious to separate them-selves. Nothing made the leading figures of the twentieth-century discipline in Britain more nervous than the spectre of gentleman amateurs, dazzled by scientific instrumentation, collecting and classi-fying in a museum context.[13] The revolution which Malinoswki claimed as his own established new goals for his followers. They set their sights on a position as scientists within the academy; and, in their drive for professional recognition, these new scholars sought to effect a radical break between past and present. Hence explicitly visual projects built around teamwork, such as the 1898 Torres Straits expedition, were defined as archaic and largely dismissed as relics of an earlier nine-teenth-century project.

More recently, visual technologies harnessed to anthropological en-deavour have, all too uncomfortably, conjured up images of the journalist, or worse, the tourist; and, of course, as anthropological cinema or television it lies dangerously close to entertainment. As we know, modern anthropology has always had a problem of professional legitimation.[14] What is its claim to expertise or specialist knowledge? What are the foundations of 'ethnographic authority'? Visual technologies as an integral part of a late twentieth-century anthropology are an unsettling reminder of the continuing salience of these questions.

The sheer strength of feeling provoked in anthropologists by visual images is certainly unusual. It alerts me to something else. Images are condemned as seductive, dazzling, deceptive and illusory, and are regarded as capable of wreaking all sorts of havoc with the sobriety of the discipline. This exaggerated response, what Lucien Taylor calls 'iconophobia', is interesting, perhaps the manifestation of a puritan spirit running through anthropology as modern project.[15] For the suspicion and fear of images, expressed by Rivers and Radcliffe-Brown as much as by many contemporary anthropologists, evokes the historical struggle of the Reformation, which resulted in the elevation of the word and the authority of its interpreters. It is hard not to think of the Lady Chapel at Ely Cathedral and its rows of images smashed by the hammers of Cromwell's men: 'Defaced images often had their eyes scratched away, as though, by breaking visual contact between image and viewer, the suspect power of the image might be defused . . . To deface or smash an image is to acknowledge its power'.[16]

Anthropology and the crisis of ocularcentrism

The ambivalence surrounding vision within modern anthropology may be considered to be a reflection of a broader intellectual climate, what Martin Jay calls the 'crisis of ocularcentrism'.[17] He suggests that, until the twentieth century, vision within Western culture enjoyed a privileged status as a source of knowledge about the world. Sight was elevated as the noblest of the senses. Over the course of the last hundred years, however, Jay traces the systematic denigration of vision by European intellectuals. The slitting of the eye with a razor in Luis Buñuel's surrealist film, *Un Chien Andalou*, is perhaps the most stark and shocking expression of the modernist interrogation of vision.

The case of anthropology is an interesting one. For the early twentieth-century anthropologists, people like Boas or Rivers, worried about vision and its status as a source of knowledge about the world. But as the discipline subsequently evolved and consolidated, vision ceased to be problematised at the same time as it assumed a new significance at the heart of a fieldwork-based enterprise. There is then a curious paradox at the heart of modern anthropology. On the one hand, the discipline manifests features of the more general ocularphobic turn of the twentieth century. This is represented, for example, in the marginalisation of visual technologies from fieldwork practice and the relegation of visual materials to a peripheral or illustrative role in the generation of ethnographic knowledge. On the other hand, the turning away from an explicit acknowledgement of the role of vision within fieldwork enquiry, as implied by Malinowski's fieldwork revolution, was inseparable from the cultivation of a distinctive ethnographic eye. It was encapsulated in the phrase 'going to see for yourself'.[18]

Anthropology's current crisis of ocularcentrism has brought the question of vision to the centre of debate. It may be interpreted as an expression of the discipline's (belated) modernist turn. For during the 1980s the problem of what Johannes Fabian calls 'visualism' became a focus for anthropological anxieties about vision.[19] Fabian and others (for example, David Howes) developed critiques of the discipline's 'visualist bias'. Observation was identified as a dominant trope in modern anthropology, one which leads the fieldworker to adopt 'a contemplative stance', an image suggesting detachment, indeed voyeurism, '"the naturalist" watching an experiment'. The knowledge garnered by taking up such a stance on reality is ultimately organised, according to Fabian, by means of a whole series of visual metaphors. The effect is objectifying and dehumanising. Both history and coevality with the subjects of anthropological enquiry are denied.[20]

The problem of anthropology's 'visualist bias' has provoked a number of different responses. These are, of course, inseparable from the more general reflexive mood within the contemporary discipline prompted by the growing political pressure exerted by anthropology's traditional subjects, and by the belated collapse of the paradigm of scientific ethnography. For example, there has been a growing emphasis upon voice, 'the native's voice', dialogue, conversation, what the film-maker, Trinh Minh-ha calls to 'speak nearby'.[21] Other anthropologists have sought to escape the tyranny of a visualist paradigm by rediscovering the full range of the human senses. It has led to the development of sensuous perspectives toward ethnographic understanding.[22]

Although the recent attack on vision does not preclude the development of anthropologies which foreground vision, that is projects taking vision as an object and method of enquiry, it certainly makes the task much more difficult. But, as Paul Stoller reminds us, the particular kind of detached, objectifying vision now condemned by the term 'observation' was not in fact a prominent feature of Malinowski's ethnography. He points to the distinctive 'sense' of Malinowski's writing, commenting: 'Since Malinowski's time, however, anthropology has become more and more scientistic. Vivid descriptions of the sensoria of ethnographic situations have been largely overshowed by a dry, analytical prose.'[23] I believe that here Stoller touches upon the question which lies at the centre of this book. There are a number of kinds of anthropological visuality or ways of seeing making up the modern project. The category 'observation' is only one of these; and even this, if, for example, given a gendered inflexion, may mean something different from the stereotype enshrined in much critical discourse.[24]

Visualizing anthropology

It is my contention that anthropology, as a European project, is marked by an ocularcentric bias. Vision, the noblest of the senses, has been traditionally accorded a privileged status as a source of knowledge about the world. It was encapsulated in the commitment of modern ethnographers to going to 'see' for themselves. For in rejecting 'hearsay', the reliance on reports from untrained observers, the fieldworkers of the early twentieth century reaffirmed the association of vision and knowledge, enshrining it at the heart of a new ethnographic project. But in suggesting the centrality of vision to modern anthropology, whether explicitly foregrounded or not, I follow Jay in recognising ocularcentrism's shifting forms and emphases. Indeed, anthropology is characterised by what I call its distinctive ways of seeing.[25]

My investigation of anthropological ways of seeing is built upon the acknowledgement that vision operates in two distinctive, but interconnected, ways. First of all, vision functions as a methodological strategy, a technique, within modern ethnographic practice. Secondly, vision functions as a metaphor for knowledge, for particular ways of knowing the world. In this latter sense vision may be understood to be about different kinds of anthropological enquiry. We might ask then – what vision of the anthropological project animates the work of particular individuals? For, as we will discover, the modern project has different visions contained within it. It is sometimes conceived to be about the accumulation of scientific knowledge, a process by which the world is rendered knowable; but in other cases it may be concerned with ethnographic understanding as a process of interrogation, a means of disrupting conventional ways of knowing the world; or, modern anthropology might be considered to involve transformation, intense moments of personal revelation.

Different anthropological visions as metaphors for particular conceptions of ethnographic knowledge are ultimately underpinned by what I call a 'metaphysic'. By this I mean the set of beliefs by which anthropologists approach the world. These, too, constitute 'vision' in a metaphorical sense; that is, they are interpretations of the world which find expression through the substance and form of the anthropological work itself.[26]

'The technique of a novel always refers us back to the metaphysic of the novelist', writes George Steiner, the literary critic. In developing what he calls a philosophical rather than a textual orientation to certain key works of literature, Steiner seeks to examine the interplay between form and what he calls 'the world view'.[27] I will pursue a similar approach here as the means by which I may explore the operation of vision in modern anthropology. Hence my concern is to try and reach an understanding of the 'spirit' of the work under consideration rather than to attempt a detailed textual exegesis. Like Steiner, I am interested in the dynamic relationship between vision as technique and as metaphysic. Vision, as understood to mean forms of knowledge or the metaphysics underpinning any anthropological project influences how vision is used as a particular methodological strategy ('every mythology . . . is transmuted through the alchemy of the particular artists and by the materials and techniques of the particular art form').[28] But equally, the techniques employed in the exploration of the world shape the metaphysic by which the ethnographer interprets that world.

Seeking to illuminate anthropology's 'hidden' visual history in this way is important, I believe, in understanding how certain epistemological assumptions continue to influence practitioners working in the discipline today. For the ethnographers's eye is always partial. As the art critic Herbert Read observes:

we see what we learn to see, and vision becomes a habit, a convention, a partial selection of all there is to see, and a distorted summary of the rest. We see what we want to see, and what we want to see is determined, not by the inevitable laws of optics or even (as may be the case in wild animals) by an instinct for survival, but by the desire to discover or construct a credible world.[29]

The organisation of the book

The Ethnographer's Eye has two parts. The first part is built around an investigation of the different ways of seeing at work in the evolution of the modern project. It involves what I call the 'visualization' of the discipline. It requires a radical shift in perspective. I suggest the recontextualization of anthropology, placing its early twentieth-century development alongside changes in the visual arts which found expression, and above all cinematic expression, during the early decades of the century.

Over the last decade anthropology has been much discussed as a particular kind of literary endeavour. What happens if we imagine it differently – as a form of art or cinema? Such a proposal may seem fanciful, perverse even, though it is not without its precendents.[30] By suggesting that we 'see' anthropology as a project of the visual imagination, rather than 'read' it as a particular kind of literature, I believe that we can discover contrasting ways of seeing and knowing within the early modern project. The 'visualization' of anthropology I propose is built around a particular example. I take three key figures from the classic British school (1898–1939) and place their work alongside that of their artistic and cinematic counterparts. I consider the work of W.H.R. Rivers alongside that of Cézanne and the Cubist artists (as the precursors of cinematic montage – Griffith, Eisenstein and Vertov); I place Bronislaw Malinowski in the context of Robert Flaherty's development of a Romantic cinema; and, finally, I seek to explore Radcliffe-Brownian anthropology by means of its juxtaposition with the interwar school of British documentary associated with John Grierson. In looking both ways at once, so to speak, I attempt to develop a way of seeing cinema, *anthropologically*, and a way of seeing anthropology, *cinematically*.[31]

The relocation of anthropology within the context of art and cinema enables us to identify three distinctive forms of anthropological visuality. I call these ways of seeing: *modernist, romantic* and *enlightenment*. Each one is underpinned by different epistemological assumptions about the nature of anthropological enquiry – for example, that ethnographic knowledge is generated by means of the interrogation of conventional ways of understanding the world; that it depends on an intense, visionary experience; and that it requires the painstaking accummulation of data to be organised into a comparative schema. Vision as metaphysic and technique are intertwined. A modernist way of seeing in anthropology may be linked to a *genealogical* approach; a romantic vision to *experiential* techniques; and finally an enlightenment project is organised around a *classificatory* method.

By tracing the rise and fall of these different anthropological visions, we will discover an interesting historical movement. For in the period of British anthropology's early twentieth-century evolution, namely in the period beginning with the 1898 Torres Straits expedition to the outbreak of the Second World War, there is a shift from the predominantly modernist vision associated with the work of Rivers to a very different kind of way of seeing, one that I identify as an enlightenment project and which is expressed in the Radcliffe-Brownian version of scientific ethnography. Malinowski, the romantic visionary, stands as a mediating figure between these two poles. But the movement from one pole to the other, occurring over the course of barely a decade, actually inverts the broader historical movement conventionally understood as a progression from the age of the enlightenment through romanticism to modernism. The reversal of this historical development in the case of anthropology suggests that the new discipline was moulded by a flight from the modern age.

The second part of *The Ethnographer's Eye* comprises a series of case studies. I look closely at the work of Jean Rouch, David and Judith MacDougall, and Melissa Llewelyn-Davies. Vision is central to these projects. It is explicitly foregrounded through the use of image-based technologies as the means by which ethnographic enquiry is pursued. Drawing on the notion of ways of seeing outlined in the book's first part, I seek to explore the interplay between vision as method and metaphysic. The emphasis of my approach shifts from the speculative or 'ideal' to the 'real', and the detailed examination of particular instances of anthropological work.

My purpose is to try and establish how far vision may function as an analytical focus for addressing questions of technique, epistemology and form within the modern discipline. For, in investigating the particular visual techniques used by Rouch, the MacDougalls and Llewelyn-Davies, I attempt to expose changing conceptions about the nature of the anthropological task.

The question of contemporary anthropological practice is critical to *The Ethnographer's Eye*. Why do we work in certain ways? How do particular visions animate the methods we use as ethnographers, whether or not we use a camera as an integral part of our anthropological engagement with the world? My interest in exploring ways of seeing at work in the discipline's development is not just about looking differently at the past. Indeed, I consider it a challenge to convince students that the history of twentieth-century anthropology matters at all. Why should a young film-maker today want to think about someone like W.H.R. Rivers, an obscure figure from history? It is my hope, however, that by approaching differently questions about the evolution of the modern discipline, it will be possible to engage creatively with the past as an integral part of our own contemporary work. The development of such a self-consciousness is important in any attempt to imagine anthropology as a project creatively engaged with the birth of a new century.

Montage and *mise-en-scène*

The exploration of anthropology's ways of seeing involves an experimentation with form. The cinematic aesthetic of montage is the organising principle of my initial thesis, the book's first half is unashamedly speculative. It is inspired by a modernist vision. Taking up Marcus's challenge, I use montage to disrupt the conventional categories by which visual anthropology has come to be defined and confined. Montage, defined as 'the technique of producing a new composite whole from fragments' by the *Oxford English Dictionary*, involves radical juxtaposition, the violent collision of different elements in order to suggest new connections and meanings. It enables me to explore a series of imaginative connections and offers new perspectives on the history of twentieth-century anthropology. I use vision here to illuminate the past, suggesting rather than arguing for the recognition that contrasting interpretations of the anthropological task comprise the modern discipline.

Eisenstein, the great theorist and practitioner of montage, once said: 'If montage is to be compared with something, then a phalanx of montage pieces, of shots, should be compared to the series of explosions of an internal combustion engine.'[32] In characterising the technique in this way, he draws attention to the particular kind of energy and episodic movement that bursts forth from a collision of shots. Certainly montage is the cinematic form most closely associated with the Russian film-makers who sought to create a new, revolutionary cinema as an integral part of the great political, social and intellectual upheaval which followed the events of 1917. Film-makers such as Vertov, Eisenstein, Pudovkin and others were passionately committed to overthrowing conventional ways of seeing and knowing the world. They recognised that what we see is inseparable from how we see. Their radical cinema, in breaking the invisible relationship between perception and the world, instead foregrounded this relationship; and thus made possible very different constructions and interpretations of what was conceived as a fundamentally fluid social reality.

Anthropology's own late twentieth-century revolutionary moment has led to calls for greater experimentation and for the development of new forms for the communication of ethnographic understanding. Montage is identified as a key technique by George Marcus, one of the leading figures in this movement, who draws attention to what he calls 'the cinematic basis of contemporary experiments in ethnographic writing'.[33] In presenting an argument about anthropology and cinema, it seems appropriate then to exploit montage as one of cinema's distinctive techniques; but, equally, my use of such a form, like the Russian film-makers, is motivated by a desire to break up the conventional ways by which we have come to construct anthropology as a twentieth-century project.

If montage underpins the initial conception of the book, its cinematic opposite, the *mise-en-scène*, animates the approach I pursue in its second part. The former expresses the bold, expansive and recklessly generalising spirit with which this enquiry was launched. The latter, however, in its focus and particularity is an expression of the academic caution which subsequently followed the initial euphoria. As the book progresses, its thesis becomes more closely and conventionally argued. The *mise-en-scène*, foregrounding relationships within a particular camera frame, is now the cinematic metaphor by which I ground my speculations through a case study approach. The motif of 'continuous space' is suggestive of a different kind of interpretative approach, one which validates context or 'situated knowledge'.[34]

By self-consciously playing with these opposing cinematic principles, I seek to evoke also the distinctive interplay of panorama/scope and close-up/detail given new aesthetic expression by the invention of cinema. Anthropology exists within the broad landscape of the modern world; and yet as a form of engagement, it is also distinguished by its attraction to detail, its tight focus. The form of the book is an attempt to evoke the movement of the ethnographer's eye, always tracking between panorama and close-up in much the same way as the camera itself.

Part I

Visualizing anthropology

1 The modernist moment and after, 1895–1945

Introduction

In December 1895 Auguste and Louis Lumière presented their newly patented cinematographe to a public audience for the first time. They showed ten short films, each of which lasted barely a minute. But with this programme, cinema was born. The first London screening took place in February 1896; and by the end of that year the Lumière films had been seen in New York and widely across Europe and Asia. Public interest was stimulated as much by the instrument itself as by what it could do, that is record actuality, the world in movement. John Grierson commented in 1937:

When Lumière turned his first historic strip of film, he did so with the fine careless rapture which attends the amateur effort today. The new moving camera was still, for him, a camera and an instrument to focus on the life about him. He shot his own workmen filing out of the factory and this first film was a 'documentary'. He went on as naturally to shoot the Lumière family, child complete. The cinema, it seemed for a moment, was about to fulfill its natural destiny of discovering mankind.[1]

Some three years after the first Lumière screening, Alfred Cort Haddon organised a fieldwork expedition to the Torres Straits islands from Cambridge. He gathered together a group of six scientists and they set out to study the native peoples of a small group of islands lying to the north of Australia. The Torres Straits expedition of 1898 marks the symbolic birth of modern anthropology. Given the great potential ascribed to the cinematographe, it would have been surprising if these late nineteenth-century anthropologists had failed to respond enthusiastically to its development. For they, too, were committed to 'discovering mankind'. Moreover, Haddon and his team were scientists; they were searching for new methods and techniques appropriate to a new subject matter. Certainly Haddon himself was enthusiastic about technology, and he was quick to include a cinematographe among the team's advanced instruments. By 1900 he was urging his Australian colleague,

Baldwin Spencer, to take a camera with him as an integral part of the fieldwork equipment he planned to use in the northern territories of Australia: 'You really *must* take a kinematographe or biograph or whatever they call it in your part of the world. It is an indispensable piece of anthropological apparatus.'[2]

The close coincidence of dates linking the symbolic births of cinema and of modern anthropology is intriguing. It forms an important starting point in my attempt to 'visualize' anthropology, since it prompts a number of important questions concerning their connection as modern projects, and it inaugurates the series of imaginative connections which I trace through the first part of the book. My exploration of the links between early anthropology and cinema is anchored in a particular interpretation of the historical conditions in which they evolved as twentieth-century forms. It is my intention here to highlight some of the key features of the period 1895–1939, as this period is the context for the emergence of the different ways of seeing which characterise early modern anthropology. Moreover, these forms of anthropological visuality are associated with certain ethnographic practices or techniques.

Cinema and modern anthropology developed in a period of remarkable change and innovation. The two decades preceding the outbreak of the Great War were distinguished by the numerous challenge to many established ideas in art, science and politics. Stephen Kern writes:

From around 1880 to the outbreak of World War I a series of sweeping changes in technology and culture created distinctive new modes of thinking about and experiencing time and space. Technological innovations including the telephone, wireless telegraph, x-ray, cinema, bicycle, automobile, and airplane established the material foundation for this reorientation; independent cultural developments such as the stream of consciousness novel, psychonanalysis, Cubism, and the theory of relativity shaped consciousness directly. The result was a transformation of the dimensions of life and thought.[3]

This is the brilliant moment of modernism –

[the] art of a rapidly modernizing world, a world of rapid industrial development, advanced technology, urbanization, seculariziation and mass forms of social life . . . it is the art of a world from which many traditional certainties had departed, and a certain sort of Victorian confidence not only in the outward progress of mankind but in the very solidity and visibility of reality itself has disappeared.[4]

Cinema and anthropology were both a part of and an expression of these currents which so distinguish the early twentieth century. They took shape as distinctively modern projects during an expansive phase in world society, one marked by fluidity, movement and experimentation. Their consolidation, however, was achieved in a different climate. The optimism which had fuelled innovation across all areas of social and intellectual life was extinguished by 1918. The Great War transformed the landscape of the twentieth century. The world which came after was characterised by division, violence, repression and despair.

This shift from an era of openness and experimentation to one which was more closed found expression in the emerging projects of anthropology and cinema. Specifically, it was manifested in the process by which each developed specialised practices known, on the one hand, as *scientific ethnography* and, on the other, as *documentary film*. The rise of these new genres was built upon a number of critical distinctions focusing around the notions of reality and truth. Perhaps the most striking feature of this shift from innovation to consolidation is that the early promise of synthesis was not achieved. Cinema and anthropology diverged and developed as separate traditions. And yet, as we will discover, they share a remarkably similar process of evolution.

The Lumière films

Watching the Lumière programme today, a century after its first public presentation, it seems easy enough to agree with Grierson's statement. The films still appear fresh. There is a tangible sense of discovery, a curiosity and vitality in the camera's attraction to the drama of everyday life. It is said that Louis Lumière's method was to take his cinematographe out into society, setting it down in front of whatever interested him. Even though we can now recognise how carefully he had in fact selected his subject matter, the symbolic importance of the camera being *in* society should not be overlooked. Indeed, Lumière himself draws attention to it, filming his brother carrying a camera and tripod over his shoulder as he disembarks from the boat at the end of a sober procession of statesmen. The unexpectedness of Auguste's appearance, coupled with his jaunty confidence, is remarkably prescient of Vertov's cameraman in *A Man With A Movie Camera* (1929).

Certainly we have to treat with greater caution Grierson's claim for the 'naturalness' of this process. It is a view which echoes other descriptions of Lumière as a technician or inventor, rather than a film-maker with an aesthetic.[5] For from first viewing it is clear that his films are neither random uncut footage nor are they offering an unmediated view of reality. Both the subject matter and the presentation reveal conscious discrimination.

The films which constitued the first Lumière programme were documents of processes – for example, workers filing out of a factory, men demolishing a wall, statesmen disembarking from a boat. As many critics note, what is most distinctive is that most of the films, despite being less than a minute in length, show a whole action, an entire movement with a beginning, middle and end.[6] Moreover, the action takes place within the centre of the frame. There are, however, two brief and tantalising moments of doubt. The first occurs in *Demolishing a Wall*, when Lumière runs backwards through his cinematographe sequences of the men we have just watched demolishing a wall. Suddenly we glimpse all kinds of new possibilities, ones which in a very different and fluid world of revolutionary upheaval become central elements of a cinematic vision. The second rupture occurs in *A Boat Leaving Harbour*. Dai Vaughan, film editor and critic, highlights its moment of spontaneity when something unexpected (a large wave hitting the boat as the rowers move from the harbour into the open sea) suddenly breaks through into Lumière's controlled world, transforming both the action and the characters.[7]

Despite Lumière's attraction to the filming of actuality, or what Grierson refers to as 'documentary', there was a curious paradox in his practice. For although Lumière took his camera out into society and recorded real life in movement, he did so from a static point. His camera was fixed while the world was animated around it. Of course it is possible to argue that the limits of the available technology prevented him from experimenting with a mobile camera, that his cinematographe was heavy and cumbersome and had to be mounted on a tripod. But a closer investigation of how a camera is used reveals something more profound than mere technological limitation.

Auguste and Louis Lumière were men of their time and class. They were late-Victorian bourgeois gentlemen; they were committed to science and technology; they believed in progress and in the ever-increasing knowability of the world. Their instrument, the cinematographe, symbolised such an outlook; how they used it as a recording device is revealing of the fundamental stance which the Lumière brothers had toward the world in which they lived. Their films are a celebration of scientific invention. They are also a celebration of work and the family. More profoundly, they are an expression of confidence in the order and coherence of the world. It is this confidence which finds distinctive expression in the substance and aesthetic of the Lumière films. Form and content are inseparable.

In many important ways the Lumière brothers were nineteenth-century men with a twentieth-century instrument. Hence the films they made owe much to earlier forms, especially to the theatre. For even though Louis Lumière took his camera into society, he recreated, in society, the theatre stage. Thus his camera always remained at a distance, framing the whole action as a tableau; people move in and out of the frame as if on stage. The basic unit of each film remains the scene, rather than the shot.

The Lumière films are usually described by critics as 'primitive' cinema. But in drawing a distinction between these early forms and later 'classical' cinema, another striking feature emerges – exhibitionism. Tom Gunning argues that the first films were primarily about 'showing', or display, rather than about 'telling', the narration of stories.[8] He calls this early cinema 'the cinema of attractions', employing Eisenstein's phrase to highlight the visibility of the cinematic apparatus and the distinctive relationship established between the film subjects and the audience. For unlike the later films, which create self-enclosed narrative worlds and carefully disguise the relationship between action on screen and spectators, cinema before 1906 is, according to Gunning, explicitly exhibitionist. Thus people perform for the camera, they show themselves off and, at the same time, show off the recording instrument itself. The audience is addressed directly, and it participates as a collectivity in the enjoyment of the spectacle displayed on acreen. Gunning argues that

it is the direct address of the audience, in which an attraction is offered to the spectator by a cinema showman, that defines this approach to film making. Theatrical display dominates over narrative absorption, emphasizing the direct stimulation of shock or surprise at the expense of unfolding a story or creating a diegetic universe. The cinema of attraction expends little energy creating characters with psychological motivations or individual personality. Making use of both fictional and non-fictional attractions, its energy moves outward towards an acknowledged spectator rather than inward towards the character-based situations essential to classical narrative.[9]

Haddon and the Torres Straits expedition

Alfred Cort Haddon, the organiser of anthropology's first fieldwork expedition was, like Louis Lumière, a man of his time. He, too, straddled the nineteenth and twentieth centuries; underpinning his advocacy of a new methodology built upon the use of advanced scientific instrumentation were older conceptions about the history of mankind. Hence, a closer investigation of the Torres Straits expedition reveals a mixture of Victorian ideas with modern innovative practices; and nowhere is this more starkly exposed than in the expedition's use of the camera and cinematographe.

Haddon's conversion to anthropology had taken place a decade earlier, when during 1888–89 he travelled as a biologist to study the flora and fauna of the Torres Straits islands which lay off the northeast coast of Australia. In the course of his research, Haddon discovered that the natives were 'cheerful, friendly and intelligent folk', and he began to form friendships with a number of them. He also became convinced that native life was under threat. At the moment he had discovered it as an area for serious scientific study it seemed to be disappearing before his very eyes. Whenever Haddon asked local people about their past he was told it was 'lost'; and he resolved to make records of vanishing cultural practices before it was too late.[10] In planning his return to the Torres Straits islands, Haddon recognised that a comprehensive, scientific study of native life was beyond any single fieldworker; rather it required a range of different skills and expertise.

The Cambridge scientists (Haddon, Rivers, Myers, McDougall, Seligman and Ray) spent almost eight months working in the different islands of the Torres Straits. They conducted tests; they interviewed native subjects; and they collected information on local customs and practices. The huge mass of data was eventually published, under Haddon's editorship, as a six-volume series. The visual quality of the Torres Straits ethnography is indeed striking. Each of the volumes is filled with photographs, native drawings and other visual materials as important counterparts to the written text, and Haddon returned to Cambridge with a number of filmed sequences which he had shot with the cinematographe.

Vision was a central question in the Torres Straits expedition. It was the focus of a substantial part of the scientific enquiry into native life, and it formed an important theme underlying the mode of enquiry itself. Vision was inseparable from the question of method. As I have suggested above, it is in the visual dimensions of the Torres Straits expedition that we may discern what is both archaic and prescient in the emerging modern fieldwork-based anthropological project.[11]

For many years Malinowski's claim to have instigated the modern revolution in anthropology was accepted. Now, however, the Torres Straits expedition and other related projects, are recognised as the precursors of a new, distinctively twentieth-century project. At its centre was the practice of fieldwork. Haddon and his colleagues acknowledged that it was no longer adequate to sit like Sir James Frazer in a college study, and interpret or speculate on the basis of information supplied by an array of missionaries, explorers and colonial officials. It was important to go and see for oneself, to collect one's own data in the field and to build theories around such first-hand information.[12] Increasingly, then, there was a fusion into a single person of the previously separate roles of fieldworker and theorist. Emphasis was increasingly laid upon direct observation. What the ethnographer saw himself or herself in the field later became an ultimate standard of proof. They had, after all, uniquely 'been there'.[13]

At first, however, these central questions concerning observation and data collection were not straightforward; and members of the Torres Straits team shared with their scientific contemporaries a profound concern about method. For, as Schaffer reminds us, the symbolic shift from a college armchair to the fieldsite which inaugurated anthropology's modern phase obscures an important feature – the fact that the leading figures were laboratory scientists, rather than literary intellectuals.[14] Men like Boas and Rivers, for example, were concerned to recreate a newly developed laboratory culture in the field. Thus they carried with them into their study of native culture the techniques and technology of late-Victorian science. The Torres Straits scientists included in their fieldwork apparatus, not just a camera and cinematographe but also

light tests, spring balance, chronometer, sphygomanometer, time marker, color tests, eye tester, diagrams, brass box, wools and types, Galton's whistle, obach cells, ohrmesser, whistle and mounting, scents, syren whistle, handgrasp dynamometer, induction coil and wire, marbles, dynamograph, pseudoptics, diaspon, musical instruments, as well some other bits of equipment and materials necessary for running and repairing them.[15]

Underlying this impressive array of instrumentation was the problem of objectivity which dominated Victorian science. Investigators increasingly worried about their influence on the object of investigation. 'Policing the subjective' was an intellectual, practical and moral problem; and in a Victorian world of self-restraint and technological innovation, machines offered to minimise intervention. Moreover, they worked more effectively and efficiently than fallible human observers.[16]

The concern about objectivity was discernible in nineteenth-century anthropology. By 1840 it was recognised that there was a problem in the acquisition of reliable fieldwork data. The growing discomfort with their continuing dependence on untrained amateurs to supply accurate information to armchair theorists led to the introduction of photography as an important scientific tool. Anthropologists shared the widespread belief that the camera guaranteed a greater objectivity, and it provided evidence against which other reports, essentially 'hearsay', could be judged.

Photographs of 'types' or 'specimens' played a prominent part in mid-nineteenth-century anthropological debate, when questions of race were paramount. During this period, the physical characteristics of people were taken to be indicators of their place in an evolutionary hierarchy.[17] The distinctive features of this kind of photography reveal the prevailing scientific anxiety about human contamination. For the generation of standardised data for analysis involved the suppression of both the subjectivity of the observer and the observed. The 'type' was always devoid of a complicating cultural context and classified on the basis of measurable physical features. Moreover a single person, deprived of their individuality, stood for a whole group; and the photographs, usually frontal and in profile, denied any relationship between the person in front of the camera and the one behind it. But as one commentator notes, the use of the camera to acquire anthropometric evidence, which focused on bodies rather than on people, could be more accurately acquired from the dead than the living. In the view of Im Thurn, photography could be more productively employed to document living people in social activity.[18] Later photographs offered glimpses of social and cultural context, usually through the presentation of individuals in 'typical' native dress.

The photographs published in the *Reports of the Torres Straits Expedition* are strongly reminiscent of a mid-nineteenth-century style of anthropological photography. For example, in the first volume, *General Ethnography*, there is a series of portraits taken by Anthony Wilkin, the expedition's photographer. Individuals are photographed in close-up; most are presented in both profile and in frontal pose; the photograph reveals only their head and shoulders; and the background is completely neutral. Haddon, too, was an active photographer in the field, as the volumes published under his editorship reveal. It is important to remember, however, that the visual data which he assembled was placed alongside the vast range of other materials that the Cambridge team of scientists collected in the course of their researches. The emphasis on the development of sophisticated scientific methods for the collection of data meant that photographs provided just one source of information and, in the context of the Torres Straits expedition, the materials produced through the use of visual technologies were always to be judged against those generated by other fieldwork strategies.[19]

Haddon's use of the cinematographe is different from his use of a stills camera, and it is perhaps more interesting. In this work, he presents living people engaged in social activity. Among the fragmentary sequences which have survived, about four minutes in total, the greater portion is devoted to the performance of ceremonial dances. The remaining footage, which documents three men lighting a fire, immediately brings to mind Louis Lumière's film, *The Card Players*. But there are other striking similarities between Haddon's Torres Straits film and the Lumière shorts. For like Lumière, Haddon's aesthetic as a filmmaker owes much to older theatrical conventions. His camera remains fixed while the world is animated around it; the action takes place in scenes comprising a single unchanging shot (rather than through a series of shots of different lengths and focus – the great innovation of D.W. Griffith); and there is an explicit acknowledgement of the camera by the native performers. Indeed, the action appears to have been staged for the purpose of the recording itself. Hence, we can describe the Torres Straits footage as an example of 'primitive' cinema or what Gunning calls 'the cinema of attractions'.[20] There is a marked emphasis on display or exhibition. The audience is shown something rather than told something.[21] But with Haddon's film we have to recognise the absence of a direct connection between the film's actors and its audience, for Gunning's use of the concept of a cinema of attractions is largely based on the notion of a shared social context. In many cases members of the audience were themselves the subjects of the early films, and they took delight in watching themselves or friends perform for the camera. The culture and behaviour of the Torres Straits islanders, however, would undoubtedly appear as exotic and 'primitive' to European viewers of 1900; and being situated outside the world of the film, the audience would inevitably be engaged in a sort of voyeuristic spectatorship. Certainly at the time there was considerable popular interest in faraway places and peoples. For a discussion of early ethnographic film and its audiences, see Alison Griffith's forthcoming book, *The Origins of Ethnographic Film*. Haddon himself seemed not to have been unduly concerned about the possible conflict between recording for scientific or preservation purposes and for commercial screening.[22]

Haddon was essentially a salvage anthropologist. He shared the widely held nineteenth-century view of the inevitability of progress; but inseparable from this perspective was an acknowledgement that valuable aspects of mankind's history were being destroyed with the advance of civilization. According to Gruber, the recognition of the threat which faced native peoples and their customs came both suddenly and traumatically to European intellectuals. By the mid-nineteenth-century, the 'vanishing savage' had become a powerful symbol, inspiring much scientific endeavour. In this climate, and given the urgency of the perceived task, it was not surprising that Haddon was determined to use the most advanced scientific instruments in his documentation of a 'dying' culture.[23]

The ideas which underpinned Haddon's salvage anthropology influenced in important ways his use of technologies, and especially visual technologies, in the field. Fundamentally, he believed that native culture was in decline. It no longer was functioning as a coherent unified whole, as a series of practices which sustained social life; rather it had disintegrated into fragments and isolated relics. Moreover, for Haddon, culture was visible. It was located at the surface of social life, and external appearances were taken as relatively unproblematic. Stills photography, as a recording method, was particularly compatible with these assumptions. It captured the apearance of things, or as John Berger puts it: 'photographs quote from appearance'.[24] They arrest moments from the past as 'traces', asserting a direct connection between the image and its referent in the world. In this sense the photographs from the Torres Straits expedition share a similar status to the forty packing cases of cultural objects which Haddon shipped back to Cambridge for museum display and presentation. For while these photographic and material artifacts are irrefutable as 'evidence', their meaning is always ambiguous. They are objects out of time and place, expressions of a fundamental discontinuity between then and now, there and here, between the moment of photography or collection and contemporary viewing or displaying. But such items are imbued with nostalgia, for they are powerful symbols of a vanished or vanishing way of life, what James Clifford calls 'a present-becoming-past'.[25] Salvage anthropology looks backwards. It is the past of a society, not its present or future, which has meaning and authenticity.

But if photography effectively serves such a paradigm through its documentation of discrete items and static states of being, isolating moments in the past, moving film is about connections, processes, and the linking of the past with the present and future. Berger writes:

Photographs are the opposite of films. Photographs are retrospective and are received as such: films are anticipatory. Before a photograph you search for *what was there*. In a cinema you wait for what is to come next. All film narratives are, in this sense, *adventures*: they advance, they arrive.[26]

With this contrast in mind, I think it is important to look again at the film footage which Haddon shot during the 1898 Torres Straits expedition. His use of the Lumière cinematographe reveals culture as lived, as performance. It appears as a continuous and coherent series of actions carried out by living people in real time and space.

Haddon's project then, while remaining trapped at one level within a nineteenth-century paradigm, also contains strikingly modern aspects. This mixture of the old and the new, the static and the mobile is expressed particularly sharply in the visual dimensions of his work. Although the role Haddon assigned to stills photography in the Torres Straits expedition reinforced the salvage paradigm of his work, the simultaneous use of moving film threatened to undermine the central elements of such a paradigm.

Anthropology, cinema and the Great War

Despite the early promise of synthesis symbolised by the Torres Straits expedition, cinema and anthropology quickly diverged. Each developed independently of the other, even though there were close parallels in their evolution as modern practices. Indeed, it is the speed with which the active use of both the camera and the cinematographe was effectively banished from the new ethnographic practice which strikes many commentators as especially puzzling. The two leading figures of the Torres Straits expedition, Haddon and Rivers, have been blamed in different ways for the disappearance of visual material from the modern discipline. It is argued that Haddon's advocacy of the use of photography and film was harnessed to a late-Victorian vision of disappearing cultures, while Rivers pushed anthropology away from the observable dimensions of social life to a concern with invisible abstract principles. But there is an interesting paradox here. For both men were undoubtedly committed to a 'visual' anthropology, even if their interests were markedly different. Importantly they shared with their scientific contemporaries a profound concern with the question of vision.

The camera did not solve the problem of objectivity in late nineteenth-century science. It merely entered into the debate.[27] Over time, the truth value of photographic evidence became increasingly problematic; and by the turn of the century what Martin Jay calls 'the crisis of ocularcentrism' permeated all areas of intellectual activity. Ironically though, as Jay points out, it was the development of the camera, 'the most remarkable technological extension of the human capacity to see, at least since the microscope and telescope in the seventeenth century, [that] helped ultimately to undermine confidence in the very sense whose powers it so extended'.[28]

D.W. Griffith shattered the camera's static pose. He broke up the controlled and ordered world of Haddon and the Lumière brothers, and confronted his audience with the violence and turbulence of the age in which they lived. For within the space of two decades, the late-Victorian optimism, a belief in the inevitability of progress which fuelled technological innovation, had been replaced by profound despair. European civilization lay in ruins. The Great War opened up a horrifying chasm of violence and destruction. Griffith's controversial film, *The Birth of a Nation*, released in 1915, cast a long shadow over this troubled landscape, standing as the powerful and shocking symbol of a world in turmoil.

If we place the Lumière and Torres Straits films alongside some of Griffith's most important work, *The Birth of a Nation* (1915), *Intolerance*

(1916) and *Broken Blossoms* (1919) we can appreciate how far cinema had travelled in twenty years. In the early footage shot with a cinematographe, we watch a series of self-contained worlds evoked as whole, continuous and coherent. They appear to be ordered in time and space. As I have noted, the way in which the new technology was used at the turn of the century owed much to the older, established aesthetic of theatre. Hence both Lumière and Haddon presented social activity as if it took place on a theatre stage – people performed for the camera; actions were whole and continuous and unfolded within a scene; the spectacle or display was organised according to the principle of perspective which converged everything onto the eye of the beholder; the audience was fixed in its position, and it was located outside the action. These limitations in technique were, I suggest, an expression of the particular vision of society with which Lumière and Haddon worked. It was one inseparable from the more general historical context in which they were located. Nevertheless, it is important not to overlook the importance of their taking the camera into society. Even if they recreated the theatre and the laboratory in the field, both Lumière and Haddon recognised the importance of developing new techniques for exploring social life. Fundamentally this meant they were committed to going out to discover people on their own terms. This was a new project, and it was one which set the early film-makers and anthropologists apart from the established intellectuals, who increasingly loathed 'the people' and feared the emergence of 'mass society'.[29]

Griffith plunges us into a very different world from the one created through the use of the cinematogaphe by Haddon and Lumière. It is characterised by movement, complexity, interconnection, violence and conflict. It is not just the vision underlying Griffith's films which is an expression of the turbulence of the early twentieth-century world; this turbulence is also manifested in the cinematic technique itself, in the use of montage. There are a number of examples which point to the growing development of montage as a technique in early cinema; but, like Haddon and Lumière, I take Griffith to be a symbolic figure. For Griffith took the distinctive language of cinema to a new stage in his mature films.

At its simplest, montage indeed means juxtaposition, and, as such, it foregrounds relationships rather than discrete entities; it emphasises processes rather than static states of being; and it draws attention to the generation of meaning through processes of contrast rather than those of continuity or development. Using montage as a technique means that the world cannot be represented as complete or stable; rather it is evoked as a mosaic, a shifting pattern made up of unstable pieces. The world is never offered up as whole but can only be approached as partial (what you see always depends on where you are), and its meaning is neither self-evident nor fixed but is endlessly generated through the different relationships which may be created between elements.

James Agee, the American film critic and writer whose collaboration with Walker Evans produced the remarkable photographic essay, *Let Us Now Praise Famous Men* (1941), wrote of Griffith:

> As a director, Griffith hit the picture business like a tornado. Before he walked on the set, motion pictures had been, in actuality, static. At a respectful distance, the camera snapped a series of whole scenes clustered in the groupings of a stage play. Griffith broke up the pose. He rammed his camera into the middle of the action. He took closeups, crosscuts, angle shots and dissolves. His camera was alive, picking off shots; then he built the shots into sequences, the sequences into tense, swift narrative. For the first time the movies had a man who realized that while a theater audience listened a movie audience watched. 'Above all . . . I am trying to make you see', Griffith said.[30]

One of D.W. Griffith's greatest innovations in cinema was to *move* the camera. The camera could now be located anywhere within a scene; it no longer watched from a fixed place outside the action, but instead it was anywhere and everywhere *within* the action. Indeed the camera itself became part of the action. Moreover, by using it in this way, Griffith stripped the camera of its human qualities, for he exploited its capacities for seeing in ways that the human eye cannot see.[31] The basic unit of Griffith's new cinematic language was the shot, rather the scene with its origins in an older theatrical form; and action was no longer conveyed as whole and continuous (as in the Lumière and Torres Straits film footage), unfolding within a single, extended and unchanging shot. Action was broken down into a series of fragments, and movement generated through their manipulation during editing. But just as a single action can now be broken down into parts, so too can the overall narrative itself.

The controversial scenes of the Ku Klux Klan at the climax of the film *The Birth of a Nation* contain all the key features of the distinctive language which Griffith was developing for cinema. We can see here the extraordinary movement of the camera; the sophisticated tempo created through the pace and rhythm of the editing; and the complexity of the film's overall construction through the intercutting of different narrative threads to suggest actions connected in time while separated in space. It is this breathtaking virtuosity harnessed to a deeply disturbing vision of society which provokes such profound unease around any screening of *The Birth of a Nation*, rendering the film as problematic for audiences today as upon its release in 1915.[32]

Film critics have sought different solutions to the problem of their ambivalence towards *The Birth of a Nation*. Most commonly they have sought to separate form from content, to consider the techniques of shooting and editing apart from the film's ideological dimensions; but such a task is, I believe, impossible. These innovations in cinema cannot be separated from a broader context. The core of Griffith's original work lies in the period of the Great War and the Russian Revolution, and his vision and method were moulded by these historical circumstances. The content of *The Birth of a Nation, Intolerance* (1916) and *Broken Blossoms* (1919) reflects the turbulence of the world in which he worked. His techniques were the aesthetic counterpart to this, an expression of the climate of experimentation in which modernist artists, poets, writers and composers sought to break decisively with the old nineteenth-century forms. This radical rejection of the past posed anew questions of subject and object, the nature of the human personality, and the place of the individual within society and history.[33]

Griffith, then, must be understood in this context. But his modernism was limited. He remained wedded to archaic forms, particularly nine-teenth-century melodrama, through which he sought to resolve the tremendous conflicts he recognised at the core of the modern world. Increasingly Griffith found it difficult to contain these explosive forces within the familiar formal conventions. His sense of movement, com-plexity and interconnection found expression in the audacity of the changing camera positions and the extraordinary tempo of his editing; and yet Griffith's movement was confined to the static world of the studio or location set. Lumière and Haddon had *fixed* their cinemato-graphe in the midst of social life; Griffith *moved* his camera but only in an artificially constructed world (the studio) located outside society. It was the Russian film-maker, Dziga Vertov, who, in the aftermath of the 1917 revolution, explored the creative connections between a camera in movement and a world in movement.

George Marcus, an anthropologist today who has drawn attention to the 'cinematic basis' of recent experiments in ethnographic writing, identifies three key features of montage as a technique: 'simultaneity; multiperspectivism; discontinuous narrative'.[34] These features are closely tied to a particular vision of modern society as urban, industrial, fragmented, interconnected and in perpetual motion. Cinema is an expression of this new era. Anthropology, however, as a modern project is the mirror opposite. It is built upon a profound rejection of industrial civilization. In place of a complex, mobile twentieth-century world, anthropologists discovered 'simple' societies – small-scale, isolated, integrated, and fundamentally non-industrial native communities which were located outside time and history. The techniques and technology used to explore them were archaic – that is, they too were non-industrial, and as such they can be understood to be the formal counterpart of the visions which animate much of twentieth-century anthropological enquiry. It is ironic that in the guise of science, the new ethnographers pursued their enquiries by means of personal experience and a note-book.

The First World War profoundly shaped the emerging discipline of anthropology. It divided the experimental period of its early modern evolution from the later phase of professional consolidation and specia-lisation. Rivers and Malinowski are the two figures considered here who may be identified with these two phases in the project's development. Rivers died in 1922, the same year in which Malinowski published his most influential anthropological work, *Argonauts of the Western Pacific*. This coincidence of events symbolises the beginning of anthropology's professional consolidation, the transformation of its identity from that of a 'cinderella science' to a fully fledged scientific discipline.[35] The process of transition was initiated, but not completed, by Malinowski. Ironically, though, of the two men Rivers was the more serious scientist. Malinowski's primary concern was to establish what Clifford in *The Predicament of Culture* has called 'ethnographic authority' – the demarca-tion of an area of expert knowledge acquired through specialist practice. Such a claim was built upon the clarification of a number of key distinctions – for example, between anthropological analysis and travel-lers' tales; observation and hearsay; depth and surface; science and speculation; knowledge and belief.

It is interesting that a similar process may be discerned within cinema during the 1920s. There was a concern with the clarification of certain principles as the basis for particular practice. These, too, focused around the claim to a particular relationship with 'truth'. The move towards the establishment of a distinctive cinematic project crystallised around the term 'documentary'. It became particularly associated with the tradition established by the British film-maker John Grierson, who used the term as the basis for his development of a national cinema.[36] Documentary cinema's claim to a unique identity shared much with that of its anthropological counterpart, scientific ethnography; that is, it hinged upon a series of oppositions – revelation and exploration, reality and fiction, objective and subjective, society and the individual, educa-tion and entertainment, and most crucially, truth and fiction.

The process by which these key categories emerged as the foundation for distinctive projects in anthropology and cinema was not, however, straightforward. There was often a discrepancy between the principles expounded and the practice itself, as the legacies of Malinowski and Flaherty, perhaps the two most critical figures in the emergence of scientific ethnography and documentary film, reveal. It is no accident that critics never seem to tire of their work. The status accorded to Malinowski and Flaherty in the evolution of the two traditions is never stable. The endless re-evaluation of their contribution stems from the fact that their projects were built upon a blurring of the ideal and the real. There was always a discrepancy between what they claimed to do and what they actually did. Although I suggest that this confusion is actually integral to their particular way of seeing, both figures might also be considered as transitional. Their work straddles the two distinctive phases in the evolution of modern anthropology and cinema, and it contains elements from both. The early phase was characterised by openness and innovation; the later one by specialisation and consolidation.[37]

It is important to acknowledge that the establishment of the two specialised practices, scientific ethnography and documentary cinema, took place in a climate transformed by the Great War. The optimism which had buoyed all the creative attempts to break with established practices in social, political, intellectual and artistic life gave way to pessimism and despair. The Russian Revolution of 1917 is the watershed. Within less than a decade the explosion of creative energy generated by the revolution had been brutally repressed by structures of totalitarianism; but the dramatic shift in power away from people and toward enhanced and expanded state bureaucracies was a more general feature of the 1920s and 1930s.

It is my argument that the emergence of the distinctive traditions of scientific ethnography and documentary cinema cannot be separated from an understanding of this broader context. During the interwar years we can identify a process by which their original radical impulse was steadily compromised. Hence the early commitment to exploring the lives of 'ordinary' people which, in turn, necessitated the development of new methods of enquiry (principally abandoning the studio, the laboratory, the study in favour of going into society to 'see' for yourself, to understand people within their own context of life) was gradually transformed into a different kind of practice. This process of transformation was also reflected in the changing visions which came to animate interwar anthropology and documentary cinema. With hindsight, both projects have come to be seen as compatible with a certain kind of state power; their harshest critics share the view that each placed itself in the service of the state, whether at home or abroad.[38] Certainly it is difficult to avoid the conclusion that the drive for professional consolidation led to political compromise and adaptation, even though individuals within each of the projects remained committed to a radical agenda. Leading figures like John Grierson or Radcliffe-Brown were engaged in making visible peoples previously excluded from conceptions of humanity. They were also committed to revealing the fundamental rationality of these people. But, it may be argued, the visions of society expressed through their work, and the kinds of visual techniques employed, were also perfectly adapted to the needs of a state seeking to order, control and confine its subjects. The commitment to truth and to reality as the foundations of documentary cinema and scientific ethnography begins to shade into propaganda.

The achievement of professional consolidation which the practitioners of both documentary cinema and scientific ethnography sought was not, in fact, secured until after the Second World War. Despite the striking similarities in their early twentieth-century evolution, the two projects moved in opposite directions after 1945. The anthropologists gained a foothold in the expanding universities, becoming increasingly concerned with theoretical and disciplinary consolidation; while the film-makers sought to break with the established ways of working (indeed blurring some of the key distinctions upon which documentary practice rested) in order to forge closer links with society. This divergence of anthropology and cinema forms the context for my exploration of different ways of seeing in the second part of this book. It underlies the emergence of a new field, visual anthropology.

2 Anxious visions: Rivers, Cubism and anthropological modernism

> The more horrifying this world becomes (as it is these days) the more
> art becomes abstract; while a world at peace produces realistic art.
>
> Paul Klee, 1915

The emergence of anthropology as a twentieth-century project was influenced by the work of W.H.R. Rivers, perhaps the most interesting member of Haddon's team of scientists who left Cambridge for the Torres Straits islands in 1898. Despite his importance, Rivers has until recently remained a shadowy figure in the intellectual histories of the discipline. The ambivalence which surrounds his contribution to the establishment of a modern, scientific and fieldwork-based anthropology is echoed in the uncertainty associated with the work of his cinematic counterpart, D.W. Griffith. Both figures are celebrated and reviled in equal measure. The radical impulse of their work in anthropology and cinema is tempered by the continuing presence of features considered archaic, indeed deeply embarassing, to present-day practitioners.[1] In linking Rivers at the outset to Griffith, one of the pioneers of the new cinematic form, montage, I wish to signal the kind of interpretation I intend to pursue here. What is important for our purposes in seeking to 'visualize anthropology' is the modernist vision which animates their work.

The essay which follows is exploratory and speculative. I make no apology for the idiosyncratic range of sources upon which I draw; rather I take as my model the spirit of experimentation which marks the modernist moment itself. The thesis I develop of Rivers' significance for contemporary anthropology depends upon the disruption of the intellectual context in which he is conventionally located. Hence, instead of placing his work within the context of late nineteenth-century science, I will suggest that certain of its key features may be understood differently if placed alongside innovations in the practices of art and cinema during this period. For it is interesting to note that Rivers' career overlaps significantly with that of Cézanne and the Cubist artists as well as with

Griffith. Situating Rivers within such a nexus of relationships makes it possible for us to discern a distinctive way of seeing at work within his anthropology. I suggest that Rivers' project for anthropology contains at its core a modernist vision. It finds expression in the metaphysic (that is, in the interpretation of the world) and method (in the means for exploring the world) characteristic of his enquiry.

Although I use the term 'modernism' to describe the key features of Rivers's anthropology, specifically its anxious, reflexive and fractured qualities, I want also to draw attention to its distinctive phases. Rivers' early modernism, at the turn of the century, finds its most concrete expression in the kinship diagram. His late modernism is to be found in the work he carried out at Craiglockhart hospital with patients suffering from shell shock during the First World War. If the early modernist phase evokes connections between Rivers and the Cubist artists, it is the latter which suggests interesting links with the work of D.W. Griffith and the Russian film-maker, Dziga Vertov.

The significance of Rivers' contribution to the intellectual life of the twentieth century is now being slowly acknowledged.[2] Within anthropology the erosion of confidence in the Malinowskian myth of the fieldwork revolution has forced a re-assessment of the discipline's early phase; gradually, Rivers is being restored to his rightful place as a key figure in the evolution of modern anthropology. His significance stems not just from his pioneering fieldwork methods, but also from his development of a new conceptual approach.[3]

My own recent engagement with the work of Rivers stems from an unusual source. It was stimulated by Pat Barker, a contemporary novelist, who places Rivers at the heart of her trilogy about the Great War. Drawing on established literature and her own documentary research, Barker creatively explores the complex personality of Rivers within this historical context. It was reading Barker's novels, *Regeneration* (1991), *The Eye In The Door* (1993) and *The Ghost Road* (1995), which prompted me to develop the approach I call 'the visualization of anthropology'. For, as a novelist, Barker works in interesting ways with vision and visualization. They lie at the heart of her interpretation of Rivers. She draws attention to their significance in Rivers' life, not just as intellectual problems but as a source of personal fascination. Such concerns are evoked, perhaps most strikingly, by the title of the second volume of Barker's trilogy, *The Eye In The Door*. Increasingly I became fascinated by the resonances of such a metaphor. Indeed, as I discovered, eyes are scattered everywhere across the novels. Barker often refers to Rivers' habit of drawing his hand across his eyes; but eyes are also found on the battlefield; they are picked up and held in the hand;

they watch, secretly but tangibly present, within different scenes. By allowing Barker's visual metaphor take hold of my own imagination, I found that it offered me new ways of thinking about the role of the twentieth-century ethnographer. How were the two main characters of the novels, Rivers and Prior, contrasted? Was the eye in the door that of the ethnographer? What was involved in looking inside, to the self, or outside, spying into the world? What did the image of the eye in the door suggest about vision and anthropology?[4]

The novels of Pat Barker reawakened my curiosity in a figure I barely knew from my own anthropological training. But equally it was her exploration of Rivers' character within the historical context of the First World War which raised questions in my mind about the very different kinds of ethnographic enquiry being pursued by the early twentieth-century figures. Returning to a consideration of the more conventional sources, I felt intuitively that Rivers was central to my project of 'visualizing' anthropology, not least because his life's work was centrally concerned with vision.[5] Without fully grasping the details, I knew that Rivers' approach to vision contrasted sharply with that of his contemporary, Malinowski. This marked the beginning of my use of the phrase 'ways of seeing', borrowed from Berger's classic work. As a concept it enabled me to interrogate the category 'vision', and to contrast the epistemological and methodological assumptions implied in the different anthropological visions of the early twentieth century.[6]

From Rivers' earliest enquiries in experimental psychology and anthropology at the turn of the century to his treatment, during the First World War, of patients deeply traumatised by their battlefield experiences, his intellectual project had at its core the exploration of visual processes in human experience. Although his interests and methods of investigation changed in the course of four decades, there is a remarkable consistency of focus. His enquiry was driven by a fascination with vision and his own loss of vision or loss of the ability to visualize. For Rivers, vision was a faculty associated with what he called the *protopathic* or more 'primitive' aspects of human personality. The more developed cognitive faculties in human personality he associated with the 'epicritic'. He understood his own experience as evidence that the protopathic had been suppressed by the development of different and progressive cognitive processes.[7]

An investigation of this central thread in Rivers' work, namely the relationship between the protopathic and epicritic, immediately evokes in my own mind the continuing ambivalence which surrounds the role of vision and visual imagery within anthropology today. It can be argued that Rivers' early position on vision as evidence of the protopathic or primitive elements in human personality has remained an important, if unacknowledged, theme in the later project. In the broadest sense then, I take Rivers to be critical to the development of a new visual anthropology, since the change which took place in his understanding of vision during the course of his career is suggestive of possibilities for its re-integration into contemporary anthropology.

But in a narrower sense, Rivers' work is important because of the modernism of its vision. It was, however, subsequently overlaid by other ways of seeing as manifested in the different ethnographic approaches developed first by Malinowski and later by Radcliffe-Brown. Today these anthropological visions no longer hold unquestioned dominance within the discipline; and, as a consequence, the modernist impulse of Rivers' work takes on a new salience. The work of several contemporary anthropologists may be interpreted as the embodiment of the open, experimental spirit which animated Rivers' anthropology at the turn of the century.[8]

The modernism of Rivers' project is, I believe, reflected in his lifelong fascination with questions of vision, and his anxiety about its operation and status. Following Martin Jay, we can recognise that Rivers' preoccupations were shared more widely by modernist intellectuals at the turn of the century. The eye, traditionally regarded as the noblest of the senses, was increasingly the focus of doubt and scepticism – even violent humiliation.[9] But in addition to the general 'ocularcentrism' of Rivers' project, his modernism also had a concrete manifestation – the kinship diagram.

If Rivers is celebrated at all by present-day anthropologists, it is for his invention of the genealogical method. The historian George Stocking identifies the genealogical method as the 'major methodological innovation' of the 1898 Torres Straits expedition.[10] It enabled the ethnographic fieldworker, in the absence of linguistic fluency, to grasp quickly the internal dynamics of the society under investigation. The method was developed by Rivers while a member of Haddon's Torres Straits team of Cambridge scientists. Rivers' own special area of research concerned questions of vision and perception, but in the course of fieldwork with the native peoples of the Torres Straits islands, he began to collect oral genealogies, recognising that kinship relationships were an important means for understanding social organization. Moreover, given the perceived urgency of the expedition's work, genealogies seemed to offer a short-cut route into the workings of pre-literate society. They were, as Langham states, 'a means of gaining insight into the abstract via the concrete'.[11] The method involved a two-stage process. First of all, informants were asked for the proper names of relatives. Secondly, the fieldworker compiled the different terms of relationships for addressing these individuals. The kinship diagram became the visual, abstract expression of these underlying principles of social organization. As Bouquet points out, however, there is an interesting paradox here. For Rivers associated the concrete with the visual, and in turn with the 'primitive' or protopathic; and yet his development of a more advanced, scientific, epicritic model was itself a visual representation.[12]

Rivers' development of a kinship-based method is now widely acknowledged to have marked a fundamental shift in the focus of anthropological work. It symbolized a movement away from older preoccupations with religion and belief towards a new concern with kinship and social organization. Two other important changes were also contained within the new approach pioneered by Rivers – a shift from biology to society; and an abandonment of the construction of hierarchies comprising discrete units in favour of the analysis of systems of relationships. As Langham notes, there was less and less interest by fieldworkers in quantative information – how many people were doing various things – and growing interest in relationships between tasks done.[13]

The kinship diagram quickly became established as a central motif in modern anthropological analysis. It lent a certain scientific authenticity to the new monograph, replacing photographs as the visual counterpart to text. Until recently, however, its theoretical status provoked little comment. Yet as Bouquet's critical analysis has revealed, Rivers' innovation may be understood as a highly specific cultural motif, one expressive of an English middle-class conception of the world. In developing her investigations further, Bouquet draws attention to the distinctive visual form of the genealogical diagram. She locates it within a broader conceptual field: 'visualizing kinship in the form of a genealogical diagram in twentieth century anthropology, derived from the prevalence of tree imagery for secular, religious and scientific purposes in eighteenth-and nineteenth-century (and earlier) Europe.'[14]

I want to suggest that Rivers' kinship diagram can be interpreted in a different way. Thus instead of understanding it as a new version of an old European motif, the tree as the visual symbol through which knowledge may be laid out and organised, it might equally be understood as evidence of the fleeting modernist moment within anthropology. For Rivers' conception of social organization involved a radical break with the existing languages of representation. Following the art critic John Berger, we might say that Rivers, like the Cubist painters, reduced the visible world to a simple, abstract form (the kinship diagram) in order to construct a more complex view of reality than had previously been attempted.[15] We may consider this new abstract form as an expression of Paul Klee's observation: 'Art does not render the visible; rather, it makes visible'.[16]

The movement towards the abstract representation of knowledge which can be discerned in Rivers' work on kinship at the turn of the century may be seen as an integral part of the more general trend in the arts and sciences of that period. Modernism represented a decisive break with nineteenth-century realism and with the desire to reproduce meticulously the external appearance of things. The nature of reality itself, as solid, stable and visible, was now in doubt. For the collapse of confidence in the Victorian idea of progress precipitated a crisis about knowledge, and it stimulated radically new ways of exploring the world.[17]

Picasso's painting of 1907, *Les Demoiselles d'Avignon*, is widely acknowledged to be a defining moment in modern art. It marks the beginning of Cubism: 'I paint objects as I think them, not as I see them', Picasso once declared.[18] Critics have traced the seeds of this revolutionary new visual language to developments in European painting from the mid-nineteenth century. In particular, as Kern reminds us, it was the Impressionist artists, in leaving their studios to paint outdoors, who first began to explore the instability of the external world; but Cézanne, whose artistic innovations were driven by 'perpetual doubt', stands as the key figure in the transition from representational to abstract art.[19] According to the art critic, Herbert Read:

Cézanne's intention was to create an order of art corresponding to the order of nature, independent of his confused sensations. It gradually became obvious that such an order of art has a life and logic of its own – that the confused sensations of the artist might crystallize into their own lucid order. This was the liberation for which the artistic spirit of the world had been waiting.[20]

In his search for objectivity, Cézanne sought to see the world as an object, to discover the fundamental nature or structure of things as a means of transcending his own 'confused sensations'. As Read observes, Cézanne's art is critically about the discovery of structural order within the field of our visual sensations.[21] His work then was marked by both flux and order, representation and abstraction, the two tendencies held together in a creative dialectic. But despite the importance accorded to Cézanne as a precursor of the new abstract impulse distinctive of twentieth-century art, critics continue to mark off the Cubist moment as representing a decisive break with everything that had gone before.[22] As an explosion, it lasted barely a decade. If *Les Demoiselles d'Avignon* is conventionally taken as a symbol of its beginning, most commentators mark its end with the outbreak of war in 1914. So what was so radically new in Cubism?

Cubism involved a fundamental break with perspective, the central principle of European painting since the Renaissance. The eye was no longer situated at the centre of world; rather modern artists offered a series of multiple perspectives. Like Cézanne, the Cubists were driven by a desire for objectivity, their art anchored in a need to understand the world; and, as such, it became a rigorously conceptual, and not sensational, art. The visible world was reduced to simple forms, but these were not static, fixed entities. For abstract art constitutes a series of complex relationships or interactions – between form and space, surface and depth, abstraction and representation. Although there was a strong pull towards total abstraction in work of Cubist artists, there was an equally strong attraction to representational art. For example, the human figure and everyday objects remain a central element in Picasso's work, but they exist in a new and dynamic relationship.

John Berger interprets Cubism as the artistic counterpart of the transformations in scientific thinking.[23] He draws particular attention to the growing clarity of form, abstraction, and to the increased concern with structures, movement and machines. Specifically, Berger makes the *diagram* the emblematic form of modernity. He contrasts it with the other motifs which he takes to be expressive of European art's different phases.

The metaphorical model of Cubism is the *diagram*: the diagram being a visible, symbolic representation of invisible processes, forces, structures. A diagram need not eschew certain aspects of appearances; but these too will be treated symbolically as *signs*, not as imitations or re-creations. The model of the *diagram* differs from that of the *mirror* in that it suggests a concern with what is not self-evident. It differs from the model of the *theatre stage* in that it does not have to concentrate upon climaxes but can reveal the continuous. It differs from the model of the *personal account* in that it aims at a general truth.[24]

The conception of the diagram raises questions then not just about the relationship between the visible and the invisible, about fluidities of form and space; it also foregrounds the interactions between different signs, and between the subjective and objective. Although, as we will discover, Radcliffe-Brown, like the later abstract artists, turned the dynamic 'Cubism' of Rivers into a sterile intellectualism, there was nothing inherently static about the Cubist moment itself. Relationships are central to a diagrammatic conception of the world. As Berger reminds us, the Cubist painters were concerned with the interjacent, with processes rather than static states of being; their creative impulse was fuelled by a need to break up all conventional categories and oppositions.[25]

One of the key elements in Berger's analysis of the Cubist movement is his emphasis on the optimistic moment of its birth. The early dynamism of modern art is, for him, integrally linked to the sense of a new beginning which modernism, and its radical break with the past, seemed to promise. The first two decades of the twentieth century were years of expansion and experimentation; but the optimism was swiftly dashed as the appalling slaughter of the Great War brought modernism's brilliant beginning to a sudden and brutal end.

Certainly it can be argued that Rivers' most creative period coincided with Cubism's birth. He was born in 1864; and his career evolved through the period of change and innovation in scientific thought and method which paralleled developments in late nineteenth-century art, as symbolised by the work of Cézanne. However, Rivers' own intellectual breakthroughs in anthropology and psychology came later. His early modernist work, the kinship diagram, is contemporaneous with that of Picasso and Braque. The later modernism, which I identify with Rivers' investigation during the Great War into the operations of protopathic and epicritic elements of human personality, overlaps significantly with the cinematic innovations of Griffith, and later with those of Eisenstein and Vertov.

It is interesting to speculate that the visual innovation which Rivers' kinship diagram represents is a corollary of changes which followed the abandonment of the studio by the Impressionist painters. For perhaps, like their artistic counterparts, once anthropologists began to leave their Oxbridge colleges for the rigours of fieldwork, they recognised the need for new forms of visual representation which could evoke the complex social realities they now encountered. The early fieldwork ethnographers, people like Rivers, Haddon and the Torres Straits team, must have seen the world as radically different once they began to confront and investigate it at first hand, rather than through its reconstruction in the comfort of their studies. Specifically, it might be argued that this experience hastened the demise of the old perspectival visual mode by which nineteenth-century ethnology was metaphorically organised. Perspectival vision focuses everything upon the eye of the beholder; the human eye lies at the centre of the world. In an important sense, this motif found expression in the elaborate schema drawn up by the nineteenth-century anthropologists who divided and ranked humanity, with all its separate classes converging upon the notion of European civilization as the apex or focal point. But as several commentators have noted, with the Torres Straits expedition the rigidity of these classification schemata begin to break down, and ethnographers became increasingly concerned not with conjectural history but with the dynamics of contemporary societies.[26]

The modernism of Rivers' vision finds its most concrete expression in his kinship diagram. I suggest that we consider it as a form analogous with Cubist painting. For as a *diagram*, it shares with modern art an emphasis on flatness, pictorial depth or perspective is abandoned; it is made up of a multiplicity of perspectives or viewpoints; it draws attention to relationships or processes; it does not describe what can be seen, but rather it is an abstract representation which evokes the complexity of the visible.

Although Rivers' kinship diagram may be understood as tangible evidence of the modernist impulse of his work, there are other aspects of his intellectual project which are important in identifying the particular way of seeing animating his anthropological enquiry. I have already noted that he shared with his artistic and scientific contemporaries a profound concern with vision. Like Cézanne, Rivers' project can be described as one driven by perpetual doubt. Specifically he was concerned with the interplay between the subjective and objective, sensation and thought or judgement, vision and abstraction. If Rivers' early work connects him to the Cubist artists at the turn of the century, I believe that his later work overlaps in significant ways with the cinematic experiments associated with Griffith, Eisenstein and Vertov.

The question of vision lies at the centre of Langham's particular reading of Rivers.[27] He contends that his fascination with it stemmed from an awareness of his own inability to visualize, to see images in his mind's eye. Rivers could remember that as a child he had the capacity to visualize, and occasionally as an adult he was reminded of this hidden aspect of his personality through dreaming; but, in developing what he believed to be the rational 'civilized' part of his personality, the 'primitive' or protopathic was gradually suppressed beneath objective or rational cognitive processes. The process by which reason curbed the subjective 'totalising' tendencies of the protopathic became an important focus within Rivers' work, at first as a study of nerve regeneration and later as crucial to his treatment of patients suffering from 'shell shock' during the First World War. It also, according to Langham, underlay the development of the genealogical method in Rivers' anthropological work. For here, too, Rivers was engaged in understanding an analogous relationship between visible phenomena and abstract representation. It was symbolised in the two-stage process of genealogical investigation.

Langham understands Rivers' own personality as having two dimensions: the protopathic associated with the concrete, with emotion, subjectivity and vision; and the epicritic expressed through abstraction, objectivity and rationality. He argues that the hierarchical relationship between them was modified in the course of his life. The first phase of Rivers' intellectual work was driven by a desire for objectivity; and yet integral to this scientific work was the recognition of subjective intrusion. The problem then for Rivers was how to ground or suppress the subjective in the objective. Thus Langham describes Rivers' early career as 'conservative', since it was distinguished by the strong desire to suppress the subjective aspects of his personality ('the dog beneath the skin'), in favour of the pursuit of objective, scientific knowledge. Later, he contends that Rivers became less concerned with curbing the subjective dimensions of his personality. Instead he began to explore it actively in the context of his treatment of patients traumatised by trench warfare, who had been sent home from the battlefield suffering from 'shell shock'

Martin Jay writes:

The Western front's interminable trench warfare . . . created a bewildering landscape of indistinguishable, shadowy shapes, illuminated by lightning flashes of blinding intensity, and then obscured by phantasmagoric, often gas-induced haze. The effect was even more visually disorienting than those produced by such nineteenth century technical innovations as the railroad, the camera or the cinema. When all that the soldier could see was the sky above and the mud below, the traditional reliance on visual evidence for survival could no longer be easily maintained.[28]

The First World War battlefield was the graveyard of the eye. Confidence in sight as the noblest of the senses and a privileged source of knowledge about the world was finally destroyed. For Rivers, the problem of vision was posed in new ways by the war. It was central to his approach in seeking to alleviate the condition of the deeply disturbed patients he encountered as a doctor at Craiglockhart hospital. One of most striking manifestations of shell shock was the intense visual symptoms of the condition. Rivers' patients were haunted by vision in the form of nightmares, memories and hallucinations. The protopathic had re-emerged as a powerful, uncontrolled, and totalising force which swept over their normal cognitive processes.

The work which Rivers carried out at Craiglockhart was a development of research begun at the turn of the century in the famous Rivers-Head experiment. In 1903 Rivers had performed an experiment on his friend and collaborator, Henry Head, in his rooms at St John's College, Cambridge. It involved the severing of the nerves in Head's upper arm; and over a period of five years they studied the process of nerve regeneration, the recovery of feeling and sensation. This was characterised by a twofold process. First the protopathic faculty was restored. The associated feeling and association had a primitive, totalising quality.

Later the epicritic faculty, characterised as rational, discriminating judgement, returned. Rivers' war work led him to understand anew the relationship between these two dimensions of personality. Normal sensibility involved not the replacement of the protopathic by the epicritic, but a partial suppression of the former and an integration of the two levels.

Rivers' investigation of the question of vision in the context of the war was distinguished by a unusual degree of personal reflexivity. In his late writing, *Instinct and the Unconscious* (1920) and *Conflict and Dream* (1923), he studied the workings of the unconscious through reflection not just upon the symptoms of his patients but upon his own experiences too. The concerns which mark what I call Rivers' late modernism are a continuation of his earlier experiments encapsulated in the kinship diagram. For again he was seeking to explore the relationship between image and abstraction, the subjective and objective, inside and outside understood in complex and dynamic ways rather than as the opposition of simple bounded categories. The First World War, and Rivers' own particular location within it, brought about an important transformation in his thinking. The two scientific projects which Rivers had pursued separately, anthropology and psychology, he now recognised as the indispensable parts of a single concern with the nature of the human condition.

I suggest that Rivers' attempt at the end of his life to bring into a creative relationship these different aspects of a single enquiry was matched by the work in cinema being pursued by his contemporary, D.W. Griffith. Griffith's mature films – *The Birth of a Nation* (1915), *Intolerance* (1916) and *Broken Blossoms* (1919) – were produced in the same period of Rivers' late writings. Moreover, Griffith was using the camera to probe into the same spaces as Rivers. His development of a distinctive cinematic language built upon close-up and panoramic shots, a mobile camera and montage may be interpreted as the expression of the world in which he lived.[29] That world was one of war and revolution in which all established structures were breaking down, posing anew questions of subject, society and history. Although Griffith, like Rivers, recognised that the old categories were no longer adequate, his modernist project was also never fully realised.

The modernist vision was perhaps most fully realised in Dziga Vertov's film, *A Man With A Movie Camera* (1929). Here, in the aftermath of the Russian revolution and before the brutal supression of its creative spirit by Stalin, Vertov linked a new way of seeing with the possibilities of a new society. I like to imagine *A Man With A Movie Camera* as the cinematic expression of Rivers' project. It embraces the

movement and complexity of modern society, offering no single, privileged vantage point upon fluid contemporary realities, only a series of
overlapping perspectives, shifting view-points in which seeing involves a
discovery of the self as inseparable from the discovery of the world. The
camera eye searches, questions and interrogates. It is both human and
mechanical, at once an observer and a participant. Vertov's vision is
profoundly subversive of the conventional ways of seeing and knowing
the world.

Rivers died suddenly and unexpectedly in 1922. His death occurred
in the same year as the publication of Malinowski's classic monograph,
Argonauts of the Western Pacific. This text established a new and different
kind of anthropological project to the one pioneered by Rivers. The
contrast between these two key figures in anthropology's early modern
phase is expressed most sharply in the distinctive ways of seeing, in the
modes of anthropological visuality, which animate their work. Rivers
and Malinowski operated with very different notions of vision at the
level of both method and metaphysic. Although the Malinowskian way
of seeing quickly established itself as dominant in the emergent project,
Rivers' modernist spirit was never completely extinguished; it continued
most noticeably in the work of Gregory Bateson.[30] Following the recent
collapse of scientific ethnography, however, a new experimental phase
has emerged. Today I find it impossible to respond to work produced by
Michael Taussig, George Marcus or Michael Jackson without thinking
of W.H.R. Rivers.

3   The innocent eye: Flaherty, Malinowski and the romantic quest

Seeing comes before words. The child looks and recognises before it can speak. But there is another sense in which seeing comes before words. It is seeing which establishes our place in the surrounding world; we explain that world with words, but words can never undo the fact that we are surrounded by it. The relation between what we see and what we know is never settled.

John Berger, *Ways of Seeing*

The First World War brought to an end the period of remarkable creativity in modern painting, particularly in Cubism. The ghastly horror of trench warfare and the sheer scale of human destruction shattered for ever Europe's optimism and belief in inexorable progress. Rivers, as a doctor responsible for treating severely traumatised soldiers sent home from the battlefield, found himself at the very centre of the crisis precipitated by the war. This experience is widely acknowledged to have brought about a transformation in his own personality.[1] Malinowski, however, was marooned on a Pacific island for many of the war years. He was engaged in the fieldwork which formed the basis for the principles of scientific ethnography he subsequently laid out in his 'Introduction' to *Argonauts of the Western Pacific* (1922). The sharply contrasting relationship of Rivers and Malinowski to the Great War is important in understanding the different ways of seeing which characterise their anthropological projects. Both men were profoundly affected by the collapse of European civilization. In the case of Rivers, it stimulated an attempt to synthesise the separate branches of his scientific project, anthropology and psychology, in order to locate complex subjectivity within society and history. Malinowski, however, sought to put the shattered pieces back together again in a different way, rediscovering humanity among those peoples previously denied it by European intellectuals. Here he found wholeness and integration within the timeless present of 'primitive society'.

Like Rivers' project, vision is also central to the kind of anthropology which Malinowski endeavoured to develop. It is manifest in the intensely visual quality of Malinowski's prose. But it is a vision which sharply contrasts with the fragmented, multiperspectival, and above all *anxious* one of early anthropological modernism. It is built upon *innocence*, upon the cultivation of the ethnographer's innocent eye. For the Malinowskian project was, at its core, a *romantic* one. The fieldworker became a visionary, a *seer*.[2]

Malinowski is the second, critical figure in our attempt to 'visualize anthropology'. There is a curious paradox, however, in his contribution to the development of the professional discipline. Although Malinowski laid down the principles of a new kind of academic practice, scientific ethnography, as a systematic process of social enquiry, his own method was entirely idiosyncratic. I think that it is important to consider this not just an expression of his own irrepressible personality nor as a deliberate attempt to mislead, but as integrally related to, or a significant expression of, the kind of vision with which he operated. For the Malinowskian vision is built around the notion of anthropological understanding as an intuitive and uniquely personal moment of insight. Indeed it might best be described as one which involves *revelation*, or the transformation of commonplace understandings. The fieldworker has to learn to 'see', to penetrate beneath the surface appearance of things. Despite the subsequent overlaying of more formal and abstract conceptions of ethnographic knowledge associated with what I call Radcliffe-Brown's *enlightenment* project, the cultivation of a Malinowskian 'innocent eye' continues to underlie much contemporary fieldwork practice.[3]

Malinowski was, of course, pre-eminently a writer. His literary aspirations became important in establishing twentieth-century anthropology as a distinctive kind of textual activity. Malinowski's demand for recognition as an author is, of course, famously captured in his declaration: 'Rivers is the Rider Haggard of anthropology; I shall be its Conrad'.[4] But perhaps of all the classic ethnographers, Malinowski was also the most *painterly*. By this I refer to the strikingly *visual* quality of his texts. Readers of *Argonauts of the Western Pacific*, above all, *see* the world of the Trobriand islanders; and what they see in their mind's eye are vivid, concrete details, images of native life, rather than its abstract representation. The visual intensity of Malinowski's descriptive writing has prompted much critical comment following the recent literary turn in anthropology.[5] This feature is, I believe, one of the manifestations of the particular way of seeing which animates his method and his conception of anthropological knowledge.

My approach in seeking to expose the distinctive features of Malinowski's way of seeing, in particular the centrality of innocence, is built upon the juxtaposition of his classic work with the cinematic project pursued by his contemporary, Robert Flaherty. Such a juxtaposition opens up a field of tantalising possibilities, for the links between their projects in anthropology and cinema seem to be both manifest and obscure at the same time. Certainly the two men are forever linked by the historical coincidence of their work. In 1922, Flaherty released his film, *Nanook of the North,* and during the same year Malinowski published *Argonauts of the Western Pacific.* Moreover, each was subsequently hailed as the founder of a new genre – on the one hand, documentary cinema, and, on the other, scientific ethnography. Now, of course, both men having enjoyed almost mythical status within their respective schools, they share the contemporary fate of fallen heroes. This closeness, and yet the absence of any tangible historical evidence linking Flaherty to Malinowski, has been a source of considerable frustration among visual anthropologists. The paradox can, however, be explained. Following Clifford (1988), we can recognise that Flaherty represented everything which Malinowski, as the new scientist of society, set himself against. He was an explorer, an amateur whose immersion and long-term engagement with Inuit society rivalled the scientific method being pioneered by the new ethnographers.[6]

It is now widely acknowledged that Malinowski and Flaherty were exploring the same terrain, using remarkably similar approaches and techniques, and producing richly textured ethnographies.[7] My concern, however, is to examine the distinctive vision which animated their work. It was one they shared. Both Malinowski and Flaherty are figures who provoke intense critical attention. Much recent commentary has interrogated the key humanist assumptions underpinning their work and exposed the serious discrepancies between certain claims to knowledge and actual practice.[8] My purpose in looking closely at a number of distinctive techniques which characterise the work of Flaherty and Malinowski is somewhat different. I want to identify the romantic impulse which animates their engagement with the world. Hence, in seeking to investigate the contours of this vision, I will be concerned with the ideal qualities of their particular projects rather than with the problematic status of the claims for documentary cinema and scientific ethnography.

'The first time you met Flaherty, and indeed on all other occasions, you noticed, before anything else, his eyes. They were a limpid, brilliant blue, lying like lakes in the broad and rugged landscape of his face', writes one biographer, Paul Rotha.[9] Another commentator on Flaherty's work, Arthur Calder-Marshall, drew attention to what he judged to be the particular quality of his vision, publishing his biography under the title *The Innocent Eye* (1963). Certainly many film critics have noted

Flaherty's reluctance to embrace the era of sound, resolutely remaining a silent film-maker in the face of technological development and the rise of the 'talkies'. Such observations about the work of Flaherty indicate some of the important features we must consider in any examination of his cinematic vision. For Flaherty's project was, above all, about vision. But he was seeking to recuperate it, to cleanse and purify it, to make it whole and universal again. His cinematic project is marked by its humanist impulse. It finds expression in the way of seeing which he cultivated as a means for transcending the corruption and decay of European civilization. The eye which had seen everything had to be made innocent again.[10]

Flaherty's cinematic project developed in the aftermath of the Great War. This context is, I believe, critical in understanding the conception of vision which underlay the films he made over the course of three decades. His first film, *Nanook of the North* (1922), is the most celebrated. It established Flaherty's reputation as a film-maker committed to a different kind of cinematic project from the one emerging in Hollywood.

Although *Nanook* became the prototype for all of Flaherty's subsequent work, it was his second film, *Moana* (1926), which acquired the descriptive term 'documentary'. In a review of *Moana*, 'being a visual account of events in the daily life of a Polynesian youth and his family', John Grierson wrote of the film's 'documentary value'.[11] Grierson's use of the term 'documentary' to characterise Flaherty's film-making approach is conventionally understood to mark the emergence of the distinctive cinema in which both Flaherty and Grierson were critical figures.[12] The new documentary film-makers drew inspiration from the early cinema of Lumière. The camera was taken out into society. It was used to film people within the context of their everyday lives.

Flaherty's engagement with the Canadian Arctic began many years before he made *Nanook of the North*, the film which launched his career. His early expeditions into the area were as an explorer and mining prospector, and he lived for long periods of time with Inuit communities. This first-hand experience of native life became the foundation of his particular documentary approach. Explaining his intentions as a film-maker, Flaherty once said: 'I wanted to show them [the Inuit] not from the civilized point of view, but as they saw themselves, as 'we, the people'. I realized then that I must go to work in an entirely different way.'[13] Reading this statement by Flaherty must evoke in every anthropologist's mind the famous declaration at the beginning of Malinowski's *Argonauts of the Western Pacific*: 'the final goal, of which an Ethnographer should never lose sight . . . is, briefly, to grasp the native's point of view, his relation to life, to realise *his* vision of *his* world.'[14]

Today such sweeping declarations make uncomfortable reading for anyone pursuing ethnographic enquiry; what I want to draw attention to here is Flaherty's acknowledgement of the need to work in new ways as the basis of a different kind of cinema. We may interpret Flaherty's break with established practice as analogous to the Impressionist painters who left their studios for the outdoors or Haddon with his team of Torres Straits fieldworkers, since he recognised that serious engagement with a new subject matter necessitated a revolution in method and technique. In making native peoples the focus of his cinematic project, Flaherty sought to understand the world of his subjects through his own direct experience of it. He lived with those whose humanity he sought to express on screen. All of his major works, but especially *Nanook of the North*, were the result of an intense, long-term engagement with people and the landscape in which they lived. This way of working, a filmmaking approach akin to ethnographic fieldwork, sharply distinguishes Flaherty from his contemporaries, not least from cinema's pioneer D.W. Griffith, whose remarkable formal innovations were achieved entirely within the static world of the Hollywood studio. There is, however, an interesting paradox. For Griffith learned to *move* his camera in the static world of the studio, while Flaherty held his camera *still* in the flux of social life.[15]

A number of issues are immediately raised by Flaherty's distinctive approach as a film-maker. First of all, he made his own *experience* of Inuit life as critical a part of his understanding as his observation of it. By experience he had in mind something quite specific. It involved the surrendering of conventional norms and expectations such that one was exposed to the world in an entirely new way. The white explorer was to render himself vulnerable and dependent upon the humanity of the people with whom he lived. Flaherty once described this process:

In so many travelogs the film-maker looks down on and never up to his subject. He is always the big man from New York or from London. But I had been dependent on these people, alone with them for months at a time, traveling with them and living with them. They had warmed my feet when they were cold, lit my cigarette when my hands were too numb to do it myself; they had taken care of me on three or four different expeditions over a period of ten years. My work had been built up along with them; I couldn't have done anything without them. In the end it is all a question of human relationships.[16]

I find this statement of Flaherty's fascinating. It perfectly expresses the necessary process of personal transformation which is the precondition for the new kind of ethnographic understanding he seeks to place at the heart of his documentary cinema. The film-maker must not be just separated from his familiar world and relationships; he must, in addition, be prepared to submit himself to the experiences of disorientation, vulnerability and ignorance.

Flaherty's conception of experiential knowledge is achieved through the return to a state similar to that of childhood and the innocence of childhood. In this way the film-maker learns to 'see' again. Again Flaherty's own comments on his earlier attempts to capture Inuit life on film are I think interesting. Of the footage destroyed by fire in 1916, he said: 'It was a bad film; it was dull – it was little more than a travelogue. I had learned to *explore*, I had not learned to *reveal*.'[17] This distinction between exploration and revelation is, I believe, central to understanding Flaherty's cinematic project. It lies, too, at the core of the Malinowskian model of ethnographic fieldwork.

It has become commonplace to refer to the 'simplicity' of Flaherty's cinema, to the absence of sound or creative use of sound, the under-developed narrative structure of the films and the 'primitive' editing built around continuity rather than radical juxtaposition. It was as if Flaherty was using one of the most advanced technological instruments of his day in service of an older art form. Unlike his contemporaries, such as Griffith or more especially the Russian film-makers like Eisenstein or Vertov, Flaherty did not exploit the 'magical' qualities of the camera; rather he sought to humanise it such that, as Rotha notes, 'the lens was an extension of eye and arm; when he moved the camera it followed precisely his own vision'.[18]

Each one of Flaherty's films is distinguished by its texture, its depth or layering, rather than by its movement. The details of everyday life are the basis of construction. There is a remarkable intimacy and intensity in the individual observations but, always, the details are anchored in an exploration of context: 'The camera cannot see everything at once but it makes sure not to lose any part of what it chooses to see.'[19] From these foundations, Flaherty builds a series of tableaux to evoke a whole, integrated and, fundamentally, humanistic world in which 'the dramatic power . . . is lodged in static representations rather than in any sequenced relationship of events.'[20] The effect for the viewer is like watching a series of still photographs in which people and objects are placed within a landscape, and relationships within the frame are foregrounded over those stretching beyond it. In his much cited essay, the film critic André Bazin draws attention to the fundamentally differ-ent visions of the world which are implied in the techniques distin-guishing the cinema of Flaherty from that of Eisenstein and Vertov. The former kind of cinema is built upon a respect for the integrity of reality. This does not involve a process of simplification, a mirroring of surfaces; rather it involves the opposite. It reveals the complexity and ambiguity of reality. By rejecting the technique of montage, Flaherty (and other film-makers such as Bresson) preserves what Bazin calls 'the spatial unity of an event', enabling 'everything to be said without chopping the world into little fragments'.[21]

At the centre of Flaherty's own film-making practice was the idea of 'non-preconception'. It involved a rejection of any self-consciously imposed form upon what was observed. Instead the shape of characters and events, and the rhythm of the film, were expected to emerge from the material itself.[22] The origins of these techniques, Rotha claims, lay in Flaherty's adaptation of a particular Inuit aesthetic; but I suggest that it may be understood more generally as an expression of the romantic impulse of his project. For Flaherty's particular visual techniques cannot be understood without reference to his particular vision of the world. The elevation of individual sensibility as a critical element in his cinematic method also, I believe, lies behind Flaherty's lifelong refusal to adapt his style to changing technologies. The refusal to burden himself with technology is inseparable from his commitment to first-hand experience as the basis for knowledge. He was committed to ensuring that the film-maker was exposed to his subjects as completely as possible. The sophisticated apparatus of cinema, specifically the camera as a machine, potentially stood in the way of the cultivation of this essential bodily and spiritual vulnerability which made possible moments of revelatory understanding.

Fatimah Rony, a recent critic of Flaherty's cinema, describes it as 'taxidermic'.[23] It brings the dead to life; and as such I am reminded again of Berger's differentiation between photography and cinema. The former exercises a pull toward the past, while the latter propels forward.[24] For in seeking to recuperate humanity, Flaherty is forced to deny history and agency to his ethnographic subjects. Hence, as Rothman notes, Flaherty's use of the camera in *Nanook* contains both an acknowledgement and a repudiation of a shared humanity.[25] Flaherty cannot resolve the contradictions established by his own presence in the pre-industrial worlds he seeks to evoke through his films. Following Berger we can recognise that his profoundly nostalgic vision is built upon a diminishment rather than an interpretation of reality.[26]

The romanticism of Flaherty's project involved a turning away from the world which had produced cinema. The latter was industrial, urban, machine-driven, imperialist, complex, colliding and chaotic. Flaherty was trying to recover something which was whole and integrated, what Rony calls 'a more authentic humanity', among peoples previously denied such humanity by European discourse.[27] His cinema was, in essence, visionary. It involved a process of transformation in film-maker, subject and audience alike; and through it Flaherty sought to transcend the divisions and corruption of the world in which he lived. He used the site of cinema, a liminal place situated outside conventional time and space, to evoke a particular experience. His films make an appeal not to rational intellect but to sensibility and emotion. We may interpret Flaherty's distinctive visual techniques as working to engage his audience *empathetically*, enabling it to find its own place within the world of the film and experience the sense of 'being there'. In surrendering him or herself to this experience, the viewer moves beyond the barriers of language or culture to grasp a new universal humanism.

Flaherty's films are characterised by their visual detail, the camera's fascination with people engaged in the material processes of everyday life. There is a subtle interplay between the camera's focus and its range, the intimate shots of individual characters (their faces often filling the screen) and a broader landscape. Flaherty seeks to render not just a cinematic sense of the space his protagonists inhabit, but also the distinctive temporal quality of their lives. Hence his tendency is toward extended individual shots that are then assembled such that they simulate whole, continuous action. Flaherty's work is based upon a repudiation of montage as the method by which the new whole is assembled from fragments. Unlike Eisenstein, who drew attention to the process of cutting, celebrating the juxtaposition of shots and jolting his audience, Flaherty draws his viewers into an experience of social reality which unfolds in front of the camera, rather than being reconstructed through editing.[28]

The kind of light which infuses Flaherty's project I imagine as an interior one, nurtured from the inside, so to speak. Hence it is not about illumination, a fierce, penetrating beam which dispels an area of darkness as I characterise the enlightenment project (the light of reason). Flaherty's conception of documentary cinema is built upon the idea of revelatory knowledge in which subjective transformation is inseparable from, and the precondition for, knowing the world differently. The new humanist understanding which Flaherty seeks to evoke through his romantic cinema is dependent upon the recovery of vision. We learn to see again.[29]

Malinowski's project for modern anthropology was, I believe, built upon a vision remarkably similar to the one which animates the cinema of Flaherty. Although Malinowski liked to credit himself as the pioneer of a new fieldwork-based ethnography, we now recognise that his contribution to the modern discipline is more accurately described as a continuation of, rather than a radical departure from, practices already established in early twentieth-century anthropology. In another sense, however, the role Malinowski accorded to vision as a fieldwork technique suggests a distinctive conception of anthropological knowledge. It contrasts sharply with the way of seeing I associate with W.H.R. Rivers. Again it was not perhaps new. I interpret it as involving a looking backwards, connecting 'modern' anthropology to an older tradition of romanticism rather than harnessing it to the modernist energies of the time. Malinowskian anthropology was founded upon a return to experience rather than on the development of ever-more sophisticated skills or scientific technology for the collection of fieldwork data. Indeed, like Flaherty's documentary cinema, scientific ethnography was built upon a profound rejection of the apparatus and ethos of industrial civilization. Vision was central to Malinowski's notion of ethnographic enquiry; but, in elevating it to a new importance as a source of knowledge about the world, he sought, like Flaherty, to recuperate sight and to restore the eye to its original state of innocence.

I noted earlier that the new kinds of ethnographic practice emerging after the 1898 Torres Straits expedition were built upon an explicit rejection of reported speech or 'hearsay'. Throughout the nineteenth century there had been growing unease among anthropologists about the status of the data supplied to them from the field by missionaries and travellers. The development of the camera, contrary to much opinion, did not solve this problem. The new technology merely generated a different kind of data – visible evidence. Scientists continued to worry about the objective status of data and, increasingly, to worry about the status of vision itself.[30] Haddon and his Torres Straits team shared the preoccupations of their scientific colleagues. Having been trained as natural scientists, their investigations of a new subject matter, humanity, betray all the concerns about method and evidence which distinguished their earlier scientific research.[31] Haddon's rejection of second-hand reportage resulted in one of the first fieldwork expeditions, establishing the practice that anthropologists had literally to go into society and see for themselves. Moreover, integral to the scientific enquiry carried out in the Torres Straits islands was an investigation of vision itself. Vision as a question of epistemology, technique and presentation was central to the Torres Straits work; but, like their intellectual counterparts, the Cambridge scientists remained cautious about equating vision with knowledge, the visible with objective data.[32]

The anxiety about vision and its status which was integral to the birth of modern anthropology as a fieldwork-based enquiry disappeared in the wake of the Malinowskian revolution. The latter, while being constructed upon the methodological foundations laid by Haddon and

Rivers, implies a different way of seeing. Malinowski's project for modern anthropology is, I suggest, essentially visionary; and the particular fieldwork techniques with which it is associated must be understood in this context.

If Malinowski's claim to be the revolutionary hero of modern anthropology no longer forms the unquestioned foundation of the discipline's intellectual history, it is nevertheless important to acknowledge the distinctive innovations he made to ethnographic enquiry. Most significant is, of course, the insistence on an intensive fieldwork model as the methodological basis of the new anthropology. A single researcher was now expected to became engaged in the long-term study of an unfamiliar society. In advocating such practice, Malinowski broke decisively with the extensive, teamwork model of early twentieth-century anthropology, in which a group of researchers combined different skills and interests to survey a wide socio-geographical area. This shift from an extensive ethnographic approach to an intensive one emphasised the fieldworker's participation in, and observation of, everyday social life. These two aspects, participation and observation, became inseparable parts of the new ethnographic approach. In characterising Malinowskian anthropology as visionary or romantic, I want to draw attention to this central role accorded to *experiential* knowledge. Ethnographic understanding emerges from experience, bodily and sensory, as much as from observation and intellectual reflection.

The question of vision is posed in a specific way within such a model. The Malinowskian ethnographer, unlike his predecessors, is expected to leave the verandah, to go out into society and *see* for himself or herself; but, given the circumstances in which such an ethnographer works, cut off from the familiar world, alone and immersed within a strange society, this fieldwork strategy implies something else. For it is not just about observing the world around oneself. It is involves learning to 'see' in a visionary sense. For the radical disruption of context makes possible certain experiences which may transform the fieldworker from a mere enquirer or observer into a 'seer'.[33] The disorientation and confusion that the fieldworker confronts may be harnessed creatively, enabling him or her to grasp with a new clarity the world rendered unfamiliar and unknown. I interpret Geertz's characterisation of the literary style which is associated with a Malinowskian approach in this light. He describes it as being based upon convincing the reader that one has 'actually penetrated (or . . . been penetrated by) another form of life, of having, one way or another, truly "been there"'. In this way Geertz draws attention to the unusual quality of a certain kind of ethnography in which the subjective element is an integral part of the world being described. The visionary quality of the fieldwork experience is conveyed within the writing itself.[34]

Malinowski, perhaps more than any of the classic ethnographers, realised most concretely the sense of having 'been there' in his writing. At the same time, the model of fieldwork which made this experience possible involved a shedding of all the technical encumbrances which distinguished the earlier team-based ethnographic research. The Malinowskian ethnographer was 'the lone ranger with a notebook'.[35] As I have noted before, it has always seemed puzzling to contemporary anthropologists why the active use of visual media disappeared so quickly from the twentieth-century project despite its presence at the birth of the new fieldwork-oriented practice. Moreover, as a number of commentators have noted, Malinowski himself took many photographs whilst in the field.[36] I suggest, however, that it is the particular way of seeing animating the Malinowskian project which renders the camera, and other scientific instrumentation, obsolete.

The image of the new fieldworker that Christopher Pinney suggests is a compelling one. It is his contention that the camera disappeared from the modern anthropological project at the very moment when the ethnographer's experience began to simulate the photographic process itself:

The anthropologists' exposure to data . . . occurred during a period of inversion from his normal reality, a stage which is formally analogous to the production of the photographic negative when the all-important rays of light which guarantee the indexical truth of the image are allowed to fall on the negative's emulsion.[37]

But, in another sense, the experience of the new fieldworker was radically different from the photographic process. Its foundations lay in romanticism. It depended upon the cultivation of human sensibility or passion. By necessity such an approach involved the repudiation of technology, mechanical skill and the trappings of industrial civilization.

Malinowski's inconsistencies as a fieldworker have now been fully exposed to view, but it is misplaced to judge him by the standards of men like Rivers or Boas. For, like Flaherty, his notion of ethnographic understanding was an essentially mystical one. Although he sought to establish the systematic principles of modern fieldwork, he shared with Flaherty the frustrating habit of blurring the distinction between what he said he did and what he actually did. But these idiosyncracies must be interpreted as an expression of the visionary impulse of his work. The process of ethnographic understanding was secret, personal and embodied. Malinowski's approach was predicated on the distinction between *exploration* and *revelation* which I identified as central to Flaherty's project for documentary cinema.[38] For, like the film-maker, the Malinowskian ethnographer was expected to be alone in the field. She or he must be exposed and vulnerable, returned to a prelinguistic state akin to that of childhood, as the necessary precondition for being able to break through to a different level of understanding.

The romantic or visionary nature of Malinowski's project finds expression, I believe, in the distinctive quality of his texts. As I noted earlier, the reader, above all, 'sees' in their mind's eye the world of the Trobriand islanders. Geertz describes Malinowski's style as 'I-witnessing':

> One grasps the exotic not by drawing back from the immediacies of encounter into the symmetries of thought, as with Levi-Strauss, not by transforming them into figures on an African urn, as with Evans-Pritchard. One grasps it by losing oneself, one's soul maybe, in those immediacies. 'Out of such plunges into the life of the natives . . . I have carried away a distinct feeling that . . . their manner of being became more transparent and easily understandable than it had been before' (Malinowski 1922 21–22).[39]

We may recognise here Malinowski's sense of fieldwork as a sort of initiation. For after establishing the conventional processes of data collection, what one might call, following Flaherty, *exploration*; he then exhorts the fieldworker to put aside his or her notebook and participate in the social life around them. Participation (or 'plunges' into native life) opens up different kinds of ethnographic understanding. Society is *revealed* to the ethnographer in new ways; and this experience, of seeing as if for the first time, disrupts the conventional separations of self and other, the subjective and the objective, the particular and the universal.

If Flaherty created a special place within the cinema for the emergence of a new kind of humanist understanding, Malinowski was instrumental in devising an analogous literary form, the monograph. This also works to separate commonplace or everyday experiences from the deeper levels of meaning embedded in the text. Unlike Frazer, Malinowski and his successors wrote for a specialized audience, anthropologists who themselves had undergone the ritual process of fieldwork. The writing itself thus implies a distinction between exploration and revelation. Hence Malinowski's texts, like Flaherty's films, are deceptive. They are seemingly open but are, in fact, also closed. Their secrets are available only to other initiates, to those willing to engage empathetically with the world described in the text. Moreover the worlds evoked in Flaherty's cinema and Malinowski's monographs appear to have been 'found' rather than made. For the Malinowskian ethnographers share with Flaherty the paradox of presenting ideas as if they emerge from life.[40]

I have already indicated that I believe Malinowski to be essentially painterly in his depiction of the world. His monographs are unusually visual, drawing on the techniques of the artist to create a rich, textured picture of native society. It is one which he constructs from what he sees, from the details of everyday life and activity around him, from the intense observations of the strange world in which he has been set down. I suggest that we consider Malinowski's style as painterly, rather than cinematic, because of the distinctive texture or layering which characterises his descriptive prose. The vision of Trobriand society presented in his monographs consists of a series of tableaux or scenes, their relationship to one another largely generated through his own restless movement across the canvas as an ethnographer of native life. The new functionalist approach which Malinowski developed emphasises context and the relationships which may be explored within a certain designated field or frame. This kind of ethnography, expressed through the classic monograph, evokes Flaherty's approach to Inuit society as its cinematic counterpart. For both forms of representation celebrate the wholeness or integrity of native life existing within an artificially demarcated space. The vision which animates the work of Malinowski and Flaherty involves a repudiation of montage, the formal expression of the movement, complexity and contradiction of the twentieth-century world. Marcus's identification of key features associated with montage (for example, de-territorialisation and the existence of simultaneous realities) have no place within the simple, non-industrial worlds recuperated by an eye that can see again.[41] In isolating these worlds from time and history, both Malinowski and Flaherty, like the painter according to John Berger, gather up native life and deliver it the reader/viewer: 'painting brings home. The cinema transports elsewhere.'[42] This analogy with painting may, however, be pursued further in relation to their projects of scientific ethnography and documentary cinema. Flaherty's development of a particular film aesthetic built around texture rather than movement, experience rather than analysis (mirrored by the literary style of the Malinowskian monograph), may be understood as an attempt to hold on to the idea of an aura surrounding the original work of art.

The German critic, Walter Benjamin, argued in his famous essay of 1936 that the mechanical reproduction of images destroys the special power or aura which was attached to original works of art.[43] Hitherto the special mystery of art was mediated by specialists who alone had travelled to the site of the painting for contemplation. After the invention of the camera, however, the images travelled to the spectator. Torn from context and endlessly reproduced, the particular power of the original artwork was destroyed by the technologies of industrial civilization. Both Flaherty and Malinowski seek, I suggest, to recreate through their work something akin to the aura of the original work of art. Hence we confront the irony contained in their use of modern forms to recover something archaic.

4 The light of reason: John Grierson, Radcliffe-Brown and the enlightenment project

The final part of my attempt to 'visualize' anthropology in the period of its early twentieth-century development addresses the question of an enlightenment way of seeing. For scientific ethnography has at its centre a distinctive vision of the world. It is one, I will suggest, that finds its counterpart in the documentary cinema of the interwar years. I propose to examine the features of this enlightenment vision through a consideration of the work of John Grierson and Radcliffe-Brown. Juxtaposing two key figures in this way extends the range of symbolic connections which I have already pursued in relation to anthropology and cinema using the examples of Lumière and Haddon, Griffith and Rivers, and Flaherty and Malinowski.

At the outset I must confess that although I recognise both Radcliffe-Brown and John Grierson to be central figures in the creation of new forms, neither quite stimulates my imagination in the manner of their predecessors. Perhaps my own intellectual training under Edmund Leach presents a fundamental obstacle in appreciating the paradigm of scientific ethnography at the heart of Radcliffe-Brownian anthropology, or 'butterfly collecting' as Leach once famously described it.[1] I recognise that one of the problems in trying to respond creatively to the interwar documentary film-makers and anthropologists is that their work is about consolidation rather than innovation. This, by its very nature, limits its experimental scope and range of imaginative possibilities.

Radcliffe-Brown and Grierson were driven by their desire to secure a professional identity for their new project of social enquiry. Hence there was a concern to articulate principles of practice, to lay down rules and to demarcate a specialist arena of operation which excluded others whose work covered similar ground or made certain truth claims about their relationship with the 'real'.[2] Such distinctions (for example between knowledge and belief, exploration and revelation, amateur and professional) may be discerned in the projects of Flaherty and Malinowski; but, as I have suggested, the romantic impulse of their cinema and anthropology works against the clarification of concepts. Indeed, it involves a deliberate blurring of boundaries, the subversion of discriminatory or dualistic ways of knowing the world.

The case with Grierson and Radcliffe-Brown is different – and not just by virtue of their particular personalities and interests. For central to my interrogation of the vision which underpins their work is an awareness of the social, political and intellectual conditions shaping it. The world in which these two men operated was markedly different from that in which the earlier, more expansive phases of anthropology and cinema emerged. By the late 1920s, the revolutionary moment in art, science, politics and intellectual life had been effectively extinguished. The open, experimental context in which Malinowski, Rivers and Vertov flourished had given way to an era of intensified state power and nationalism as another war approached. The features which emerged to be defining principles of scientific ethnography and documentary cinema cannot be understood apart from these historical currents. They profoundly influenced the evolution of these new forms, establishing at the same time a difficult legacy, one marked by suggestions of political compromise or political collusion which few contemporary anthropologists and film-makers can ignore.

The enlightenment vision of the world which animates the interwar work of Radcliffe-Brown and Grierson is distinguished by an emphasis upon order, integration, rationalism and knowledge. It involves *illumination*, rather than *revelation*. Such a way of seeing has at its centre the belief that the world is ultimately knowable, that it may be rendered transparent through the exercise of 'the clear light of reason'. Vision is a key strategy by which the world is investigated and ultimately controlled. Hence there is a concern with the perfection of techniques of observation. These techniques are predicated upon the Cartesian dualism which lies at the centre of an enlightenment vision – 'the world understood as an object out there, of vision requiring distance which promotes knowledge' as one contemporary artist, Antony Gormley, characterises it.[3] There is a reification of the divisions between subject and object, self and the world, belief and knowledge.

Fabian's early critique of the visualist paradigm running through modern anthropology is, of course, pertinent here.[4] His identification of the objectifying and dehumanising visual techniques at the heart of scientific ethnography also raises questions for documentary cinema. As anyone working in these fields knows, both projects are today highly problematic. For the enlightenment way of seeing which emerged at their centre became synonymous with particular forms of political control at home and abroad. Many of the harshest critics of documentary cinema and scientific ethnography have argued that the eye of observation quickly evolved into one of surveillance. It was no longer innocent and whole, but all-seeing and all-knowing. The controlling gaze transformed the world into something resembling Bentham's Panopticon.[5]

Ironically, most of the interwar figures associated with Grierson and Radcliffe-Brown believed in the radical impulse of their work. They were committed to something new, substantively and methodologically. The parallel projects in cinema and anthropology contained a challenge to prevailing social and political assumptions about people. But, as we will discover, the distinctive vision (and its associated techniques) which typified the work associated with Radcliffe-Brown and Grierson was also, in significant ways, compatible with the needs of state power. Furthermore, in their attempt to secure a professional footing for their activities, the documentary film-makers and anthropologists sought to mediate between their subjects and the different agents of state power. The question of whether either project was of any serious use to those in power is, however, an important one. As John Grierson wrote in 1931:

We know our England glibly as an industrial country but we do not know it in our everyday observations as such. Our literature is divorced from the actual, practised in the rarefied atmosphere of country colleges and country retreats. Our gentlemen explore the native haunts and investigate the native customs of Tanganyika and Timbuctoo but do not travel dangerously into the jungles of Middlesbrough and the Clyde.[6]

From the early years of his career, John Grierson sought to articulate a coherent vision for the new kind of cinema to which he was committed. Not only was he interested in establishing a different subject matter to the one emerging in Hollywood, but he was also interested in particular techniques of investigation which were appropriate to film-makers pursuing a different kind of project. Moreover, Grierson's position is strongly reminiscent of the one which distinguished the turn-of-the-century ethnographers. For the emergence of new subjects of study – people understood in the context of their own lives – stimulated innovations in documentary method analogous to those emerging in the new fieldwork-based ethnography. Flaherty was, of course, an important pioneer; but so too were the Russian film-makers who, in the aftermath of the 1917 upheavals, sought to overthrow all existing forms in order to create a revolutionary cinema. Grierson became a critical figure, synthesising these different strands and consolidating a movement around the single term 'documentary' in the context of interwar Britain. His establishment of the principles of documentary were the means by which the new cinema laid claim to a special relationship with truth.[7]

It is important to acknowledge at the outset that Grierson's interest in exploring a particular subject matter (non-fiction, people as them-selves), a set of methods (non-actors, non-studio, first-hand experience as a basis for knowledge) and certain technology (the camera as a mechanical recording device) was sharply at odds with the opinions of established literary intellectuals in Britain at the time. Prominent figures such as the poet T.S. Eliot and writers like D.H. Lawrence or Virginia Woolf viewed with fear and loathing the emergence of people as a distinctive force in society.[8] The Great War had finally shattered the old notions of civilization and humanity. Not only were people worldwide now clearly a decisive force in history, but they were also visible as never before. Looking at the films of Eisenstein or Vertov, or even Chang and Schoedsack's *Grass* (1926), I am always struck by the *presence* and *movement* of people. Many intellectuals, however, despised the camera and the new social and aesthetic form, cinema. Both were identified with popular entertainment, shop girls and suburban clerks. Charles Baudelaire condemned photography as a 'sacrilege' allowing the '"vile multitude" to contemplate its own trivial image'; while D.H. Lawrence fantasised about annihilation of people under the eye of a cinemato-graphe.[9] It was not just the sheer number of people which was terrifying; it was also their invasion of those spaces previously reserved and restricted for the 'civilized'.[10]

Grierson was unusual, then, in locating his new project of documen-tary cinema not with the established intellectuals but with 'ordinary' people. Although this position became increasingly compromised (it is difficult to imagine he had workers in mind as his primary audience), it was part and parcel of Grierson's more general commitment to the expansion of social democracy.[11] Using the technology and site repu-diated by those wedded to older versions of civilization based upon a narrow and hierarchical literary culture, he sought to find ways of giving expression to the fundamental humanity of people. He repudiated the notion of a stupid mindless mass, savages at home who, like the natives abroad, were considered to be irrational or simple brute-like creatures. Rather Grierson revealed people to be highly skilled and organised, masters of the most advanced machines of industrial civilization. They were discovered to be noble and dignified in their work and in their everyday lives. But perhaps, above all, Grierson's subjects emerge as deeply social beings.[12]

The Drifters (1929), an early film made by Grierson himself, is a useful starting point in any attempt to grasp the vision which animates the British interwar documentary movement. Furthermore, it establishes certain cinematic techniques as expressions of such a vision of the world. But, in seeking to expose what I characterise as the enlightenment orientation of the project, its distinctive way of seeing, I nevertheless remain aware of the innovative spirit and diverse range of films which are associated with the documentary movement. As John Corner reminds us, it is all too easy to fall into the trap of caricaturing and stereotyping John Grierson. It is equally easy to forget the unusual range of people with whom he worked – the poet W.H. Auden, the composer Benjamin Britten, and others such as Basil Wright, Alberto Cavalcanti and one of Britain's leading surrealists, Humphrey Jennings. Not surprising, given this eclectic collection of people, the films made by the Grierson group reveal considerable diversity, ranging from what Corner calls the 'aesthetic density' of *Coalface* to the 'maximum transparency' of *Housing Problems*.[13] My interest, however, remains anchored in the consistency of the vision which animates Grierson's documentary project. For its investigation enables us to clarify a set of beliefs, ideas and practices which were, during the same period, crystallising into scientific ethnography.

'I did what I could to get inside the subject. I had spent a year or two of my life wandering about on the deep sea fishing boats and that was an initial advantage. I knew what they felt like', Grierson wrote in an essay of 1929.[14] Echoing Flaherty's approach to cinematic investigation, Grierson initially sought to make his own first-hand experience of the North Sea fishing boats the basis for his depiction of the herring industry. *The Drifters* also introduced the theme which quickly became central to the new documentary cinema, namely work. Men were depicted within the context of their labour, working in harmony with nature, machines and with their fellow men. The process of production is presented as complex and integrated, its different parts located, through the market and network of modern communications, within the context of world society. There is a wholeness or integrity about this cinematic portrayal of working life. The film effectively synthesises Flaherty's celebration of people in the landscape with the Russian preoccupation with industry, technology and rhythm.

The Drifters combines a certain texture (density within the frame) with movement (rhythm and development). But although Grierson attempts to combine creatively these different cinematic elements, his film never quite ignites. It remains worthy and rather dull. Other key films produced by Grierson and his group during the 1930s, for example *Industrial Britain, Coalface, Night Mail, Song of Ceylon, Housing Problems, Spare Time* reveal a similar fascination not only with what people do in society but also with the articulation of these distinctive rhythms with broader currents in the modern world. Each of the films mixes the 'aesthetic' and the 'informational' in strikingly different ways, through sustained experimentation with the different possibilities presented by image, sound and editing.[15]

Despite the self-consciously innovative spirit of Grierson's documentary cinema movement, and the sheer range of films to emerge within the space of a few years, I always encounter resistance to this body of work from contemporary student audiences. Of course, the films are dated in significant ways; but so, too, are those made in the 1920s and 1930s by Flaherty or Vertov. The latter, however, continue to attract – indeed even thrill – viewers today. There seems to be a level of critical engagement sustained by Vertov and Flaherty which contrasts sharply with the response to the work of the Grierson group. This difference is, I think, significant. Its investigation is important in understanding the particular way of seeing which underpins Grierson's cinema.

The Drifters presents the viewer with a perfectly integrated and orderly vision of the world. It is a vision replicated countless times in the documentary films of the subsequent decade. For, like Grierson's 1929 film, the ones produced later also evoke wholeness or integrity. They express and encompass the full diversity of modern society – its different work processes, its different classes and genders, its different spaces. But everything is in its place. Leisure is just as orderly and meaningful as work. All the parts, whether human or not, function as cogs in a complex, well-oiled machine. Such an interpretation of the world may be described as strongly Durkheimian in its fundamental premises. At its centre is a complex division of labour, organic solidarity, built from the integration of separate parts into a whole. There is a marked emphasis on the normative – society is conceived as a 'moral order'.[16] Its individual parts exist only as expressions of the whole.

As the twentieth-century expression of an enlightenment vision, Grierson's project is concerned with knowledge – knowledge of the modern world acquired through the exercise of reason. Grierson himself was quite explicit about his belief in the educative function of documentary cinema.[17] For him it was a means for enabling people to know more about the world in which they lived; and it was integral to the expansion of social democracy. Consequently Grierson used cinema in a very distinctive way. His cinema worked against the dark, magical properties inherent in the site itself. Unlike Flaherty, who used the liminality of cinema to create conditions for identification across differences of language and culture, or Vertov who used the cinema as a site for social and political transformation, Grierson's audience was expected to emerge from the cinema knowing *more* but not knowing *differently.* He engaged his audience soberly, rationally and intellectually. Spectators were not expected to surrender themselves to an experience but rather to think. This feature of Griersonian cinema sets up the problem which confronts the contemporary audience. Hence, if we follow the spirit of Grierson's work and do not suspend our disbelief, we cannot escape an acknowledgement of the overwhelming synthetic quality of his documentary cinema. Thinking about the vision of the world expressed through the interwar films sharpens our awareness of a disjuncture within the work itself. What is presented through image and sound is not what it seems. The form is empty. The radicalism of Grierson's cinema exists only at the level of rhetoric.

Grierson's vision is predicated on a top-down perspective of the world. It is manifested not just in the substantive focus of the films, but also in their techniques. The particular styles of camera work, editing, the uses of sound, narration and narrative are never expressive of the material itself; they are always located outside, functioning as a sort of glue which fixes the different parts in their particular place and in relation to one another. The open, democratic and emancipatory impulse of an enlightenment project becomes then, in interwar Britain, a celebration of impersonal bureaucracy. For the commitment to knowledge, the banishment of darkness, ignorance and superstition, through a process of illumination or the shedding of the light of reason was effectively appropriated and transformed by the state in the name of national integration.

The particular conditions under which Grierson and his group worked, and their location within the political landscape of the 1930s, made the subversion of their project or what Winston calls 'the running from social meaning', almost inevitable.[18] As I have already suggested, it is the *synthetic* quality of the 1930s documentaries that perhaps most repels an audience today. The films appear to be about people and yet we encounter types; they appear to contain movement but in fact are static; they are located within the modern world and yet deny both history and politics. Despite all the flaws of Vertov or Flaherty, there is a certain spirit – an openness, a humanistic curiosity and playful wit in their work – to which we can still respond. It is this which is so markedly absent in the Griersonian films of the same period.

The issue concerning the radical impulse of documentary cinema and its transformation into the celebration of impersonal bureaucracy is central to understanding the kind of anthropology which emerged in the so-called 'British' school of the late 1920s and 1930s. For, during this period, the new kind of enquiry launched by Haddon and Rivers began to take definitive shape through the identification of a particular subject matter, a range of theoretical concepts and distinctive techniques of investigation. Modern anthropology's process of consolidation, its gradual professionalisation, depended upon its leading practitioners successfully laying claim to specialist knowledge and scientific expertise. Building on the achievements of his predecessors, Malinowki was a key figure in this process (even if he liked to claim the revolutionary title exclusively for himself). So, too, was Radcliffe-Brown.

Rivers' death in 1922 symbolically marked a new phase in modern anthropology's evolution. It was the year in which both Malinowski and Radcliffe-Brown published their first major works. Radcliffe-Brown's monograph, *The Andaman Islanders*, reveals not just a different person-ality at work from the cautious Rivers or the overblown narrator of *Argonauts*; it also suggests a different kind of vision at the heart of the emergent discipline. In characterising these two men, historians of twentieth-century anthropology usually draw upon the contrast made by Raymond Firth, who was himself a leading figure in this phase of the British school's evolution. Firth describes the project associated with Malinowski as 'romantic', with an emphasis upon 'imaginative insight' (what I have called 'the visionary'). Radcliffe-Brownian anthropology is identified as 'classical'. Value is placed upon 'precision, proportion and restraint'. There are no fieldwork 'plunges' here. If one figure empha-sised content and ethnographic density, the other emphasised form and structural symmetry.[19]

My own interpretation builds upon this established contrast between Malinowski and Radcliffe-Brown; but, by employing the concept 'ways of seeing', I seek to extend it, encompassing the epistemological and methodological assumptions which underpinned their projects for anthropology. Vision as method and metaphor operates differently in the work of Malinowski and Radcliffe-Brown. If the romanticism of the former involves *revelation*, it is the visual image of *illumination* which expresses the enlightenment impulse of the latter.

There is a certain elusiveness to Radcliffe-Brown. Hence the work of John Grierson and his group has an important role in enabling us to 'see' the distinctive features of the parallel project in anthropology. Specifically, the juxtaposition of the latter with interwar documentary cinema enables us to clarify a number of key issues around vision or what, following Fabian, is called 'visualism' within scientific ethno-graphy.[20] For it is my belief that Grierson and Radcliffe-Brown share, in fundamental ways, the same vision of the world. It is manifest in both the substance and form of the work identified with these key figures. But although Radcliffe-Brown was critical in articulating an enlightenment vision as the basis of the modern discipline, it is in the anthropology of his Oxford associates, Meyer Fortes and Evans-Pritchard, that we may perhaps discover its fullest expression.

Visualizing the characters of Radcliffe-Brown and John Grierson immediately throws up some striking contrasts. If there is a certain flair to the former's personality – he is variously described as a 'charlatan', 'overbearing', 'a bit of a superman'[21] – the latter seems far too sober and worthy to ignite the imagination. Moreover, if Grierson was prolific in his writing, setting up the problem of slippages in meaning,[22] Radcliffe-Brown wrote virtually nothing in his entire career. After the publication of *The Andaman Islanders* in 1922, he produced only a scattering of papers and lectures which he left to others to publish.[23] Radcliffe-Brown literally travelled lightly. He was constantly on the move. According to legend, he carried with him only his copies of *L'Année Sociologique* as he passed through Australia, South Africa, and North America before eventually being elected to anthropology's first university chair at Oxford in 1937.[24] His arrival coincided with Grierson's departure from Britain; but, despite their different trajectories, both men had worked to the same end. Their visions of anthropology and documentary film became the foundation for distinctively modern, professional projects.

From the beginning of his career, Radcliffe-Brown's intellectual interests were focused upon abstract questions concerning social structure and organisation. Unlike Malinowski, he did not flourish in the ethnographic minutiae yielded through long periods of intensive fieldwork. His original research in the Andaman islands was, by all accounts, thin and unsatisfactory. It was closer to the older survey-enquirer model of fieldwork than the subjectively denser participant-observational model. Although historians of the discipline disagree over the relative weight of influence, there is nevertheless an acknowledgement that Radcliffe-Brown's trajectory as an anthropologist was decisively shaped by his critical engagement with the work of Durkheim and Rivers.[25] For a Durkheimian approach to social life enabled him to take over some of the distinctive features of Rivers' project, not least a concern with the establishment of anthropology as a scientific enterprise, while at the same time it provided him with the foundations of a position opposed to the late Rivers. By the mid-1920s Radcliffe-Brown had cast aside questions of both history and psychology in favour of an anthropology anchored in the synchronic analysis of social structure. It became known as 'comparative sociology' or 'the natural science of society'. As Bouquet notes:

This 'natural science of society', with its systematic definition of concepts for a theoretical understanding of how societies 'functioned', contrasts sharply with Malinowski's conviction that social institutions 'hang together' – as if this were the logical outcome of competent ethnographic description.[26]

The Radcliffe-Brownian project, as it emerged during the interwar years, was marked by its explicitly normative stance. There was a concern with systems, with rules, order and stability. The ethnographic subject, Malinowski's Trobriand man with his skilled negotiation of self-interest and social obligation, disappeared behind the abstract functioning of roles and duties.[27] Moreover, as Bouquet's contrastive characterisation reveals, there was also a concern with conceptual clarification, and with the application of reason, rather than the assumption of intuitive understanding, in the identification of the mechanisms by which society's different parts fitted together. Classification and cross-cultural comparison became important principles in the pursuit of a more abstract and theoretically grounded anthropology. Society was now visualised as consisting of a series of compartments, the logic of the connection between them, the 'rhetoric of ethnographic holism', achieved through the development of a particular kind of narrative device.[28] For just as Grierson and his group conceptualised society as a series of parts making up a whole (work, leisure, housing), so too did the structural-functionalist ethnographers whose monographs were divided into sections dealing with economy, kinship, religion and politics. In each case, the achievement of 'holism' or closure is predicated upon a denial of subjectivity, agency and history.

Despite the critical role Radcliffe-Brown played in the articulation of structural-functionalism, what I call anthropology's enlightenment way of seeing, it is the work of Evans-Pritchard which more fully articulates such a vision. It is here, too, that the Griersonian vision resonates most strongly at the level of metaphor and method. For Evans-Pritchard is not only preoccupied with the question of order; he also accords a central role to vision as an observational technique, a strategy by which society may be 'seen', thus indicating a certain conception of scientific knowledge.

The anthropology of Evans-Pritchard is built upon the idea of illumination. The world is ultimately knowable. It is rendered transparent through the exercise of the light of reason: 'All this drastic clarity – luminous, dazzling, stunning . . . blinding – is . . . not just an adjunct of Evans-Pritchard's ethnography, not a stylistic quirk or a bit of rhetorical decor laid on to make the facts less wearying; it is the very heart of it', Clifford Geertz writes. Geertz allows light to play across Evans-Pritchard's ethnographic canvas in a number of interesting ways. He characterises his literary style as 'intensely visual', containing 'clean, well-lighted judgments' and 'flat, unshaded assertions'.[29] Evoking Fabian's notion of visualism in its 'mathematical-geometric' (rather than the 'pictorial-aesthetic') form, Geertz suggests:

The vignette, the photograph, the sketch, the diagram – these are the organizing forces of E-P's ethnography, which moves by means of decisively imaged ideas, which coheres more as a landscape coheres than as a myth does (or a diary), and which is dedicated, above all things, to making the puzzling plain.[30]

In seeking to accumulate anthropological knowledge through the development of a new kind of scientific enquiry, the project associated with Radcliffe-Brown and Evans-Pritchard shares a passing resemblance to the enterprise launched by Rivers at the turn of the century. Indeed, in certain respects, structural-functionalism might be considered as a significant advance on the latter, given the absence of the embarrassments of diffusionism and psychology which subsequently became associated with Rivers' anthropology. My interpretation is different, however. I suggest that the dynamic Cubism of Rivers' project was appropriated by Radcliffe-Brown; and in decisively casting off any concern with questions of history or subjectivity, he transformed it into a sterile intellectualism.[31]

The consolidation of scientific ethnography took place around an enlightenment vision. As a way of seeing, it had originally been an expression of the pursuit of science and knowledge harnessed to new democratic and humanist ideals. By the second decade of the twentieth century, however, the radicalism of such a project had been subverted. Science and reason, appropriated in the name of democracy, were now strategies of control employed by the agents of state power. The anxious, fragmented, multiperspectival modernist vision of Rivers is transformed into 'the gaze', the disembodied eye of observation. Vision is returned to its status as a privileged source of knowledge about the world, what Fabian terms 'visualism'. Its interrogation and problematic status are replaced by a new confidence. Society is 'observed' and turned into an object to be studied. A variety of visual metaphors (diagrams, grids, maps, etc.) serve to objectify knowledge. Both history and agency are denied to those now under the scrutiny of the ethnographer's eye.[32]

Fabian's identification of the visualist bias running through modern anthropology is often adopted as a wide-ranging and totalising critique of the disicipline. I believe that it is most valuable in understanding the distinctive features of the Radcliffe-Brownian project which emerged in, and were moulded by, the particular social and political conditions of the interwar years. The fundamentally static and normative vision of the world expressed in structural-functionalism, strongly reminiscent of Griersonian cinema, was compatible with the prevailing ethos of social consensus by which politicians sought to create a coherent sense of national identity in the face of economic depression, social unrest and approaching war. Indeed it might be argued that however far the film-makers and anthropologists thought they had travelled from the centre, they nevertheless continued to reproduce it in every level of their work.[33]

The political compromises of the interwar film-makers and anthropologists were, of course, also much more blatant than these more subtle accommodations of vision. Both groups were unashamedly in pursuit of state support for their new enterprises. From Grierson's courtship of sponsors such as the Empire Marketing Board, the Gas Board and the General Post Office to Malinowski's and Radcliffe Brown's attempt to find patrons in the Colonial Office, there is little evidence to suggest that possible conflicts of interest were uppermost in their minds. The primary concern of the documentary film-makers and the anthropologists was the attainment of professional recognition. To this end they sought to prove their value by making themselves useful.[34]

The claims made by the documentary film-makers and anthropologists to be offering something new in the guise of 'education' or 'science' were, however, built upon a curious paradox. Each group was anxious to claim a special relationship with reality and truth through the demarcation of a distinctive sphere of operation and range of expert knowledge. For Grierson this involved separating his documentary cinema (as the creative treatment of actuality) not just from fiction film but from other kinds of non-fiction film.[35] Radcliffe-Brown and his associates, too, in claiming to employ special techniques and concepts as the means of elevating their work beyond mere description, also implied the creative treatment of actuality. Hence in the name of reality, science and truth, the film-makers and anthropologists reinserted fiction at the heart of their enterprise.

Despite the sharp critique which may be made against the political compromises and collusions of the interwar anthropologists and film-makers, it is easy to overestimate the significance of these tiny groups operating in the interstices of the national and colonial state. In fact, these groups were made up of a curious collection of misfits and outsiders, marginal people who carried no real clout with the British establishment. Of course their very marginality may have made them useful as mediating figures between potentially difficult subjects at home and abroad and the agents of a state which struggled to contain them. But although they worked hard to promote their new enterprises, neither the documentary film-makers nor the scientific ethnographers achieved the professional status they so desired until after 1945. Their failure during the interwar period, however, was – to adapt Winston's wry observation – due not to Politics but (office) politics.[36]

Part II

Anthropological visions

5   Cinema and anthropology in the postwar world

Rome, Open City, Rossellini's classic film, opened in 1945. It is a landmark in modern cinema. Made in the final months of the Second World War using film stock acquired through the black market, its distinctively new subject matter and aesthetic form may be seen as reflecting the birth of a new phase in world society. For the end of the war marked the disintegration of the old imperial powers and the rise of a different world order shaped not just by the Cold War but by a resurgence of popular democratic movements across Asia, Africa, Europe and the New World.

The impact of Rossellini's film derives from its moving portrayal of Italian resistance to German occupation. He locates humanity among the people of Rome – Pina, Francesco and Don Pietro, who are organised with others against the cruelty and barbarism which Fascism, war and invasion has brought about. Moreover, Rossellini seeks to express his vision of society through the very form of the film. He innovates with established cinematic techniques. *Rome, Open City* is notable for its documentary aesthetic; Rossellini's use of the city itself as integral to the revelation of character and development of the narrative; his employment of non-professional actors; his commitment to realistic dialogue and the details of everyday life. Evoking through the use of such devices an open, collective and humane world, Rossellini contrasts with it a static and artificially constructed studio world of dark, closed interiors where brutality lurks.[1]

Rome, Open City is a useful starting point for a consideration of the relationship between anthropology and cinema in the postwar period. For, irrespective of whether it actually represents the decisive break often claimed, Rossellini's film raises important questions concerning individual and society, reality and artifice, truth and fiction, substance and form which go to the heart of these projects as they evolved after 1945. The end of the war in Europe marked a new era in the development of cinema. There was a crisis in Hollywood, subsequently accelerated by the expansion of television as the new form of mass communication. European cinema underwent an important renaissance, its creative renewal being marked by the emergence of film criticism as an arena of intellectual investigation. Documentary cinema, as a particular kind of social enquiry, was an integral part of this changing landscape. In exploring its key concerns after 1945, I will suggest that the innovative features of documentary cinema and television were driven by a new and creative engagement with social life. Anthropology, however, while subject to the same forces sweeping through the postwar world, moved in a different direction. Its consolidation in the universities coincided with the loss of its traditional subject matter, 'primitive society'; but as an academic discipline built upon the paradigm of scientific ethnography, its expansion was predicated upon abstraction and specialisation. Hence, unlike the postwar film-makers who abandoned professional hierarchies in order to engage anew with people in society, their anthropological counterparts retreated from the world, reifying a set of concepts, methods and forms rooted in a different phase of intellectual endeavour.

The changing ways in which practitioners of cinema and anthropology engaged with the postwar world are the focus of my concerns in this introduction to the second half of this book. An awareness of the different strategies used by film-makers such as Rossellini, De Sica, Antonioni, Rouch, Drew, Leacock and others to interrogate contemporary social realities is important in clarifying key concepts which animate projects of anthropological visuality which emerge during this period. Ironically, it is at this time after 1945, when anthropology and cinema are moving in opposite directions, that we find attempts to realise the promise of synthesis contained within the shared moment of their symbolic birth. On the one hand, there is the emergence of 'visual anthropology' as a specialist field within the academic discipline. On the other hand, new projects growing out of a self-conscious exploration of visual techniques within ethnographic enquiry raise issues of epistemology, method and form which go to the heart of anthropology itself. It is the latter, specifically the work carried out by Jean Rouch, David and Judith MacDougall, and Melissa Llewelyn-Davies which is the subject of critical attention in this second half of the book.

The three case studies are an attempt to take further questions I posed at the outset of the book concerning the nature of anthropological knowledge. An examination of the role of vision or, more broadly, what I called anthropology's 'ways of seeing' highlighted the relationship between method and metaphysic at the heart of the modern discipline. Now I draw upon such a framework to examine how technology, technique and forms of knowledge are intertwined within contemporary work. The critical perspective I develop with respect to Rouch, the MacDougalls and Llewelyn-Davies, takes seriously their anthropology, despite its refusal to conform to the discipline of textual forms. Indeed it is the explicitly visual orientation of their work that throws into sharp relief the underlying assumptions animating their different projects of ethnographic investigation.

The significance of Jean Rouch, David and Judith MacDougall and Melissa Llewelyn-Davies as figures within contemporary anthropology partially stems from the coherence and extension of their ethnographic projects. In each case, their films constitute a distinctive corpus marked by a high degree of innovation and reflexive experimentation. This unusual combination of continuity and change makes their projects especially interesting, exposing as it does the shifting nature of anthropological enquiry. Central to my interpretation of the innovative quality of this work is its location within particular social and political contexts. Hence I explore the experimental impulse in Rouch's cinema against the backdrop of African independence. I seek to understand how the politics of nationalism and the rights of native peoples have shaped the Mac-Dougalls' project. Finally, I trace the different ways in which Llewelyn-Davies's engagement with the Maasai people has been mediated through the politics of gender.

My approach toward understanding the pursuit of ethnographic knowledge by means of visual techniques and technologies is built upon a different cinematic metaphor from the one of montage, the organising principle of my initial thesis. If the first half of the book is built around juxtaposition, the self-conscious disruption of context, the latter half is animated by Bazin's notion of deep-focus photography. Hence, I follow Bazin in elevating composition (the *mise-en-scène*) over cutting (montage), since as a cinematic metaphor it evokes the subtle, complex nature of the context from which the projects of Rouch, the MacDougalls and Llewelyn-Davies emerged. Such an orientation, with its roots in an appreciation of the cinema of Flaherty, Renoir, Rossellini and Welles, is especially appropriate given both the form and substance of the argument which follows. For, in opposing the artifical and contrived nature of montage that sees the world fractured into pieces and reconstituted according to the subjective view of film-maker, Bazin argues for an approach toward reality which, in emphasising its width and depth, is able to reveal its fundamental ambiguity. His biographer, Dudley Andrew, notes that the attempt to evoke 'the integral unity of a universe in flux' leads Bazin to conceive cinema as a process not of creation but of exploration and discovery.[2]

The new engagement with reality at the centre of Bazinian cinema brings about a transformation in the conventional relationship between film-maker and audience. It does not involve the erasure of the vision of the author; rather, there is an abdication of a particular kind of direction. As Andrew explains:

Of neither Flaherty nor Renoir can we say that the film-maker has erased his own vision. He has instead erased his direction of the action while retaining his style of vision as witness to that action. The audience may then watch an actual event and a considered perspective oriented toward that event.[3]

My intention in adopting a Bazinian perspective for this part of the book stems from an interest in engaging readers differently. My thesis is built upon the evocation of a certain kind of spatial density concerning relationships between anthropology, cinema and the postwar world. I am anxious to avoid reductionism in my discussion of the particular case studies while, simultaneously, arguing for the centrality of context to any interpretation of the kind of anthropology pursued by Rouch, the MacDougalls and Llewelyn-Davies. By 'filtering' or revealing elements that may constitute the social and historical conditions of their work, I seek to stimulate what David MacDougall terms the 'exploratory faculty' of the reader. I invite the reader to imagine a complex web of interrelationships existing between anthropology, cinema, television and the social and political circumstances of the postwar world rather than any series of direct correspondences.[4]

Italian neorealism

The trauma of war, Occupation and Liberation brought forth a new cinema in Italy. Its key figures, Rossellini, De Sica and Visconti, along with scriptwriters Zavattini and Fellini, sought to effect a decisive break between their own work and the bombast and grandiosity of earlier Fascist film.[5] Their concern was to approach the world differently, to see it as if for the first time. As Fellini puts it: 'neorealism is a way of seeing reality without prejudice, without conventions coming between it and myself – facing it without preconceptions, looking at it in an honest way – whatever reality is, not just social reality but all there is within a man.'[6] This new stance toward life necessitated its own aesthetic. The innovations in cinematic form and technique pioneered by Rossellini and the other Italian neorealist film-makers were animated by a new vision of the world, one which emerged from the ruins of war. At its core was a commitment to people in society as the force for civilization.

Any appreciation of the immediate postwar cinema movement in Italy owes much to the writing of André Bazin. From the very beginning of his attempt to develop a coherent critical perspective toward the appreciation of film, Bazin's concern was to move beyond a mere description of techniques to address more fundamental questions of epistemology and the nature of reality. His exploration of the subtle interplay between interpretations of the world and forms of aesthetic expression was central to his practice as a critic; and, as such, Bazin's approach offers a broad critical framework by which we may highlight the changing features of documentary as they unfolded after 1945. For many of the key features which Bazin identified in Italian neorealist cinema found their fullest expression within a new conception of non-fiction film – at first as direct cinema in America and, later, as observational cinema, a particular form of anthropological visuality.[7]

Bazin's approach to understanding the work of Rossellini, in particular his classic films *Rome, Open City* (1945), *Paisan* (1946) and *Germany, Year Zero* (1947), depended upon the location of his cinema within the social and political moment it expressed. Bazin recognised that Rossellini's work was contemporaneous with the world which brought it into being, i.e. it was part of what it documented, rather than a comment upon it. Hence it was both part of a particular moment and a manifestation of it. Although, as Bondanella reminds us, Italian neorealist cinema encompassed a considerable diversity of style and subject matter, it contained at its core what we might call, following Raymond Williams, a break towards realism.[8] As a movement, its leading figures were animated by their desire to reject artifice, convention, established practices and forms in their attempt to rediscover the world. The new engagement sought with reality was, of course, dependent upon the use of artifice. Indeed, drawing attention to the interplay of illusion and reality was one of the hallmarks of classic Italian neorealist cinema.[9]

The foundation of Bazin's approach to neorealism privileged an understanding of its metaphysical orientation over its methodological innovations. Describing the films of Rossellini and his contemporaries as examples of 'revolutionary humanism', Bazin identified the centrality of people in the world, the authenticity of their lived experiences as the basis of cinema's postwar renaissance.[10] Hence the characters of the classic neorealist films were conceptualised within the landscape as concretely as in the earlier documentary cinema of Robert Flaherty, the creativity and vitality of their lives finding expression in the collective struggle to rebuild society from the ruins of war. In the early neorealist work, images of bomb-scarred cities were integral to the unfolding of the drama itself, the backdrop against which a different future could be imagined and be constructed. The later films, in particular De Sica's *Umberto D* (1951), also drew crucially upon landscape as fundamental to the understanding of character and action; but, in this case, it was used to strikingly different effect. The city becomes, as Millicent Marcus puts it, 'a fragmented, decentered space with few familiar landmarks and no sense of cohesion'.[11]

The expression of a neorealist vision of the world depended upon the use of a different range of cinematic techniques. Specifically, it required commitment to methods that we, as ethnographers, might call 'participant-observation'. For the neorealist film-makers, in being positioned differently towards contemporary life, were themselves implicated in that which they were seeking to explore. This was manifest in the use of the technology itself: 'The Italian camera retains something of the human quality of the Bell and Howell newsreel camera, a projection of hand and eye, almost a living part of the operator, instantly in tune with his awareness', Bazin writes.[12] The intimate connection with the world was forged through the intense observation of the details of everyday life. The amassing of such details, evocative of the world's density or texture, was conveyed cinematically through the use of long takes and deep-focus photography. The employment of such techniques (as Orson Welles so brilliantly demonstrated in *Citizen Kane*) was inspired by a conception of cinema as about ambiguity, involving revelations of the real rather than any explanation of it.

The development of a new aesthetic which conveyed, by its situating of people in the world, the emergence of phenomenological cinema, was built upon a different notion of the role of the director and – importantly – of the audience. Hence, although Visconti, Rossellini and De Sica remained critical to the realisation of a certain cinematic vision of the world, their relationship to that world and to their audience was significantly different from the roles as conventionally understood. The film-maker's role was less about directing and presenting the action, and more a process of filtering in which the audience itself was actively engaged in the creation of meaning: 'I try to interfere the minimum amount possible with the image, my interference is only to find the point of view and to say what is essential, no more', Rossellini once explained to an interviewer. He continued

You can suggest and tell people what you have had the possibility to collect, observe, and to see. You can even give, but very smoothly, your point of view which is there as soon as you have made your choice . . . My purpose is never to convey a message, never to persuade but to offer everyone an observation, even my observation.[13]

Rossellini's war trilogy inaugurated the postwar renaissance of cinema, but the drama and optimism inherent in the 'cinema of Reconstruction', which portrayed people united in their heroic struggle to rebuild society, was quickly exhausted. De Sica's film, *The Bicycle Thief* (1948), as Marcus notes, already represented a significant shift away from the vision of the world evoked in *Rome, Open City* or *Paisan*. His later film, the story of an old man and his dog (*Umberto D*, 1951), was a bleak expression of isolation and despair. For Bazin, ironically, the film was suggestive of new possibilities for neorealism. He envisaged 'a cinema of "duration"', by which he meant a final break with film as spectacle or drama. In its place a cinema would be constituted from 'the succession of the constant instants of life, no one of which can be said to be more important than another, for their ontological equality destroys drama at its very basis'.[14]

Despite Bazin's later identification of this as a new moment in the evolution of cinematic language, other Italian film-makers were by the early 1950s anxious to escape the confines of neorealism. Specifically, they were interested in pursuing a project of interior exploration. During the 1950s, Antonioni, Fellini and their contemporaries elsewhere (most notably Bergman and Resnais) embarked upon an investigation of memory, history, emotion and consciousness – the nature of subjectivity itself; and their new project for cinema unfolded amidst the politics of the Cold War, McCarthyism and the threat of nuclear annihilation.

The postwar Italian films reframed a number of key questions concerning the relationship between society and subjectivity, reality and illusion, documentary and fiction which had crystallised over the previous three decades. This subversion of established categories within cinema cannot be considered apart from the changing social and political conditions of the postwar world. For, although the years after 1945 were marked by the growing threat of nuclear war as the super-powers faced each other across a divided Europe, there was at the same time an explosion of popular forces across Africa, Asia and the Caribbean. It is important to recognise that the period of the Cold War, while conventionally understood as characterised by tremendous repression and fear, was also a period of immense political vitality. We have already seen how the immediate postwar Italian film-makers sought to engage more directly with the new political energies at work in society. By making their cinema an integral part of this moment, Rossellini and his associates reinvented the form itself. The particular qualities associated with subsequent moments of experimentation – British Free Cinema, *cinéma vérité*, direct cinema and the French New Wave – must likewise be understood. They, too, reflected the desire by film-makers to engage with new currents in social life; and, in so doing, their experimentation with form became inseparable from their exploration of new subject matter.

The Free Cinema movement which emerged in Britain during the 1950s represented an attempt by film-makers to locate their work more securely in the changing conditions of postwar society. Although the work of Lindsay Anderson, Karel Reisz and Tony Richardson involved a rejection of earlier cinematic conventions in favour of a freer style expressive of the energy spilling out from a young postwar generation, it perhaps remained more imitative of Italian neorealism than any significant development beyond it.[15] Moreover, as with their Italian counterparts, the British film-makers tinkered with the established categories of fiction and documentary but failed to pursue their innovations to the point of final dissolution. De Sica and Zavattini hinted at the possibilities. Their ambition could not be fully realised, however, until the documentary form itself was pushed to its limits, rather than being used and transcended in the search for a new kind of fiction film.[16]

Cinéma vérité

The release of *Umberto D* in 1951 marked the end of neorealism as a creative moment in postwar cinema. It revealed both the limitations and future possibilities of neorealist film. On the one hand, the cinema of Antonioni and Fellini represented movement away from neorealism's fundamental premises (about the nature of reality, the relationship between individual and society, and the logic of narrative). On the other hand, direct cinema, which emerged a decade later in America, may be interpreted as an extension of the kind of neorealist project envisaged by Zavattini (and Bazin). Despite these very different responses to the end of cinema's immediate postwar renaissance, it is clear that throughout the 1950s the categories of fiction and documentary continued to be unstable. Indeed, if the challenge to these conventions was initially articulated by Rossellini and others in the area of fiction film, a number of other challenges originated in documentary cinema.

Documentary, as it had evolved during the 1930s, was, of course, deeply affected by the postwar changes in the conception of cinema. The blurring of boundaries which Italian neorealism represented revealed as much about the artifice of documentary as about the reality of fiction. Thus, while many conventional histories place the eruption of the French New Wave as the next significant moment in cinema's postwar development, it is important to be aware of those changes occurring within documentary cinema during the years between *Umberto D* and the release of Francois Truffaut's *400 Blows* (1959). Not only did these changes shape ideas and practices across cinema as a whole; they also formed the basis for the emergence of anthropological cinema.

Many of the postwar documentarists shared with their Italian counterparts a fundamental commitment to people in society. Again, there was a concern to break with those styles compromised by war and propaganda, and to engage anew with life through the subversion of hierarchies built into the conventional relationship between film-makers, subjects, audiences and technology. The development of what became known as *cinéma vérité* and direct cinema was rooted in these changing ideas about the nature of the documentary project. Despite an overlap in the film technologies characteristic of these new approaches (namely, lightweight portable cameras and sound recording equipment), each one was underpinned by a different epistemology, set of techniques and aesthetic form.[17]

One of the problems that I have confronted in exploring, from an anthropological perspective, the evolution of cinema after 1945 arises in connection with *cinéma vérité*. This may seem something of a paradox, since *cinéma vérité* is perhaps most clearly identified with the work of an anthropologist, Jean Rouch. But, in seeking to establish the features of this distinctive approach which emerged during the 1950s, it was difficult to locate it properly with respect to an earlier Italian neorealism and a later French New Wave. Clearly, as the conventional film histories revealed, it belonged chronologically between those two moments; but the new configuration of key questions preoccupying postwar film-makers was not, I felt, satisfactorily explored with reference to Rouch. All too often issues concerning technology became an obstacle inhibiting any further investigation of the fundamental premises of his cinema – and its location in Africa.[18]

I suggested earlier that out of neorealism, two contrasting projects developed. The first, perhaps most fully realised by Antonioni, involved a break with the assumption of the social determination of individual subjectivity implied in the postwar Italian films. Although landscape remains integral to the nature of Antonioni's cinematic enquiry, his strikingly new configuration of people in the world serves to evoke not human solidarity and connection but the isolation, alienation and failure of communication which lies at the heart of modern existence. The other response to neorealism was represented by the direct cinema movement. In contrast, it was built upon a reaffirmation of the central relationship between individual and society – now explored within the context of contemporary American life.

Certainly Rouch's cinema was neither that of Antonioni nor of the American film-makers around Robert Drew; but it seemed, interestingly, to contain an unusual synthesis of these contrasting responses to neorealism. For his films of the 1950s were crucially about individual and society, but that relationship is not an external projection – manifested as people doing things in the world (direct cinema or what Bazin imagined as a kind of 'reconstituted reportage'), the nature of subjectivity revealed through the social context of their action – rather it involved the reconfiguration of this relationship from the inside out. In the latter sense then, Rouch followed a similar path to that of Antonioni in his commitment to a cinematic exploration of interiority; but his work was located in West Africa not in Europe, and he came up with a strikingly different vision of both subjectivity and the world.

The *vérité* approach pursued by Jean Rouch unfolded within the conditions of West African independence politics. As an experiment in film-making, it was contemporaneous with the critical challenge to established ideas and practices in cinema led by Francois Truffaut. Indeed 1954 was the year which marked both the making of Rouch's most controversial film, *Les Maîtres Fous*, and the publication of *A Certain Tendency in French Cinema*, Truffaut's manifesto against what he called 'le cinéma de papa'.[19] The attack upon key assumptions about reality, character and narrative launched by Truffaut and his colleagues at *Cahiers du Cinéma* stemmed from a self-consciously articulated intellectual position. Rouch's subversion of such notions, however, was driven by his own film-making practice. It was in the very nature of his work, in its particular location and subject matter (the migrant experience) that Rouch not only developed a kind of cinema which was neither documentary nor fiction, but he also re-discovered the modernism of earlier French cinema through its transposition into an emergent independent Africa.[20]

The origins of the term, *cinéma vérité*, have been the subject of much debate. Its adoption, however, as the description of film-making techniques rooted in capturing life as it is lived – undirected, unscripted, unfolding – made explicit the connection between the kind of project Rouch began to pursue during the 1950s and that of the Russian revolutionary film-maker, Dziga Vertov (*kino-pravda* or cine-truth). Each figure was committed to plunging the camera into the midst of a world in flux. The spontaneous, improvised quality of their films, emerging from a new positioning of film-maker and subject, technology and society, was expressive of the more general condition of fluidity in social and political life. The cinematic challenge to notions of reality, character and narrative which the work of both Vertov and Rouch represented was inseparable, then, from their direct engagement with conditions of revolutionary upheaval. The high degree of reflexivity characteristic of such *vérité* projects was evidence indeed of a fundamentally different orientation toward the world. If the conditions of revolutionary change laid bare the provisional, ideological and contestable nature of social reality, then the camera was exposed, too, as an instrument involved in the *creation* of realities rather than understood as an instrument for the *discovery* of reality.

The distinctive techniques associated with *cinéma vérité* grew directly out of the attempt to create a film-making approach which expressed the complex subjectivities of people emerging as a new force in world society. From the beginning of his project, Rouch sought to free his camera, to make it mobile, embodied, spontaneous, emancipatory and improvisatory:

The only way to film is to walk about with the camera, taking it to wherever it is the most effective, and improvising a ballet in which the camera itself becomes just as much alive as the people it is filming. This would be the first synthesis between the theories of Vertov about the 'cine-eye' and those of Flaherty about the 'participant camera'. I often compare this dynamic improvisation with that of the bullfighter before the bull. In both cases nothing is given in advance, and the smoothness of a faena (strategy of play) in bullfighting is analogous to the harmony of a traveling shot which is in perfect balance with the movements of the subjects.[21]

Engaging with life in a completely new way as a film-maker, Rouch, like Vertov, confronted the limitations of existing technology. Importantly, it was not the development of lightweight cameras and synchronous sound-recording equipment which made possible *cinéma vérité*. It was the evolution of *cinéma vérité* which demanded these technological innovations.

It is significant that France and the United States, sites of the most intense political struggles in the West during the 1950s and 1960s, became the foci for experimentation in postwar documentary. Although many of the innovations pursued by Robert Drew, Richard Leacock and Donn Pennebaker in America were contemporaneous with those of *cinéma vérité*, they were profoundly different kinds of social enquiry. Certainly there was a superficial resemblance which derived from the film-makers' shared interest in forging a different relationship with life through the abandonment of conventional film-making hierarchies and technologies. But the conditions under which *cinéma vérité* and direct cinema evolved – namely, colonial independence and civil rights, respectively – were critical in establishing different concerns at the centre of these two projects. Moreover, each approach was predicated upon a radically different notion of both reality and the form of its re-presentation. If *cinéma vérité* was located in cinema itself, drawing upon its unique features as an arena for transformation, then direct cinema, as part of broader movement in American journalism, accommodated itself within a different site – television. The former was weighted toward a certain kind of experience, the latter toward information.

Direct cinema began as a rather curious hybrid form, a strange mixture of cinema (in its use of character, context and narrative) and broadcast journalism (in its commitment to inform); but television quickly became the most appropriate niche for the kind of film-making approach to which Drew and his associates were committed.[22]

Direct cinema

Direct cinema represented an important continuation of postwar Italian neorealism, especially its late phase. The foundations for such an extension within a different cultural setting had already been laid, however, by developments within American cinema. The crisis in Hollywood after the war and the collapse of a cinema audience precipitated a number of changes in film production which mirrored those occurring within European cinema. Specifically, New York emerged as the centre for a new kind of cinema. It involved a rejection of Hollywood artifice – namely, its studio-based production, star system and formulaic narratives – in favour of an excavation of the city itself as the landscape in which complex subjectivities were located.[23] Hence, in the decade after 1945, a growing number of American fiction film-makers were moving closer toward direct engagement with social life. At the same time, the leading figures in actuality film-making began to look towards the fiction film as a way of escaping from the confines of word-dominated documentary.

From the outset, the approach to actuality film-making which Robert Drew, the key figure in the development of direct cinema, fostered was built upon the casting aside of established documentary conventions or what he called its 'word-logic': that is, films assembled around a verbally articulated argument. Instead Drew and those who were grouped around him, Leacock, Pennebaker and the Maysles brothers, located themselves as film-makers in the midst of social life. Their role was to capture life as it unfolded, without direction or preconceptions: 'I am interested in one approach only', Drew once stated in the context of a discussion with other leading documentarists, 'and that is to convey the excitement and drama and feeling of real life as it actually happens through film.'[24]

Direct cinema as a new and distinctive film-making approach was established by *Primary* (1960), Drew's early film about John F. Kennedy's battle for the Democratic presidential nomination. It was followed by a series of other films, including *On the Pole* (1960), *Yanki No!*

(1960), *The Chair* (1962) and *Crisis* (1963). The commitment of film-makers like Drew, Leacock and Pennebaker to their total immersion in the drama of contemporary life and the recording of live action (rather than its re-enactment or explanation), meant a constant struggle against the limitations of film technology. Certainly it is striking to read the personal accounts of this period, since there is a palpable sense of the excitement contained within the discovery of new ways of working. But, perhaps more than anything else, there is a remarkably clear vision of the kind of films they were, as a group, determined to make and the necessity of having to invent their own technology appropriate to it. For, as with *cinéma vérité*, direct cinema was not a technologically driven innovation. The technology lagged far behind the imaginative conception of the project itself.[25]

The techniques of direct cinema were founded upon the freedom and mobility of the film-makers themselves. Film crews were small – two people recording image and sound synchronously. There was no use for lights, tripods, scripts, interviews, actors or directors. There was a strict adherence to the principle of spontaneity. Nothing was staged or repeated.[26] Working in this way, film-makers sought to insert themselves as far as they could into situations. From such a vantage point, they watched and listened with an extraordinary intensity, recording whatever details of character and context might serve as clues to an understanding of the action unfolding before them. The film-makers acted as witnesses to action, not as the provocateurs of it. Such a role demanded, moreover, that the film-makers be present at both the recording and editing of the work. In seeking to offer spectators the sense of themselves 'being there', of the audience being situated within the action itself, the film-maker's presence at every stage of the project was central to the authenticity or the 'truth' of the film 'evidence' offered.

The critical perspective toward cinema developed by André Bazin during the early 1950s serves as a valuable framework by which the particular concerns and techniques of the new documentary film-makers gathered around Robert Drew may be judged. Although there is something inescapably American about direct cinema – its energy, its attraction to action and drama, its male heroes (whether the film-makers themselves or their subjects) – Bazin's reflections on the postwar Italian films enable us to identify its origins in the ontology of neorealism. For the techniques developed by people such as Leacock or Pennebaker were expressive of an orientation toward the world which closely resembled that of Rossellini and De Sica. This stance was manifested in the aesthetic quality of the direct cinema films themselves, for example in the emphasis upon the *mise-en-scène* and their 'found' rhythm.[27]

At the centre of direct cinema lay a preoccupation with the relationship between individual and context, the central axis of Italian neorealism. The use of the *mise-en-scène* was the cinematic means by which both subjectivity and the world were conceived. Film-makers, as I have noted, cultivated an extreme sensitivity to the dynamics of situation in which they were immersed, since it was the moment of recording (and not that of editing) which was fundamental in grasping this relationship. Working in this way did not just establish a distinctive filmic space, a focusing of relationships within a scene, but it also evoked a different sort of time: 'time does not flow. It accumulates in the image like a formidable electric charge'.[28] Hence the role which direct film-makers adopted towards subjects, reality and audience closely resembled the kind of 'filter' that Bazin associated with other figures like Rossellini, Renoir and Flaherty. As Bazin's biographer, Dudley Andrew, put it:

[The] style is part of an instinct that first chooses what to watch and then knows how to watch it – more precisely, how to coexist with it. Under the subtle pressure of this approach, relationships within reality become visible, bursting into the conciousness of the spectator as a revelation of a truth discovered.[29]

The distinctive features associated with Robert Drew's documentary work were, of course, built upon a set of assumptions about reality and the nature of its apprehension. In rejecting montage as its basic principle in favour of the *mise-en-scène*, the direct film-makers were committed to 'non-preconception', that is, to an investigation of a pre-existent world rather than its creation (as, for example, predicated by the kind of approach pursued by Rouch).[30] It was by attending to the world through intense observation, specifically of people's actions within it, that the direct film-makers sought to yield new understandings of the nature of contemporary life.

Despite its origins in a particular kind of cinema, the direct approach to documentary was perhaps more profoundly shaped by television. Many of its key features harmonised with the distinctive characteristics of the mass medium with its emphasis on live action. Drew's enterprise resembled the kind of 'reconstituted reportage' imagined by Bazin as an important stage in the evolution of cinematic language; but it was not, in fact, the proper realisation of the vision imagined by either Bazin or Zavattini.[31] Direct cinema, driven as it was by Drew's commitment to commonly shared human experience and markedly ethnographic in its orientation and techniques, was important in shaping a new kind of anthropological enquiry. The emergence of observational cinema, however, represented something other than a transposition of direct cinema methods into ethnographic situations. Observational cinema brought film-makers into an active engagement with Bazin's notion of a cinema of duration. Hence, despite the points of connection with Drew's approach, it was through observational cinema that classic Italian neorealism was properly reinvented.

The consolidation of academic anthropology

I have suggested that the innovative impulse animating cinema after 1945 should be understood as evidence of a new encounter between film-makers and the world. The rediscovery of people in society as a rich, complex subject matter influenced all areas of film-making, from technology to questions of aesthetics and form. At its core, postwar cinema was profoundly subversive of existing notions about truth, fiction and reality. Its restless, questioning spirit was an important expression of broader social and political currents at work in the world after 1945.

Anthropology's consolidation as 'a form of disciplined inquiry' was contemporaneous with the period of cinematic experimentation inaugurated by Italian neorealism; but the location of scientific ethnographers within the academy and their pursuit of professional status resulted in very different trajectories from those characteristic of the postwar film-makers.[32] If a great deal of the creativity of the latter was stimulated by the repudiation of earlier work, the former sought to reify the ideas and methods of their predecessors in an attempt to legitimate their claims to a particular kind of scientific expertise. Hence in place of experimentation and reflexive self-consciousness, we discover a marked conservatism in the anthropology of the immediate postwar period. The concern of its leading figures was the establishment of professional norms as the means for sharply distinguishing the nature of their scientific enquiry from other kinds of social reporting and investigation.[33] It is ironic, however, that the ideas, techniques and forms being articulated as the foundations of the university discipline were already archaic. For the onset of the Cold War cast doubt upon science as an undertaking that was in any way straightforwardly neutral or progressive, and the movement of colonial peoples for independence represented a fundamental challenge to certain assumptions central to the creation of a 'modern' anthropology.[34]

Although the years between 1945 and the late 1960s saw the clarification of distinctive national traditions in anthropology, most notably the American, British and French schools, there were many points of connection arising from their shared history as professionalising areas of academic enquiry.[35] The postwar expansion of higher education created university posts for those anthropologists whose training had occurred during the previous decade of insecurity and uncertainty, when their teachers had struggled to foster an incipient discipline through a sort of apprenticeship model of recruitment.[36] Modern anthropology had been nurtured in the small cliques surrounding key figures of the 1920s and 30s (Malinowski, Boas and Griaule, for example). The ideas and practices associated with such people were difficult to sustain, however, until institutional legitimation provided the means by which the scientific impulse of their work could be fully realised. Once established in the universities – and Radcliffe-Brown's appointment in 1940 to an Oxford chair marked the beginning of this process in Britain – the recruitment to the discipline was formalised and carefully controlled.

Anthropology's profile as a professional mode of enquiry was dependent equally upon its intellectual and institutional consolidation. The former involved the development of theory as the framework for a cross-cultural comparative sociology. The rise to prominence of Parsons, Radcliffe-Brown and Lévi-Strauss within the American, British and French schools marked a movement away from the idiosyncratic details of ethnographic work and toward a concern with abstract structural principles. The institutional counterpart to this shift saw the creation of bureaucractic procedures by which the discipline's activities could be properly monitored and protected. It was in the course of finally triumphing over amateurism that the new university-based scientific ethnographers became narrow and specialised. Modern anthropologists were academics rather than intellectuals. Shedding the grander speculations of their predecessors, they became scientists not philosophers, and they increasingly restricted their communication to those who, like themselves, only published in specialised journals and shared an arcane language.[37]

Visual anthropology emerged as a distinctive field during the period of the discipline's postwar university expansion. For at the same time as academic anthropology asserted itself as a unified, coherent arena of enquiry, it fragmented into numerous subdisciplines whose relationship to the centre was always contradictory and unstable. But, as Joan Vincent has convincingly demonstrated, the investigation of these peripheral areas throws up a range of questions about the preoccupations of the discipline as a whole.[38] The case of visual anthropology is especially interesting. The particular nature of the synthesis pursued resulted in the exposure of issues about epistemology (science), method (observation) and form (writing) which were central, if largely unacknowledged, to modern anthropology itself. These issues were laid bare by the attempt to bring together two projects (cinema/television and anthropology) which were driven by very different impulses in the postwar world. One was predicated on the interrogation of notions of reality and the means of its apprehension through the development of a new relationship with the world; the other project, located within the academy, was built upon the assumption of the world as an object to be scientifically investigated and represented. It was the attempt to use a scientific instrument, the camera, in the service of ethnographic investigation which starkly exposed the pretensions of anthropology's claim to be a modern science, whether it was pursued by visual or textual techniques.

The rise of visual anthropology

Visual anthropology developed most fully as an area of specialist interests and techniques within American anthropology; and, as such, it contained many of the theoretical and methodological assumptions of the American discipline more generally.[39] Its emergence in the late 1950s and 1960s was particularly associated with Margaret Mead. It is important to recognise that Mead's own preoccupations and location within the profession were also significant factors in the establishment of a certain agenda for visual anthropology. There is an irony in the fact that Mead, widely perceived by her colleagues to be a populariser and unscientific, sought to use visual technologies in the name of science.

Mead's vision of a new anthropology which engaged with the potential of visual media contained interesting possibilities; but, typically, it was compromised by her tendency to simplify and to hector her professional colleagues. Certainly the scepticism with which Mead was viewed by most university-based anthropologists greatly attributed to the marginalisation of visual anthropology by those who considered themselves at the centre of the discipline. The subdiscipline was frequently dismissed on the grounds of its theoretical naivety, its commitment to a salvage paradigm and its scientistic pretensions. These were, of course, all charges which were levelled at Mead herself.

Although visual anthropology as a specialist field within anthropology did not crystallise until the late 1960s and early 1970s, Mead's interest in the ethnographic potential of photography and film grew out of her collaboration three decades earlier with Gregory Bateson. Together they had sought to develop an innovative methodology appropriate to their investigations of certain cultural practices in Bali and New Guinea. It involved the deployment of film and photography along with other fieldwork techniques (note-taking, for example) in an effort to develop a reflexive approach to ethnographic enquiry and presentation. As Bateson emphasised in his 'Introduction' to *Balinese Character*: 'We treated the cameras in the field as recording instruments, not as devices for illustrating our theses'. The use of the camera was conceived as an active fieldwork strategy. It posed rather than resolved questions. Equally important in the use which Mead and Bateson made of visual techniques and technologies was their recognition of the limitations of language in conveying or translating aspects of social life. The juxtaposition of different kinds of material was integral then to the evocation of what Bateson called 'ethos', that is, the 'intangible aspects of culture'.[40] Later, in the context of the Second World War, Bateson and Mead embarked on what was known as the 'study of culture at a distance'. At first it involved the development of an anthropological approach towards the interpretation of film (for example, Nazi propaganda). Subsequently it became a more general study of forms of visual communication understood not as descriptions but as cultural statements about the world.[41]

The potential of the early Bateson and Mead work was never fully realised, as each moved on to pursue other, separate interests. Still, Mead continued to work with the film footage generated during their Balinese and New Guinean fieldwork, editing it into a series called 'Character formation in different cultures'.[42] Typically the important questions about method, epistemology and form raised by the approach Mead developed with Bateson were not seriously pursued. Indeed, Mead reduced them to a sort of simple scientism harnessed to a salvage paradigm.

By the early 1970s Margaret Mead had become one of the key figures in the new field of visual anthropology. Other important figures included John Marshall, Tim Asch, Asen Balikci, Robert Gardner and Karl Heider, whose concerns found focus in ethnographic film. From the outset the subdiscipline was burdened by a number of problems originating in Mead's work. Hence much energy was expended in seeking to legitimate ethnographic film as a respectable form of scientific endeavour.[43] These efforts, however, merely underlined the problematic nature of ethnographic enquiry itself. For, as Winston's astute analysis of *The Ax Fight* reveals, Asch and Chagnon were making a series of claims in their film about anthropological understanding which were not, in fact, sustained by the evidence offered by their footage. Their attempt to show the different stages by which anthropological knowledge may be reached, culminating in a set of kinship diagrams (which never fails to provoke hilarity among contemporary audiences), starkly exposed the shaky foundations upon which scientific ethnography was built.[44] The use of the camera in the service of science did not in fact solve the problem of evidence; instead, it functioned to pose once more questions about the status of evidence which had so preoccupied nine-teenth-century science.

The project of ethnographic film as it initially unfolded was not concerned with the interrogation of the fundamental premises of the discipline. This was not, perhaps, suprising. Academic anthropology itself was still largely informed by the paradigm of scientific ethnography with its distinctive object (primitive society), method (fieldwork) and theory (structural-functionalism). Although a number of important critiques had begun to emerge in the late 1960s and early 1970s, it was not until a decade later that the discipline underwent a more profound revolution.[45]

The rethinking of anthropology's claim to be a science cast doubt on all its aspects – from its object of investigation to its theory of knowledge, methods of enquiry and forms of presentation. Another kind of anthropological approach built around the use of visual techniques and technologies had already rendered problematic many of these issues. Located originally within the paradigm of scientific ethnography and yet largely pursued outside the academy, the work of Jean Rouch, David and Judith MacDougall, and Melissa Llewelyn-Davies forms an important counterpoint to the textual preoccupations of their anthropological contemporaries in the academy.

An understanding of the particular nature of the synthesis achieved between anthropology and cinema/television is central to the three case studies I will consider. For, in contrast to the general and amorphous category of ethnographic film (is it a kind of cinema or television or academic presentation?), the work of Rouch, the MacDougalls and Llewelyn-Davies involved the harnessing of anthropological sensibilities to the creative exploration of the aesthetic and social features attached to different media forms. These different attempts to pursue anthropological questions by means of image-based technologies throw into sharp relief the assumptions about knowledge and technique at the heart of the discipline.

6 The anthropological cinema of Jean Rouch

> The poet makes himself a seer by a long, prodigious and reasoned disordering of all the senses.
>
> Rimbaud[1]

Les Maîtres Fous was first screened in Paris in 1955. The small audience of French anthropologists and African intellectuals invited to the film's premiere at the Musée de l'Homme was largely hostile in its response to Jean Rouch's work. Marcel Griaule called for the film to be destroyed; Africans present at the screening denounced it as offensive and racist.[2] Shortly afterwards the British government moved to prevent it from being shown in the colonial territories of West Africa. Now, forty years later, *Les Maîtres Fous*, is widely acknowledged as a classic of modern cinema; its impact, the film's power to move and unsettle audiences, has not been diminished by the passage of time.

In this chapter, I will examine the distinctive character of Jean Rouch's anthropological cinema. The question of vision as method and metaphor is central to this task. For Rouch, like David and Judith MacDougall (the focus of the next case study), is deeply committed to an 'ocularcentric' project. Vision is elevated as the noblest of the senses, and it is privileged as a source of knowledge about the world.[3] But, as we will discover, Rouch's conception of anthropological cinema is markedly different from that developed by the MacDougalls. Thus in sharp contrast to the latter's explicit, carefully controlled, well-argued and intellectually rigorous agenda, Rouch's project appears to be highly idiosyncratic and founded on intuition.[4]

The contrast between these two examples of anthropological cinema may be traced to a number of sources – individual personalities, working methods, schools of anthropology, the social contexts for film-making activities and differing historical moments in which projects were developed. Certainly such factors are important and worthy of serious attention, as my narrative will reveal; but I will suggest that the diverse character stems from fundamentally different ways of seeing. Unlike the

MacDougalls' enlightenment project, a version perhaps of what Martin Jay describes as 'Cartesian perspectivalism',[5] where knowledge comes from intense observation of a world situated outside the self, Rouch's practice unsettles the very divisions upon which such an epistemology is founded. He disrupts the boundaries between the self and the world, mind and body, the mind's eye and the surveying eye. I want to suggest that his anthropological cinema may be considered to be 'the irruption of the night light of Romanticism as the libertarian Other of le siècle des lumières, the Century of Lights, the Enlightenment'. It is at once part of the enlightenment and yet its antithesis, the shadow around the light.[6]

Rouch once commented: 'I do know that there are a few rare moments when the filmgoer suddenly understands an unknown language without the help of any subtitles, when he participates in strange ceremonies, when he finds himself walking in towns or across terrain that he has never seen before but that he recognizes perfectly'.[7] I understand Rouch to be a modern-day visionary, a *seer*. His anthropological cinema involves moments of revelation. The visionary quality of his work, with its origins in European romanticism (and one of its twentieth-century offshoots, Surrealism) and African trance and possession, are harnessed to a new, expansive humanism. The qualities that Rouch brings to the task of anthropology, his imagination, his boldness, his playful wit and his subversive, adventurous spirit stand in stark contrast to the scepticism of much contemporary intellectual discourse. Not surprisingly, for younger anthropologists seeking to rediscover human connectedness in a world confined by old forms and ideas, Rouch is a fascinating figure.[8]

It is important to acknowledge that the unique quality of Rouch's work stems from his unusual personality. Indeed, it is virtually impossible to remain indifferent to the audacity and fiercely individualistic spirit which characterises his anthropological cinema. But any assessment of its distinctiveness must also take into account other factors shaping Rouch's ethnographic sensibilities. These include his own background, the intellectual and artistic climate of interwar Paris, and the specific concerns of French anthropology. Central, too, are the social and political circumstances in which Rouch forged a new synthesis of anthropology and cinema, my own interpretation of the innovative qualities of Rouch's anthropology involves the situation of his work within the moment of West African independence. I will suggest that Rouch's creativity was intimately linked to a revolutionary moment in modern society.[9]

The final break-up of European hegemony after two world wars and the emergence of colonial peoples as an important force in world history, shattered forever the conventional metaphysics behind notions of humanity, civilization and subjectivity. Although the political optimism which surrounded the emancipation of colonial peoples during the 1950s and early 1960s quickly gave way to cynicism and despair as the old divisions of race and power reasserted themselves, the independence movements across Asia, Africa and the Caribbean must nevertheless be acknowledged as a watershed in modern history. Jean Rouch was part of that moment of transition. Moreover, I believe that he was uniquely open to it. His work, perhaps today more than forty years ago, can be recognised as a powerful expression of a new and expanded vision of universal humanity which was embodied in the revolution of colonial peoples.

I take *Les Maîtres Fous* as the starting point for my enquiry into the distinctive nature of Rouch's *visual* anthropology. It establishes a number of themes which recur in his work (for example, the notion of a journey, an interest in migrants and urban life, the phenomenon of possession), and it evokes the contours of his humanistic vision. Moreover the film locates us squarely in the historical moment of colonial independence which, I believe, inspired Rouch's greatest work. For *Les Maîtres Fous* inaugurates the celebrated series of films (including *Jaguar, Moi – Un Noir, La Pyramide Humaine, La Chasse au lion à l'arc,* and *Chronique d'un Eté*) which Rouch made between 1954 and 1960. Although a number were not completed until a decade later, Rouch had pursued, within the space of just a few years, a boldly experimental approach to cinematic form as he pushed into new areas of anthropological experience and knowledge. A number of these 1950s films form the focus for my discussion of the nature of Rouch's romantic or visionary project. I will consider several of them as a set, establishing that the relationships between the films selected are as significant as the innovative qualities of each particular work. But in identifying *Les Maîtres Fous, Jaguar, Moi-Un Noir,* and *Chronique d'un Eté* as a distinctive group, I do not wish to suggest that these films represent a progressive sequence, a linear development; rather, I conceive of them as variations on a set of themes.

Les Maîtres Fous

Les Maîtres Fous (*The Mad Masters*) documents the course of a possession ceremony held during one Sunday by members of the Hauka sect working as migrant labourers in Accra. Emerging in the colony of Niger during the 1920s as a form of resistance to French colonial rule, the cult took hold among people who had moved from their rural villages to find work in Kumasi and Accra, the commercial areas of the British-controlled Gold Coast. During the ceremony its members undergo a violent possession by spirits, assuming the identities of their colonial masters; and, as the ambiguity contained in the title of Rouch's film suggests (who is mad – the colonial rulers or their imitators . . . or both?), the cult of the Hauka questions conventional hierarchies of power and rationality.

The film opens in the heart of Accra. We are plunged into the midst of a bustling city, what Rouch in his commentary calls 'a true Black Babylon' where different peoples from across West Africa jostle with one another, sharing in 'the great adventure of African cities'. From the beginning the film conveys a sense of movement, of complexity, of the simultaneity of events. Above all, we see people *doing* things – a rapid series of snaphots of migrants working, dancing, celebrating Jesus, shouting political slogans.[10] Interestingly, Rouch describes this activity as 'noise'. He sharpens our sense of encountering a vibrant city through the rapid juxtaposition of different shots to create a mosaic or montage structure in the film's first part.[11] But suddenly, into the shifting pattern of different elements which make up this modern urban life, Rouch inserts a possession sequence from a Hauka ceremony. Dark figures, wild-eyed and frothing from the mouth, appear against a dark sky. Already disoriented by the exuberance of the city, we are almost unaware of this shift from day to night, from the city to an unknown place, from the routine of migrant work to a moment of violent possession.[12] But, returning to Accra to meet the individuals who are members of the Hauka sect, we discover that we have absorbed, if subconsciously, both the radical disjunction and fundamental similarity of different aspects of contemporary life.

The second part of Les Maîtres Fous is signalled by the journey of the sect's members from Accra to the site of the ceremony. Leaving aboard hired trucks and buses decorated with slogans such as 'Perseverance Conquers Difficulties', the migrants travel along West Africa's first tarmac road, now overgrown, which leads deep into the forest. Here lives Mountebya, the high priest of the Hauka, whose compound with its Union Jacks, altar and statue of the governor has been carefully prepared for the ritual occasion. The film documents the preliminary stages (the nomination of a new member, the confession of wrongdoing, and purification), before building progressively to a dramatic climax in which different members become possessed, taking on the identities and customary behaviour of the British governor and his retinue. The imitation and subversion of official power which this implies is subtly underlined by Rouch's juxtaposition of a sequence from the 'real' governor's presence at the opening of the assembly in Accra. For in sharp contrast to the rest of the film, this sequence is shot from a camera situated high above the official gathering; we look down on the governor and his wife, an action expressing both the conventional hierarchy of power and its subversion during the course of the Hauka possession. With the killing and eating of a dog, the ceremony reaches its peak. Dusk approaches. Slowly the Hauka members emerge from their trance and prepare to return to Accra.

The film concludes with a series of flashbacks. Rouch returns the following day to visit different members of the Hauka sect. We watch them working calmly and efficiently, restored to their everyday lives; and yet we are reminded by the intercutting of brief dramatic shots of the previous day's Hauka ceremony that other dimensions of experience and personality co-exist within a single lived reality.

Les Maîtres Fous remains today a powerful and unsettling film. Within anthropology itself there exists a certain mythology surrounding occasions of the film's showing.[13] Undoubtedly images of the Hauka at the climax of the ceremony – possessed and frothing at the mouth; dribbling saliva flecked with the blood of a slaughtered dog; their violent and uncontrolled body movements; the pieces of dog meat bubbling away in a cauldron – are among the most disturbing which remain in the memory of a film audience. Shocking as these scenes may be, however, their impact must be considered as inseparable from the fundamental inversion of conventional categories of order/disorder which the audience confronts through its immersion in the film. What I think is unsettling about *Les Maîtres Fous* is the *orderliness* of the disorder. Moreover, in significant ways, the spectators' experience of the film replicates that undergone by the Hauka in the course of the ritual. The film disturbs the body as much as the mind. Indeed, the extreme physical responses provoked in an audience seem to mirror those manifested by possessed cult members, prompting questions about the extent to which *Les Maîtres Fous* is not just *about* possession but is an occasion *for* possession. This particular work expresses concretely what is distinctive about Rouch's project of anthropological cinema as a whole. He takes the participatory ethos of modern anthropology and synthesises it with the unique characteristics of its twentieth-century counterpart, cinema. In so doing he creates a new site for possession and transformation.[14]

The transformative power of Rouch's anthropological cinema is not a matter of chance. It is, I believe, carefully orchestrated. Like the Hauka possession ceremony itself, Rouch creates effects in his audience through the combination of different ritual elements; but in his case, it involves the use of images, sound, titles and commentary. Thus once we are able to put to one side the powerful, affective qualities of *Les Maîtres Fous*, we may appreciate the film's formal precision. Although Rouch prefers to leave the creative process deliberately unexamined, rather than self-consciously exposed through critical reflection as in the case of the MacDougalls, it is difficult to accept that there is anything random or haphazard about the way in which the film's different components are interwoven. A closer examination suggests that each cinematic element has been carefully positioned in relationship to the others and to the whole; but it is through these contrived juxtapositions that Rouch opens up areas of interpretative freedom.

The notion of a rite of passage, with its classic Van Gennepian phases of separation, liminality and re-integration, is obviously central to any interpretation of *Les Maîtres Fous*. But, as I have suggested, it is an organising motif which resonates beyond the film's substantive concerns. Furthermore, when we examine this anthropological concept more closely we will discover that Rouch's subversion of the conventional attributes associated with the three stages of a ritual performance constitutes a powerful critique of contemporary social reality.

The formal development of *Les Maîtres Fous* mirrors the progression of the ritual which it documents. Its three parts symbolise the movement which takes place in both space and time between the different phases of the rite of passage. The members of the Hauka sect travel from the heart of the city to a remote place, the site of possession, before returning again to their lives as migrant workers in the city where the film began. There appears to be a neat spatial symmetry then between the first and third parts anchored in images of urban life. Moreover, this similarity appears to be underlined by the formal composition of the film's opening and closing. Both are constructed through the technique of montage, where shots are juxtaposed rather than developed historically, and where Rouch inserts, into this present, images from different times and places. On further inspection, however, we can identify a subtle difference between the first and last part of *Les Maîtres Fous*. The opening part involves a coexistence of different elements which are organised into a series of oppositions – for example, the city and the savannah, noise and silence, chaos and order, light and dark, modernity and tradition – while the concluding sequences of the city evoke synthesis, an integration at a deeper level of the disparate parts of social experience. This new state of integration is, of course, symbolised in Rouch's discovery 'by chance' of certain Hauka members working on the day after the possession, outside Accra's mental hospital.

Rouch has been much criticised for suggesting, in the conclusion to *Les Maîtres Fous*, that possession functions as a sort of therapy, that the

Hauka cult is a means by which African migrants adapt themselves to a colonial regime.[15] Such a criticism neglects, however, the subtle difference between the states of integration which mark the opening and closing of the film. At the beginning, Rouch depicts African urban life in a style which echoes the European city symphony films of the 1920s. Through montage, he evokes the rhythm and complexity of a machine in which migrants function as a skilled and varied workforce. The sheer range of jobs Rouch reveals in the first part of *Les Maîtres Fous* is remarkable; but so, too, is the integration of such a complex division of labour. Although in the latter part of the film, he appears to suggest the re-absorption of the migrants into this functioning machine, at another level and integral to it we are aware of profound resistance to 'mechanical civilization'. The members of the Hauka cult are no longer just part of a labour force, an anonymous mass of 'hands' (what Rouch calls in his quirky English 'force of the main'); they have been revealed as complex individual human subjects.[16]

According to Eaton, Rouch was committed to the use of film in ritual situations because he believed it could capture the rapidly unfolding events in a way which was impossible through the means of conventional note-taking.[17] What is striking about *Les Maîtres Fous*, though, is Rouch's rejection of montage as the cinematic technique for capturing the simultaneity and complexity of the Hauka possession ceremony itself. Thus, in contrast to the first and last part of the film, the middle section which documents the ritual performance is constructed as a narrative with a marked linear movement. Events are shown in sequence and build progressively towards the ceremony's climax. It is only when the climax is reached that Rouch abruptly changes perspective, interposing scenes from the British governor's salute in Accra. The insertion of this material underlines the conventional hierarchy of colonial society and its subversion during the course of the ritual. But it is important to recognise that the possession ritual itself is built upon division and hierarchy. Thus the middle phase of the film, what anthropologists following Van Gennep conventionally term 'liminality', is neither a fluid nor a chaotic state. It is highly structured and orderly. At one level audiences of *Les Maîtres Fous*, disturbed by the bizarre images of possessed Hauka, experience a strong sense of dislocation as conventional patterns of behaviour break down. But at another level, beyond the immediate and powerful sense of disorder is an alternative order. The Hauka ceremony inverts, rather than dissolves, the paired oppositions which are posed in the film's opening. The 'madness' of the ritual unfolds in real time. Its participants are ranked hierarchically; their actions are strictly rule bound; and the 'rationality' of *Les Maîtres Fous*'s extraordinary sequences is expressed through an established narrative form. Finally, of course, the film inverts the conventional social and political order – it is about Africans representing Europeans.

In returning to the city in the final part of *Les Maîtres Fous*, the phase of re-integration, Rouch attempts to synthesise the film's previous parts. He is seeking to evoke a new kind of integration or what might be called a 'surreality'. For in beginning with a series of conventional divisions between the city and the countryside, Europe and Africa, the conscious and the unconscious, the mind and the body, Rouch inverts these pairs as a preliminary to their incorporation into an expanded vision of social experience which is, at once, the same and different, whole and complex.

The vision Rouch expresses through *Les Maîtres Fous* may be interpreted as a rejection of the progressive political rhetoric of the time. The film was made in the midst of Africa's struggle for emancipation, and it contains a powerful critique of colonial authority. But to me it is more than just a repudiation of European domination. Rouch's critique implicates the African intellectuals who so vigorously denounced the film at its first screening. Their condemnation may be understood as a response to Rouch's implicit challenge to their political ambition as much as it was a rejection of images they perceived it as representing of a savage and irrational African psyche. For, in *Les Maîtres Fous*, Rouch questions the simple equation of independence and progress, modernity and rationality, what is called 'mechanical civilization' in the film's opening titles. The possession sequence, in its inversion and satirization of political hierarchy, may be understood as a symbol of the fundamental irrationality of all structures of government, whether colonial or postcolonial.

Les Maîtres Fous is widely acknowledged by commentators to mark a crucial moment in the development of Rouch's anthropological cinema.[18] It represents the movement away from an earlier conception of ethnographic film-making associated with the documentation of culture. Now Rouch begins to use the camera to bring about a qualitatively different kind of ethnographic understanding; but, in so doing, he may be considered to be extending, rather than breaking with, an approach closely identified with his teacher, Marcel Griaule. For central to *Les Maîtres Fous* is a distinction which James Clifford highlights within Griaule's work between ethnography as documentation and as initiation.[19] Moreover, the film stands as a striking manifestation of Griaule's recognition that ethnographic research involves conflict – it is 'inherently agonistic, theatrical and fraught with power'.[20] Indeed, as Clifford himself notes, Griaule's 'ethnographie vérité' is analogous to the *cinéma vérité* pursued by Rouch. Both express a perspective which is not predicated on the recording of an objective ethnographic reality. Instead ethnographic realities are produced in and through the ethnographic encounter itself.[21]

But, in other ways, *Les Maîtres Fous* establishes the beginning of Rouch's own distinctive project. Although drawing creatively upon earlier work in French anthropology – and, importantly, French cinema – Rouch, with *Les Maîtres Fous*, begins to forge an unusual synthesis of these traditions, transforming each element in the process. On the one hand, Rouch maps out fresh territory for ethnographic exploration – specifically, migrants, cities and movement in a West African context, a subject matter which he once described as the 'populist avant-garde'.[22] On the other hand, and inseparable from the opening up of these new substantive concerns, is Rouch's distinctive use of the camera. No longer a device for recording social reality, the camera in Rouch's hands becomes progressively more active, audacious, even aggressive as it fuses with his being, freeing him to explore new areas of human experience and knowledge.

Rouch began making *Les Maîtres Fous* in the period before lightweight, portable cameras with synchronous sound were available to documentary film-makers.[23] The film was shot silently by Rouch using a handheld camera. The sound was recorded separately by Damouré Zika, a Nigerien whom Rouch had met during his work as an engineer in West Africa almost ten years earlier. The final edited version of the film saw the addition of a commentary to its sound track. This took the form of an impromptu performance by Rouch himself. The particular formal features of *Les Maîtres Fous*, the perceived limitations of 1950s cinematic technology, often serve as explanations of the film. Certainly Rouch, like Richard Leacock or Robert Drew, his American counterparts actively re-making documentary cinema in the postwar period, was pushing against the restrictions of existing camera and sound equipment; but it is important to be wary of technologically determined explanations. To pursue such an argument, one which Rouch himself often encourages, distracts attention from more interesting questions about the interplay between freedom and constraint, chance and necessity which run throughout his work.

Les Maîtres Fous is distinguished by its intimate camera work, a reflection of the film-making style which Rouch had developed early in his career when he abandoned the use of a tripod. Characteristically he presents the evolution of this handheld camera style as the result of an accident, rather than a conscious act, an improvisational gesture forced upon him by the damage he caused to the tripod he was carrying in his equipment. Likewise, the film's other dominant technique apart from its striking images, Rouch's narration, is described as impromptu. Again it suggests a spontaneous or an unrehearsed delivery emerging in the course of the cinematic process itself – in this case during the film's screening. Already we can identify here a curious mixture of determinism and spontaneity in Rouch's practice. It appears that certain formal dimensions of his work are shaped by the constraints of technology; and yet intuition, accident and improvisation may be discerned as equally critical elements in his film-making process. As I have suggested, it is the dialectical movement or interplay between the opposing poles of freedom and constraint which generates the creative energy at the core of Rouch's anthropology. Rouch himself alludes to it in the opening titles of *Les Maîtres Fous*. He refers to the film as a 'game' in which members of the audience may become players. Such activity and participation is, of course, bound by rules; but equally it is driven by risk, innovation and improvisation.

Rouch begins *Les Maîtres Fous* with a title sequence which prepares us for, or warns us about, what is to follow. From the outset, then, we are aware that something extraordinary will be encountered in the course of the film. We are told that the acceptance of certain violent scenes is a precondition for our full participation in a ritual which the cinema itself simulates. We become players in what Rouch calls 'the game'. The problem we face, however, is that we do not know the rules of this game. Thus we are forced to depend on Rouch as our guide; he acts as the mediator between what we know in our everyday experience and the strange world we enter in the cinema's darkness. The critical role which Rouch assumes is revealed in one of the *Les Maîtres Fous*' dominant features, its commentary, which manages like the images on screen to be both comprehensible and incomprehensible at the same time.

Les Maîtres Fous, as I have noted, was shot without sound. The contrast between noise and silence, however, is one of the film's central themes. Rouch refers several times in his commentary to this contrast, which he links to the different spaces of city and savannah. I hear his own voice as part of the noise of the city, the babble/babylon where migrants live, communicating across linguistic barriers through the creation of new, improvised, hybrid languages just like Rouch's own 'bad English' or expressed in the distinctive quality of his narrations which, as Jeanette De Bouzek notes, have 'the "surreal" aspect of a cacophony of mixed voices, a collage of direct observations, "scientific" information, scholarly interpretations, reflexive reflections, reportage, and poetic translations of bits of dialogue'.[24] But Rouch's voice is also *Les Maîtres Fous*' single unifying thread, its constant beat; and, as such, the commentary becomes a ritual chant. Hence at first the narration seems to function as an obstacle to the realisation of community that Rouch seeks to create within the transformative site of cinema. Later it is transcended, yielding to a complete participation in the cinematic experience: 'Seeing comes before words', John Berger writes. But in order to rediscover the wholeness of a world which existed before language, we have to pass through language itself.[25]

In seeking to interpret *Les Maîtres Fous* I have drawn on methods of analysis developed in the study of myth and ritual. Using a variety of approaches, anthropologists have sought to identify the different elements which make up a text or performance; and in exposing the dynamic of relationships between such elements, they have revealed chains of significance and an open-endedness of meaning. Whether the film is a Hollywood movie or one labelled as 'ethnographic', an anthropological perspective proves valuable in interpreting cinema both as text and performance, as a powerful site of contemporary myth and ritual. I have attempted to exacavate some of the latent meanings embedded within the text through an examination of certain formal dimensions which characterise Rouch's film and, in this way, indicate what I understand to be the contours of Rouch's distinctive vision of the contemporary world. But, in engaging in this exercise, I have drawn on conventional patterns of intellectual argument. I have used ways of thinking and writing associated with a rational enlightenment discourse. It is precisely this mode of inquiry, one dominated by the voice of Reason, which Rouch in *Les Maîtres Fous* is determined to disrupt.

Rouch attempts to persuade us of his vision through participation in a shamanistic experience. He seeks to effect a revolution in an audience's experience of social reality, creatively combining cinema's intrinsically fantastic properties with a particular manipulation of film's different elements. Rouch's intention is made explicit in the film's opening titles:

The Producer, in showing the audience these documents *without concession or concealment* is anxious to warn them about the violence and cruelty of some scenes. But he wants to make them participate completely in a ritual which is a special solution to the problem of readjustment, and which shows how some Africans represent our western civilization.[26]

Rouch engages us, then not through an appeal to the mind, like the MacDougalls, but rather to the mind and body, through the disordering of the senses and the subversion of habitual ways of thinking as a precondition for plumbing new depths of knowledge and understanding.

In the next chapter we will discover how differently David and Judith MacDougall have used the cinematic medium as a distinctive form for the expression of anthropological knowledge. Despite an innovative approach, their films remain closely wedded to the intellectual style of literary anthropology. Rouch's own comments on them suggest a similar view: 'MacDougall's [sic] films on the Turkana are a wonderful positive approach, in which he translates his subjects' words in subtitles. The trouble for me is that the translations are books – the transformation of a written language.'[27] Thus although as spectators of the MacDougalls' work we are plunged into a dark space, we are not expected to surrender our rational faculties. Indeed, quite the contrary – we are expected to strengthen them against the experience of bewilderment and instinctive prejudice. We have to learn to think our way through what appears on screen as chaotic or incomprehensible. It requires work, effort and brainpower – or, more metaphorically, the exercise of the light of reason.

Rouch's intention, however, is to create a different kind of cinematic experience. As *Les Maîtres Fous* reveals, he takes the Hollywood model of cinema – a dark place filled with magic, fantasy and fear – and, into this space, he violently inserts the traditional concerns and subject matter of anthropological inquiry. Rouch recreates the Hauka ceremony with each screening; and with his audience freed from everyday inhibitions, disoriented as we are in an enclosed, dark arena situated outside normal time and space, the film-maker tries to persuade us to surrender conventional patterns of thought, to reconnect mind and body through a ritual experience.[28] Moreover, in making a community with our fellow spectators, we also discover a new community with those who appear on screen. We become engaged as active participants in the creation of an expanded notion of human society.

Les Maîtres Fous reveals the sharp contrast between the conception of a shared or participatory anthropological cinema pursued by the Mac-Dougalls and the one practised by Rouch. In the case of David and Judith MacDougall, their innovations in collaborative practice grew out of observational cinema. Building from an initial premise of respect and distance, they attempted to generate a new kind of participation through the notion of conversation, in which voice, rather than vision, is the means for defining and understanding the world. Rouch's participatory anthropology, however, is built upon a violation of these qualities. Moreover, it is not built around words as part of rationalist discourse, but involves exploitation of their evocative power, enabling the poet 'to see'.

Unlike the MacDougalls' penetrating light of reason, Rouch is drawn to the shadow around the light. This is powerfully symbolised by the cinema itself, the darkness which surrounds the illumination of the screen. It is an image which resonates throughout *Les Maîtres Fous*; it reappears in *Moi, Un Noir* and *Chronique d'un été*.[29]

Jaguar

At the conclusion of the Hauka possession sequence, one of the cult members declares: 'This year's festival has been a great success indeed. Next year we must have two festivals and we, the Hauka, will be very pleased.' To this Rouch adds his own observation: 'Thus from one festival another is born'. The notion of one event precipitating another forms an important principle in Rouch's own film-making practice, as William Rothman observes: 'Rouch makes his films to beget films'.[30] Unlike the MacDougalls, whose project unfolds through a series of critical reflections on practice, Rouch's anthropological cinema is much more haphazard, based on chance and intuitive connection. With *Les Maîtres Fous*, Rouch, rather like his migrant subjects, has embarked on a journey; and, as with their festival, from one of his films another is born.

Jaguar was shot by Rouch during the same period as *Les Maîtres Fous*, that is, in the mid-1950s. According to Paul Stoller, the idea for the film came from Damouré Zika (the sound recordist on *Les Maîtres Fous*); and, from the outset, it was conceived as an experiment in improvisational cinema.[31] For unlike *Les Maîtres Fous*, with its event-based logic, all that was known about *Jaguar* in advance of its making was the beginning and ending of the migrants' journey. The film was not completed until a decade later, when Rouch worked with an editor on the footage and added to it a highly distinctive sound track. The close connection between this film and *Les Maîtres Fous* is immediately revealed in the shared material which Rouch uses of scenes from Accra (for example, the wonderfully named 'Weekend in California' bar; the train crossing the city; and the gold miners descending into the shaft). More interesting to explore, however, is the way Rouch now develops the central themes of *Les Maîtres Fous*. For although through *Jaguar* he again raises questions of migration, cities and modernity, they are presented in a strikingly different configuration. Central to both works is the journey, the movement of people through time and space; but, on closer inspection, we will discover that this shared structural principle functions to create films which are the mirror opposite of one another.

In *Les Maîtres Fous*, Rouch dramatically exposes hidden layers of subjectivity, transforming an anonymous mass of migrant workers ('force of the main') into individuals, active human agents with complex inner lives. *Jaguar* may be considered as an extension of his concern with the migrant experience and the nature of individual subjectivity. This time the geographical movement itself forms the focus for Rouch's explorations of personality and society. He joins three characters, Lam, Ilo and Damoure, on their journey from Niger to the Gold Coast and back again. The different stages of their adventure give his film its three distinctive parts.

The first part introduces the film's key characters and their preparations for the road. Each one occupies a distinctive niche in village society – Lam, the herder; Ilo, the fisherman; and Damouré, with his elementary schooling, the ladies' man. The market place, a microcosm of the cities for which they are bound, is their meeting place. Here they listen to those who have returned from the Gold Coast with tales of adventure and success, and they begin to dream of their own great journey. Before embarking upon it, Lam, Ilo and Damouré take the necessary ritual precautions to ensure luck, good fortune or a 'good road'. Their separation from the familiar world of the village begins with the long trek by foot through strange places and peoples. Traversing the dramatic landscape, the three friends encounter different emblems of modernity – roads which have been cut through mountains (as one of them asks 'by God or men?'); bridges painted red; an overturned truck lying beside the road. But, as the village men discover, the connection and movement implied by these symbols are, in fact, subverted by the apparatus of colonial government. For the first part of *Jaguar* ends at the customs post. Travelling without identification papers, Lam, Ilo and Damouré are denied entry to the Gold Coast. The first barriers the young men have confronted in their epic journey are not geographical or social ones, but the political controls of colonial bureaucracy. By slipping illegally across the border, however, they demonstrate skills essential to migrant life, one built upon the exploitation of cracks in official society.

From the beginning, *Jaguar* is marked by certain distinctive formal features. For example, Rouch's camera work emphasises in striking ways the symbolic quality of the journey being undertaken by Lam, Ilo and Damoure. It may be understood as an expression of the film-maker's rejection of conventional approaches to migration which often reduce it to material considerations, to a strategy motivated by economic weakness. Rouch's camera, never still but always in movement, swooping, turning and dizzyingly mobile, is a full participant in the existential experience which migration represents.[32] It evokes the disorientation and excitement of the journey. During the opening part of the film there are several abrupt shifts from documentation to what might be described as 'surreal' sequences. In this way, through the use of striking images of light, vegetation and landscape, Rouch intensifies the sense of leaving behind a familiar world and entering an unknown territory.

Part two of *Jaguar* begins with the separation of the three friends, as each one embarks on his particular adventure in the city. Rouch formally marks this moment in the film by abandoning the structural principle which organised its first part into a single progressive narrative. Now he builds the middle section of *Jaguar* around montage, intercutting different episodes and characters to suggest the complexity, fragmentation and timelessness of modern urban life. Among the most memorable scenes of the film as a whole are those of Damouré arriving triumphantly in Accra, which opens the city sequences. Imagining himself as a political leader, riding an open-topped vehicle and acknowledging the cheers of the crowds below, Damouré, the ever confident ladies' man, imitates the style of political leaders like Nkrumah who were travelling at the time across the West African countryside and mobilising popular support for independence. As Rouch suggests here, the city is a place of dreams, of fantasy, of new identities, where anything is possible and everyone can re-make themselves. Damouré, of course, soon finds his niche. He becomes a foreman in an Accra woodyard; he takes to wearing glasses (a sign of education that is, reading) and he adopts the mannerisms of a 'boss'. Lam, in Kumasi, changes out of his old clothes and buys a *boubou* to wear in town. Almost mesmerised by the sheer visual spectacle of the city, he plunges headlong into the crowd and is carried along by its seemingly boundless energy and activity. He notes the different economic niches which migrant groups have managed to colonise; but he, too, quickly adapts, becoming yet another cog in this vast machine. Lam sets up a stall; selling whatever comes his way from clocks to combs to perfume and medicine, he services the sophisticated tastes of an urban clientele. Ilo works in the port of Accra, a *kaya kaya* or porter who struggles to survive at the margins of cosmopolitan life.

The middle part of *Jaguar* is constructed as a series of snapshots, with the film-maker cutting continually between the three friends at work and at leisure. The camera's restlessness and sharp juxtapositions are a constant reminder of the distinctive nature of the city itself.[33] There is attraction and repulsion, fascination and fear. Moreover, Rouch's camera assumes an audacious air, swaggering akin to Damouré the 'jaguar' himself. For the film-maker seems to be everywhere and anywhere, disregarding all the conventional rules of both shooting and editing as he constantly shifts his position from one character to another, from one location to another, from the street to the rooftops, cutting between them with a rapidity and confidence which is breathtaking.

From these separate, fragmented episodes of city life, Rouch concludes the film's middle section with the three friends re-united and flourishing in their own business. Ilo and Damouré have travelled from Accra to Kumasi to meet up with Lam. Now they are partners, selling from what was Lam's stall; and as a natural arena of theatre, a place for role playing, wit, verbal skill and improvisation, they show off all the strategies which as migrants they have mastered. Running their own stall is, of course, the pinnacle of their success, not just because it attracts customers but also because the friends no longer work for anyone other than themselves.

Having left for the city on foot, Lam, Ilo and Damouré travel back to the village for the rainy season by truck. This time the customs post can pose no threat to the 'modern heroes', as Rouch describes them in his commentary. For the three friends, loaded down with the symbols of their success, relive the triumphal moment of return enjoyed by the great explorers and conquerors of past centuries. Although in the final part of his film, Rouch shows how each one is re-absorbed into village life, assuming his responsibilities for harvesting or beginning to plan his marriage, the young men enjoy a new status. They are the same and yet different, now members of an elite group of men, each of whom has been away, endured the trial of strange places and peoples, and has returned with honour to commit himself anew to village life.

Rouch underlines the reintegrative impulse of *Jaguar*'s closing chapter by a return to the narrative structure and linear time which organised the film's first part. I want to suggest that this formal feature may serve as a useful starting point for an exploration of the different levels of meaning embedded within Rouch's text, specifically concerning questions of history and subjectivity. For *Jaguar*'s three parts organized into a movement from narrative to montage and back again to narrative reveals a particular interpretation by the film-maker of contemporary social reality.

At one level Rouch's film may be understood as an ethnographic record of a particular time and place. It is located in the period immediately before the establishment of independent African nations, when migration from the savannah areas to the cities of the Gold Coast was expected of young men.[34] A period in the city formed an integral part of growing up. Migration conferred adulthood on young men; and thus, like the more conventional rituals of transition (circumcision or warriorhood, for example), Rouch reveals it to be a rite of passage in the Van Gennepian sense. We may identify in *Jaguar* the different phases of separation, liminality and re-integration in the successive stages of Lam, Ilo and Damouré's journey as Rouch charts the process by which these men achieve their new status in society. The distinctive features of each phase are underlined by Rouch's alternation of the principles of narrative and montage in his construction of the film's three sections.

Unlike the liminal phase of *Les Maîtres Fous*, the middle section of *Jaguar* contains the features conventionally associated by anthropologists with the phase of transition. The city is located outside time; it is conceived as a series of fragments which overlap and intersect; there is movement but not development. We can see how Rouch's formal construction of this sequence around the principle of montage sharply contrasts with the film's other parts. *Jaguar* begins and ends in a specific place. As the origin and destination of the young men's journey through time and space, the village appears to be located in real time. It functions as a symbol of authenticity. It is the locus of the film's truth, the site for the legitimation of social identity in marked contrast to the transience and effervescence of an unreal city. Rouch uses the narrative sections of *Jaguar* to frame, or more precisely to contain, the montage sequence of its middle part. In this way, he locates the African village in history. Moreover, *Jaguar* reveals Lam, Ilo and Damouré as subjects in history, indeed making history from where they are situated in the world and not from where colonial structures have sought to place them. For the Nigerien migrants to Accra and Kumasi are part of a tradition of mitration and labour movement which predates European domination of this area. The moment of colonial independence is incidental, rather than central to their trajectories as historical subjects.[35]

Jaguar is, above all, a celebration of human agency. It is dominated by engaging personalities whose actions are the driving force in the film's development. We follow the young men as they seek to forge their own identities, mixing the old and the new, the countryside and the city, the traditional and the modern, the mundane and the fantastic with a boundless self-confidence which is reflected in the style and energy of the film itself. Importantly, Rouch and his characters do not fail in the city; rather, they demonstrate all the skills and resourcefulness of successful game players. They take risks, improvise, bend the rules, exploiting and flourishing in the cracks of official society. As the film progresses, its key characters, including Rouch himself, expand, their personalities becoming almost larger than life in order to meet the challenges posed by a fluid and complex world. By emphasising human agency in this way, focusing attention on the energies and capacities for individual self-determination, Rouch downplays the power of society and history in shaping peoples' lives. He inflates the size of the individual personality to match that of the social moment itself; and in so doing we witness the film's characters taking on the world on their terms. Thus if *Les Maîtres Fous* emphasises the oppression and confinement of urban life, necessitating violent moments of catharthis, the city in *Jaguar* appears in a radically different light. It is a place of freedom, of energy and transformation, where the self expands and individual identity can be endlessly reinvented.

Thus, at one level, *Jaguar* replicates the progressive movement implied in the Van Gennepian motif of a rite of passage. The film involves a transition from the old to the new as symbolised by the friends' journey. But at the same time, this linear movement subverts conventional assumptions concerning history and modernity. In making the village both the point of departure and arrival, Rouch rejects the modernization paradigm characteristic of contemporary African and European political discourse. Moreover, through his focus on the creativity of individual subjects, Rouch refuses to accept the inevitability of bureaucatic power as symbolised by the state. Unlike the MacDougalls, whose critique of modernization in *To Live With Herds* only serves to reify modernist categories of countryside and city, traditional and modern, past and present, the authentic and the synthetic, the vision articulated in *Jaguar* is perhaps more truly subversive. For Rouch refuses to be bound by the dualisms at the heart of contemporary intellectual and political discourse.

Jaguar, organised around the anthropological motif of a rite of passage, contains a marked linear movement, reflecting the physical journey undertaken by its principal characters. In this sense its formal structure may be characterised as a progressive narrative, albeit one which is not defined by European conceptions of society and history. But Jaguar also contains another kind of movement which is implied in the Van Gennepian concept. Cutting across the film's linear or historical development is cyclical time. It is symbolised by the return of the migrants to the place where their journey began, the village which Rouch identifies as the site of social reproduction. The return to the village, however, does not involve a rejection of the city. As the film reveals, the two are intertwined, their boundaries blurred by the continual movement of people for whom the city and countryside coexist as dimensions of a single complex social reality. Moreover, for Rouch's subjects this world is pre-eminently personal. It is one made through human agency which both pre-exists and is subversive of the structures of contemporary state bureaucracy.

Rouch's critique of the anthropological enterprise istelf is no less profound. For although the motif of the rite of passage reverberates at many levels in the film, Rouch also uses Van Gennep's concept reflexively to comment on ethnographic practice itself. Indeed *Jaguar* may be enjoyed as a satire on the anthropologist's own journey, with its heroes, their fantasies, adventures and tall tales. But more than this, Rouch questions the central paradigm around which the modern humanist project since Montaigne was built. As Michele Richman observes in an essay exploring anthropological modernism in France:

If Montaigne set a precedent for French humanism, it is because his *Essais* record the first self-reflexive mapping of the modern self, an inner voyage whose confrontation with the demonic dualisms of Western consciousness – body and soul, self versus other, intellect over sensibility, contemplation against action and male versus female – were no less formidable than the enounter with the mythic monsters awaiting explorers who trespassed the geographical boundaries of the sixteenth century. The parallel is not merely rhetorical. For the innovation of the author of 'Des Cannibales' is to have tied the discovery of the modern subjects to the exploration of a New World which would irrevocably decenter the Old. Comparisons with cultural others was neither invidious nor simply praiseworthy of difference: it was the catalyst for self-scrutiny and reappraisal of the relation of self to society through the standards of an other.[36]

Rouch takes this defining moment in history, Europe's encounter with the exotic other, and inverts its key elements to undermine the very premises upon which anthropology, among other modern disciplines, has conventionally rested. The journey undertaken by *Jaguar*'s African characters, Lam, Ilo and Damouré replicates that of the European explorers and ethnographers; but it is, crucially, the mirror opposite. Moreover, as in *Les Maîtres Fous*, Rouch presents this upside-down world within a darkened auditorium. Thus again, Rouch recognises and exploits the distinctive features of the cinema (the dark around the light, its situation outside everyday time and space) in order to confront an anthropological audience with an inverted image of itself.

The cinematic experience Rouch seeks to create around *Jaguar* differs, however, in certain interesting respects from that of *Les Maîtres Fous*. The contrast between them is related to the specific concerns of each film. In both cases Rouch attempts to replicate in his audience the experience which the film's subjects themselves undergo on screen. Thus, as we have already seen with *Les Maîtres Fous*, the film-maker recreates with each showing something of the violent nature of the Hauka ceremony itself, using the cinema to evoke a notion of expanded community through the audience's participation in a collective ritual. Given its different substantive focus, *Jaguar* engages its spectators as individuals, rather than as a collective. Every viewer has the chance to establish their own unmediated relationship with the film's distinctive characters (not least because Rouch does not position himself as crucially between us and the screen). In some ways members of *Jaguar*'s audience resemble the readers of a late nineteenth-century novel. Our cinematic journey mirrors that undergone by Lam, Ilo and Damouré; and like them, in the darkness of the cinema we create our own dreams and revel in private fantasies. By surrendering to the film, becoming participants or players in 'the game', breaking rules and taking risks, we eventually emerge, like the friends themselves, as different people. We are returned to our everyday life; but stimulated by the exuberance and inventiveness of *Jaguar*'s key characters, we too experience the sense of an enhanced personality, conscious of our capacities to be actors in society and history.

With *Les Maîtres Fous*, Rouch uses the cinema as an arena in which religious community, a sort of timeless collectivity bound by shared experience, might be generated. But equally, as *Jaguar* reveals, Rouch exploits cinema's potential as a site for historical consciousness. This film, it can be argued, expresses something of the original impulse behind the cinematic innovations of the great directors of the early twentieth century. For Griffith and Eisenstein, history as society in movement could be uniquely recreated on screen. They recognised that in the darkness of the cinema, spectators may escape from the limitations of their conventional personalities; and by projecting themselves into what they watch on screen, imaginatively participating as agents in the large and complex world which unfolds before them, a film audience is able to reach a new understanding of itself in history. Without the epic sweep of a Griffith or Eisenstein movie, I believe that Rouch's *Jaguar* evokes in its audience something similar – a sense of subjective expansion and heightened historical consciousness.

Although it is important to examine each of Rouch's films as a single text, it is also important to explore the connections between them, since collectively they reveal the film-maker's distinctive vision of modern society. As I noted earlier, *Les Maîtres Fous* and *Jaguar* were filmed by Rouch at the same time; but I suggested that the connections between them were more profound than merely the footage they shared. We are now able to acknowledge that while the two films are constructed from the same key elements, they are combined in strikingly opposite ways. *Les Maîtres Fous* began in the city, moved to the countryside and returned to the city. In *Jaguar*, however, this movement is reversed; and the film moves from countryside to city to countryside. This contrast also finds expression in the formal sequence of the two films. For *Les Maîtres Fous* begins and ends with a sort of montage, while narrative structures the central ritual section; but in the case of *Jaguar*, it is the opening and closing sections which are distinguished by a linear or narrative movement, with the middle section more loosely or episodically constructed. If *Les Maîtres Fous* is built pre-eminently around the notion of an interior journey, *Jaguar* is about real movement through time and space. If the city confines the migrants of *Les Maîtres Fous*, it is the site of freedom for *Jaguar*'s adventurers.

The question of modernity lies at the core of both films. It is subtly indicated by Rouch in the early part of *Les Maîtres Fous*, when in his commentary he draws our attention to the road along which the migrants are travelling in order to reach the compound of Mountebya, the Hauka high priest. As he tells us, it was the first tarmac road in West Africa, a powerful emblem of modernity; but, virtually abandoned, it lies neglected and overgrown. The movement of the migrants is in the opposite direction to that symbolized by the road's construction. Once the conduit for people and goods moving from the forest to the coast, it now leads only to the site of Hauka possession. But as we have seen, Rouch turns this picture upside down in *Jaguar*. What appears to be a puzzling contradiction is, in fact, one of the surrealist hallmarks of Rouch's work. His purpose is to juxtapose conventionally contrasting positions in order to subvert a certain intellectual way of thinking.[37] Thus in placing *Les Maîtres Fous* and *Jaguar* alongside each other, he refuses to take an either/or position, evoking instead a picture of contemporary reality as a hall of mirrors.

Moi, Un Noir

Moi, Un Noir offers yet another perspective on the world of migrants, cities and journeys which Rouch sought to explore through his development of an anthropological cinema. This film, like *Jaguar*, was shot silently during the late 1950s and edited some years later, when an improvised soundtrack was added. *Moi, Un Noir* raises many of the questions already established in Rouch's other work of this period; but, characteristically, their configuration and the cinematic experience provoked through this particular film are different. The distinctive features of *Moi, Un Noir* can only be fully revealed by juxtaposing it with the other films of this series.

The early sequences of *Moi, Un Noir* situate us within familiar territory. We embark on an adventure with Rouch and a handful of characters, following 'Edward G. Robinson' as he moves around the city, Abidjan, during the course of a week, from Monday to Monday. Both the tone and content of Rouch's opening commentary, as with the other films, evokes a sense in the audience that what we are about to experience is emblematic in some way of the modern world. There is an epic quality about the journey to and through the city which these Africans undertake. For Rouch's characters, never static, are revealed in new ways by the experiences undergone in the course of the film; and, as a consequence, the marginality or invisibility of their structural position as migrants in the city is transformed. Their lives, their dreams and aspirations become a drama of contemporary life.

'Every day, young people like the characters in this film arrive in

Africa's towns. They have left school or the family's land to enter the modern world. They know how to do everything and nothing. They are one of the things wrong with Africa's new towns – young people without jobs', Rouch's opening commentary declares.[38] We set off with Robinson in search of wealth, for Treichville (a suburb of Abidjan) is, as he puts it, 'the capital of money'. The city is a crowded space, a place where people and things are endlessly in movement. It offers itself as a spectacle, a source of visual fascination and desire – cars, trucks, porters, markets, bars, movies and processions. Robinson strolls through the streets. Initially he appears to be rather like a jaguar (a *flâneur*); he dreams of success and of acquiring what the city holds out as its prizes (a job, money, a car, a wife). But very quickly we learn that he and his friends are excluded from the city. They move about within it but are denied any real connection to it. We, like them, share the experience of being always on the outside looking on.

If the first part of *Moi, Un Noir* depicts a week in the life of a migrant and his fruitless attempts to make an entry into urban life, the second part follows him through a weekend when no one works and everyone enjoys themselves. Robinson and his friends visit the beach. They play in the waves and on the sand; but, despite their own exuberant activity, they cannot transform the experience of their own situation. For again, Robinson is conscious of standing outside. He glimpses but cannot grasp the happiness he seeks. What remains available to him, however, is fantasy. It becomes the means by which he is able to express his own subjectivity, his agency, his creativity in the face of the city's refusal to acknowledge him. One of *Moi, Un Noir*'s most striking sequences is contained in the middle part of the film. Here, Robinson becomes a prize fighter. Rouch's camera is the vehicle through which he acts out an extraordinary performance in his imaginary boxing ring. But it can only be a temporary release from the confines of his situation, and the film returns Robinson to confront yet another Monday as a migrant in search of work. He dreams of going home. Images of life in a Nigerien village promise the happiness which has eluded him in the city.

Again *Moi, Un Noir* is constructed around the motif of a journey. However instead of movement through space (geographical, in the case of *Jaguar* or psychological with *Les Maîtres Fous*), here there is movement through time – a week in a migrant's life. Again it might be said that Rouch uses a three-part structure to organise this cycle of work and leisure in the city; but what is striking about *Moi, Un Noir* is the absence of transformation in Robinson and his friends as they move through the different phases of Van Gennepian rite of passage. Their own journey to the city from the village is, of course, a rite of passage in itself, as Rouch revealed in *Jaguar*. In *Moi, Un Noir*, the city is not experienced as a place which frees young men who travel from their Nigerien village in search of adventure. It is not a site for the reinvention of self or for the expansion of personality – except in moments of private fantasy. For this time the city confines these young Africans, and it denies them subjectivity. With *Les Maîtres Fous*, Rouch reveals the coexistence of city and countryside; the ceremony of violent catharsis which the film's subjects undergo affirms the scope and dimensions of their complex subjectivity.

In both *Les Maîtres Fous* and *Jaguar*, Rouch uses cinema to provoke a particular experience in his audience. With *Moi, Un Noir*, cinema itself as a place of fantasy is the film's reflexive focus. The characters on screen become stars from Hollywood movies; and in watching their transformation we, the audience, confront the imaginative projection which the camera makes possible.

Chronique d'un été

Can't cinema become the means of breaking that membrane which isolates each of us from others in the metro, on the street, or on the stairway of the apartment building? The quest for a new *cinéma vérité* is at the same time a quest for a 'cinéma de fraternité'.[39] Edgar Morin, 'Chronicle of a film', p. 5.

Chronique d'un été was filmed in Paris and St Tropez during the summer of 1960. It is widely acknowledged as a key text in the development of the *Nouvelle Vague* or New Wave; and, as such, the film has always attracted a much wider cinema audience than just an anthropological one. Certainly its substantive concerns and formal innovations evoke comparisons with the work of Rouch's European contemporaries, film-makers such as Godard, Truffaut and Antonioni. From the mid-1950s Rouch had been developing a highly innovative project of anthropological cinema in a West African context. Nevertheless, in terms of his own trajectory, *Chronique* represents a significant new departure. It was Rouch's first experience of working as an anthropological film-maker in Europe. Moreover, it was the outcome of a collaborative project which he developed with the French sociologist, Edgar Morin. Rouch himself recognised that, after having focused his energies for more than a decade in Africa, his own 'odd tribe', the Parisians, had become strange to him. His experience, however, in sharing the lives of a handful of young people over the course of a summer resulted in a profoundly unsettling vision of modern society.

The opening shots – an industrial landscape at dawn, a factory siren, people emerging from the metro – signal the film's primary focus. It is what Rouch calls in *Les Maîtres Fous* 'mechanical civilization'. In some ways, *Chronique*'s opening sequence is reminiscent of the city films made during the 1920s, particularly Ruttman's *Berlin – Symphony of a Great City*. The detached camera eye which looks down on the metro station as people scurry out like ants suggests Ruttman's alienated, dehumanised industrial world; but, in also quickly shifting to street level, Rouch characteristically juxtaposes another dimension of modern urban life. *Chronique* explores the individual lives which are lived within, or through resistance to, the constraints of a vast industrial machine.

In an early sequence, a young couple put on some music. A mechanical wheel moves round, generating an unchanging, synthetic sound which comes to haunt the film, evoking as it does the distinctive experience of modernity which Rouch and Morin's enquiry progressively reveals. For every character we encounter (except the African student, Landry, and Rouch himself) is confined, struggling against the tyranny, the routine, the monotony, the regimentation of a mechanised existence. Thus, although the film's title suggests it will be a register or documentation of events as they happen, an experiment/experience that will unfold through time, we quickly discover that there is, in fact, no real movement or development in the course of the work. Rouch and Morin's Parisian subjects are marooned in a state of timeless modernity. We have already glimpsed this condition in the earlier film, *Moi, Un Noir*. Nevertheless Rouch's African characters create moments of release through fantasy, projecting their personalities into the characters of Hollywood films. But, unlike the transformative quality of Rouch's other African films of the same period, *Chronique* offers no escape beyond its own confines. We, the audience, like the film's characters, remain trapped in limbo. *Chronique* does not carry us beyond our experience of the familiar; rather, as the film-makers note in their closing dicussion, it (merely) 're-introduces us to life'. The film itself becomes the hall of mirrors which is contemporary reality.

The distinctive form and content of *Chronique* are inseparable. The film's unusually reflexive style, its episodic style, and particular hierarchy of voice and vision are integrally related to the vision of society which is articulated through the text. Rouch and Morin's much celebrated 'nouvelle experience en *cinéma vérité*' begins with a conversation. 'How do *you* live?' 'What do you do with your life?' the film-makers ask Marceline, a young Parisian. Her answer is intriguing. At first she replies simply 'Work, mostly'. But pushing her further, Rouch enquires if she has a plan for each day; and Marceline replies: 'I know what I ought to do. But I don't always do it. I never know what I'll do next day. I live on the principle that tomorrow can take care of itself. For me, adventure is always just around the corner.' This exchange is critical in establishing the film's agenda and its central device, conversation or voice. And it poses the central question which inspires the film, namely the relationship between freedom and necessity, individual and society within 'mechanical civilization'. Rouch and Morin examine this question through the concept of 'happiness'. Moreover, in making voice central (*Chronique* is pre-eminently a film of people talking), the film-makers introduce simultaneously the problem of truth or knowledge.

Chronique d'un été consists of three distinctive parts. The first, and by far the longest, section introduces particular subjects through whose experiences the meaning of happiness is explored. It also establishes the centrality of Morin and Rouch as characters in the film, and the very different agendas each one seeks to pursue through their experiment in *cinéma vérité*.[40]

Their enquiry is launched by Marceline, who begins walking around with a tape-recorder in the streets of Paris. She asks people if they are happy. The urban location for her enquiry is crucial to the film's concerns. The city is the symbol of modernity itself, a liminal place where people brush past one another, living out isolated lives in the eternal present of an urban landscape, freed from the baggage of their past and yet denied humanity by an oppressive industrial machine. The relationship between what appears on the outside and what lies inside is thus raised from the beginning; and it is, of course, at the heart of Rouch and Morin's cinematic experiment, too. Marceline's tape-recorder disrupts the anonymity of the city. It cracks open the surface of everyday life, carrying us into the contradictions at the heart of modern existence. The snatched encounters between Marceline and bemused passers-by, observed by an aloof and detached camera eye, give way to an active, intrusive camera. It becomes a tool for the interrogation of particular individual personalities; but, equally, it can 'free' people, enabling them to articulate the deep sense of dissatisfaction which pervades their lives. Gradually, we become aware of the variety of ingenious strategies which individuals develop in order to survive, to resist the pressure to become just another cog in a vast urban machine. Happiness is neither a frivolous nor a materialistic concept, and it emerges as something profound in modern society. It animates people's lives, an elusive and yet deeply desired state of fulfillment.

The juxtaposed conversations with Angelo, Jacques and Simone Gabillon, Marilou, Marceline and Jean Pierre which comprise the long first section of *Chronique* gradually reveal the contours of the prison in which they live. Not surprisingly, the film begins with the question of work, one of the most potent and tangible symbols of modern oppression; but the sense of oppression experienced by Rouch and Morin's Parisian tribe is more complex and far reaching. It touches all aspects of people's lives, not least their most intimate personal relationships.

We observe a day in the life of Angelo, a car worker at Renault. I find this extended sequence to be one of the most striking and intriguing in *Chronique* as a whole (in many ways more curious than the much-discussed sequence of Marceline in the Place de la Concorde). It is a strange, muted, almost ghost-like interlude in a film dominated by people talking. It brings powerfully to life what Angelo's words can only imperfectly suggest. The factory images are reminiscent of a heroic Griersonion vision, celebrating a harmony of man and machine; but the noise (*Les Maîtres Fous* and the city) is overwhelming. It makes conversation, human contact, impossible. Curiously, we experience the absence of voice as a kind of silence. Moreover, most of the other exchanges which unfold between Morin and the film's different characters are located in dark, confined spaces which seem to be suspended outside time. Angelo's world, however, extends in time and space. We experience its rhythm, its integrity, its discipline and regulation, the integration of work and home, man and machine such that we can begin to understand what it means when Angelo says: he lives to work.

Angelo's experience as a car worker at the Renault factory is an obvious but nonetheless powerful symbol of the mechanised existence lived out by the film's subjects. But, as the other characters we encounter in this part of the film reveal, the sense of confinement is much more complex and far reaching. It is not just a question of work or even the pressures of an impersonal bureaucratic society. Their own intimate personal relationships are also a prison – as it is starkly, indeed painfully, laid bare in the case of the two couples, Jacques and Simone Gabillon, and Marceline and Jean-Pierre. Each person struggles to retain a belief in their own unique personality. As Gabillon eloquently describes it, he tries to retain a sense of 'the real me', the individual essence or integrity existing beyond the bureaucratic bundle of papers which the modern person has become. But, suddenly and characteristically, Rouch flips the coin. We meet Marilou, a young Italian woman living in Paris. She appears to be on the verge of a complete breakdown. Unlike Angelo, for example, she is not oppressed by society, but by her isolation from society. She is forced in on herself, trapped within the tyranny of her own thoughts.

By juxtaposing Marilou with the other characters in this way, Rouch again establishes the importance of subverting opposed categories in favour of exploring their interplay. Hence what matters is not one pole or the other, individual or society; rather, it is the relationship between them which is important. Either pole is a tyranny – the tyranny of an isolated self or the oppression of mechanised existence. The same tension underlies the question of truth/fiction which is centrally posed by the film – as Rothman asks, is it 'telling the truth by lying'?[41] *Chronique* is neither real nor unreal. It is both.

The second part opens with a meeting convened by Morin. He is seeking to broaden the film's scope beyond what he calls the 'personal' to include discussion of the social and political issues of the day. This attempt and a subsequent one fail. Watching these scenes, it is hard not to recall the satire of colonial government in *Les Maîtres Fous*, when the Hauka, in trance, convene several 'round-table discussions' and the governor-general petulantly complains that no one ever listens to him. But, as Rouch's intervention reveals, social and political events do not exist in the abstract. They take on meaning when refracted through personal experience – as the awkward silence which follows the discussion of the tattoo on Marceline's arm reveals. It provokes the film's moment of 'psychodrama'. Marceline relives her memories of deportation as a Jew during the war. As with the earlier scenes of a day in the life of Angelo, this becomes a sequence extended in time and space. The camera moves alongside Marceline, framing her against the city. For almost the first time, the film opens up to reveal an urban landscape. Hitherto it has been confined to dark streets, stairways, crowded rooms. As the sequence develops, the camera shifts position and moves to face Marceline before slowly pulling away. She begins to get smaller and smaller, dwarfed by the architecture of Les Halles until she is swallowed up by that vast, dark space in the way that experience and memory threaten to overwhelm her. Marceline becomes a child again.

In the final part, the film moves to St Tropez as Parsisians leave the city for their annual summer vacation. Here we return to a familiar Rouchian theme – the African adventurer. Again, as in *Jaguar*, Rouch reverses the conventional image of the European traveller (anthropologist) among Africans; instead we accompany Landry in his investigations of the French while on holiday. He is the only character in *Chronique*, apart from Rouch himself, who appears to be free – indeed to be having fun. Rouch thinks life is fun, Morin, however, does not.[42] For even on holiday, away from the city, Rouch's Parisian tribe cannot escape the sense of confinement and routine. The seaside, unlike the village or the bush in *Les Maîtres Fous*, *Jaguar* and *Moi, Un Noir*, does not become a site of freedom. But in making a seamless transition from holidaying in St Tropez to being part of a cinema audience as the lights go up, the question is posed again – can cinema function as the site of transformation in mechanical civilization?

One of the most interesting features of *Chronique d'un été* is that it is pre-eminently a film of people talking. For me this feature of the work makes it strongly reminiscent of *The Confidence Man*, Herman Melville's experimental novel of 1857.[43] Here Melville dispenses with the established literary conventions of character and narrative, depicting a community of strangers cast adrift on a ship which moves but never arrives. People encounter each other within this state of limbo, their connection to one another exists only through the medium of words, conversation, argument, debate: 'the book has no time for the mute externals of a given world, for it is above all interested in the words that men say – and write – as they attempt to relate or exploit, communicate or manipulate, to enlighten or outwit, to tell the truth or insert a lie.'[44] It is the very 'wordiness' of the novel, as Tony Tanner points out, which raises the question of the relationship between words and 'worth' or trustworthiness.

Rouch's concerns in *Chronique* might be likened to those which Tanner identifies at the heart of *The Confidence Man* – the problem of truth, authenticity and confidence in mechanical or urban civilization. For the city, like the ship, is a sort of limbo, existing outside time and space, where people have no connection with one another except through language. There are episodes but no story; there are characters, but who are they really? There is nothing to go on, either for the film's subjects or the audience, in negotiating this world of only 'clothes, bits and pieces and talk' as Tanner puts it.[45] The question raised is how are social relationships possible under these conditions? Can society be created in conditions of fluidity? How can one know anything? But Rouch follows Melville in rejecting the search for absolutes, since it is premised upon a dichotomous vision of the world. The world in which we live is a twilight zone, an area of light and dark, truth and falsehood, reality and fiction. Moreover, as we have now seen, this is the world in which Rouch, like Melville's confidence man himself, truly flourishes.

'The eye exists in a primitive state.'

This chapter has taken the work of Jean Rouch as a case study in anthropological cinema. The handful of films which Rouch made during the late 1950s have been the focus for my attention as I have sought to expose his particular way of seeing. As a set, *Les Maîtres Fous*, *Jaguar*, *Moi, Un Noir* and *Chronique d'un été* are distinguished by consistency in theme (notably by a concern with migration, cities and modernity); by a sustained experimentation with cinematic form; and by the unusual historical context of the films' making. I suggested that Rouch's creativity and innovation was linked to the moment of colonial independence. For his work, pushing at the limits of both anthropology and cinema, may be understood as a counterpart to the fluidity in social and political structures which marked the collapse of European hegemony and the emergence of the new nations across Africa, Asia and the Caribbean.

Within the space of five years, Rouch opened up a new and distinctive field – *anthropological cinema*. In bringing together these two different traditions, Rouch was not seeking to express the concerns of traditional ethnographic enquiry through a visual form; rather, he was creating something new. He united the humanist impulse of anthropology with the transformative power of cinema, and in so doing he transcended the limitations at the heart of each project. Rouch not only created what he calls 'ethno-fiction' or 'science fiction', thereby subverting the conventional divisions within anthropology between description and imagination; but also within cinema itself, he found a way of transcending a division which has run deeply from the very beginning – namely, he found a way of fusing the realism of Lumière with the fantasy of Méliès.

Although I have drawn attention to a number of common themes which run throughout Rouch's films of the late 1950s, it is equally important to recognise that the changing form of each work subverts any consistency of meaning. The meaning of any one film both clarifies and dissolves through its juxtaposition with others of the series. Hence, as I indicated at the beginning of this chapter, I consider these films as variations on a set of themes, and not as a progressive sequence. Rouch offers different perspectives on a particular moment in modern history; but there is no social whole to be grasped. Conceptualising his work in this way enables us to understand his particular vision of the world – contemporary reality exists as a hall of mirrors. Rouch's enterprise is deeply subversive of intellectual certainties. It challenges the binary thinking by which anthropologists (and film-makers) have sought to interpret the world. Rouch's films express his refusal to accept the stability of conventional categories such as black/white, irrational/rational, village/city, truth/fiction, Africa/Europe. Rouch *plays* with these oppositions, rejecting an either/or position, always revealing the co-existence of both parts of the pair.

I use the word *play* deliberately here to emphasise another characteristic of Rouch's work. Rouch's anthropological cinema is built around the notion of play, and the film-maker himself is pre-eminently a player.[46] His presence in each film is distinctive. He hovers like a capricious spirit, he is provocative, he grins, he has fun. We feel that he is enjoying himself – unlike Morin, for example, in *Chronicle d'un été*.

Rouch's characters, too, are offered the chance to be players. And we, the audience, are invited to join in. We can also become players if we are willing to participate in what he calls 'the game' (*Les Maîtres Fous*). Playing the game with Rouch means accepting certain rules; but equally it involves exploiting spaces or cracks in the way that his West African migrants do, as they take risks, improvise and innovate.[47] Following Roland Barthes, we can recognise that pleasure or *jouissance* is an important feature of Rouch's work. For the pleasure generated through participation in this game is not merely cognitive. It is, as Barthes' concept implies, sensual.[48]

Rouch's anthropological cinema is romantic. Its animating principle is happiness (even love), rather than the pursuit of truth or knowledge which underpins the enlightenment enquiry pursued by David and Judith MacDougall. Hence one of its distinguishing features is its transformative power or what Rothman calls its 'visionary aspiration'.[49]

The distinctive hierarchy of vision and voice running throughout Rouch's films of this period is, I believe, an important indication of a certain visionary metaphysic. The relationship between image and sound in *Les Maîtres Fous*, *Jaguar*, *Moi, Un Noir* and *Chronique d'un été* is more interesting than merely a question of technological limitation. *Chronique* was the first film which Rouch shot using synchronous sound; the others were all shot silently with an improvised commentary added later. But with his 1960 work, Rouch lays bare the problem of voice.

Rouch's project involves the recuperation of vision. Central is the notion of innocence. For, as with the Malinowskian ethnographer, the recovery of sight enables one to see again or to see as if for the first time. It returns one to an original state. For unlike the MacDougalls, whose work Rouch once described as like books, Rouch seeks to expose the limitations of language (noise, babble, baylon) and to provoke a cinematic experience through which participants/players can glimpse what Rothman terms 'the transcendental, the unknowable, the unsayable'. This is what defines Rouch's project as visionary. The spectator is transformed into a seer.[50]

The process by which the eye may be cleansed involves a radical disruption of everyday modes of engagement with the world. Romantic techniques appeal to sensibility, to the emotions and to the body. In the Malinowskian case, this is brought about through the disorienting sensory experience of fieldwork. For Rouch the camera acts as a transformative agent. Hence it is not humanised. It might become part of the film-maker's body; but the body is not human when Rouch embarks on his journey, which he calls *cine-trance*. To quote Andre Breton, 'the eye exists in a primitive state.' As such the film-maker becomes fugitive, elusive, capricious like a spirit.[51] Likewise, in a darkened auditorium, something strange can happen; but only if participants are willing to play game, to become players. For cinema offers itself as a primary site for disruption and transformation.

Cinema is, indeed, an interesting site for the pursuit of a Romantic project. It contains both darkness and light. Rouch plays with light and dark in the same way that he plays with other categories (rational/ irrational, truth/fiction, self/fantasy, authentic/performance) – there is neither one nor the other but always both. The romanticism of his anthropology is built around the interplay of darkness and light. There is no progressive illumination, no movement from night to day through the exercise of the 'light of reason' as implied in the linear development of what I call the MacDougalls' enlightenment project. Instead, Rouch's films provoke moments of revelation, momentary flashes of light which penetrate the dark like the beam of projector in the cinema auditorium.[52]

7   The anthropological cinema of David and Judith MacDougall

David and Judith MacDougall have been leading figures in the project of anthropological cinema for over two decades.[1] They began working in the late 1960s, in the aftermath of the creative explosion in postwar cinema which was inaugurated by the Italian neorealist school. The impulse behind the formal, technological and substantive innovations of British Free Cinema, the French New Wave and the American direct cinema movement was a commitment to an expansive democratic project. The new film-makers broke decisively with the old categories of fiction and documentary, and with the established hierarchy of professional practice.

The MacDougalls have made their own distinctive contribution to postwar cinema. They sought to employ its new techniques in areas of traditional anthropological enquiry. The problems they encountered in attempting to synthesise the separate but related traditions of cinema and scientific ethnography precipitated a bold experimentation with method, as the location of their work shifted. The MacDougalls first began to develop their anthropological cinema in the context of East Africa, later they moved to Australia, and more recently they have made films in Europe and Asia.

Although David MacDougall made his 1993 film *Tempus De Baristas* alone, most of the work considered in this essay was carried out in partnership with his wife, Judith MacDougall. The first film, *To Live With Herds* (1971), was attributed to David MacDougall as solo director. The later Turkana and Australian Aboriginal films were jointly credited to David and Judith MacDougall as co-producers/directors. In all the films discussed here, David MacDougall is the camera operator, Judith MacDougall the sound recordist.

From the beginning, David and Judith MacDougall have had a clear sense of their own intellectual agenda. Moreover, they are unusual in making the contours of their project explicit, charting each stage of development as a response to the limitations of their previous practice. In this reflexive stance, underlined by David MacDougall's extensive writing and commentary, they stand in sharp contrast to most anthro-pologists. The MacDougalls' patient, carefully explained method of working also differentiates their enterprise from that developed by Jean Rouch. The latter, who turns the process of ethnographic exploration into a mystical or shamanistic journey, seeks to subvert the very kind of intellectual reasoning which so distinguishes the MacDougalls' work.

My concern here is to explore the nature of the vision which animates the MacDougalls' anthropological cinema. Many of its distinguishing features emerge most concretely from the juxtaposition with Rouch's enterprise, since despite points of connection, there are fundamental differences between the two in their conception of vision and knowledge. Certainly audiences respond very differently to these two examples of anthropological cinema. If Rouch captivates audiences through his energy and charismatic personality, the MacDougalls inspire respect for the structural elegance and delicate texture of their work. The former, I suggested, stands as a rather fugitive figure at the centre of a romantic anthropology. The latter, however, may be considered as key figures in the creation of an enlightenment project of anthropological cinema. The different ways in which light plays across the work of Rouch and the MacDougalls reveal the contrasting nature of their enterprises.[2]

Important as David MacDougall's writings undoubtedly are in ad-dressing issues which emerge from the development of a cinematic approach toward ethnographic realities, what I have called the 'meta-physic' underpinning the techniques he has developed in collaboration with Judith MacDougall remains largely unacknowledged in his reflec-tions.[3] By proposing that we consider their work as an expression of an *enlightenment* way of seeing, I wish to draw attention to the dominant epistemological concerns of their cinema. The question of knowledge lies at its core. The corpus of films (and writings) produced by the MacDougalls during the last twenty years is marked by a drive for clarity; or, to use a visual metaphor, there is a desire to banish darkness through the exercise of what might be called the light of reason.

What is known? How is it known? The MacDougalls' investigation of these questions involves what I imagine as a *process* of illumination, the idea of a penetrating beam of light which dispells the shadows and renders the world ultimately transparent and knowable. The shedding of light across areas of darkness is a steady, cumulative process. It does not involve the sudden, unexpected flashes of insight or *moments* of revela-tion which characterise the kind of anthropology pursued by Jean Rouch. For Rouch, whose project is inspired by the notion of happiness, thrives in the shadows between darkness and light, endlessly disrupting the categories by which intellectuals conventionally seek to explain (and contain) the world. By contrast, there is inescapably at the centre of the MacDougalls' work a strong impulse toward clarification or toward the separation of categories as necessary stages in the acquisition of knowledge. It finds expression in the *progressive* innovation which characterises their anthropological cinema.

Each film in the MacDougall corpus is a response to the perceived limitations of the last one. This linear or evolutionary conception of the work as a whole marks it off from the image of variations on a set of themes which I proposed when considering Rouch's films. The romantic cinema of the latter is not marked by a strong forward momentum. It exists rather as a playful exploration of different possibilities. The developmental impetus of the MacDougalls' work suggests an underlying conception that ethnographic realities may be rendered ultimately knowable through the improvement of the techniques of enquiry. The achievement of such a goal, as the successive phases of their enlightenment project reveal, always remains beyond reach. For the ethnographers' tireless pursuit of questions concerning truth, knowledge and reality only makes them ever more elusive and problematic – until, finally, the elusivity of meaning itself becomes the subject of the MacDougalls' last two films.

The MacDougalls' commitment to questions of knowledge rather than to those about happiness (romanticism) makes for a distinctive kind of enlightenment cinema. It is one which in significant ways runs counter to the intrinsic properties of the site itself. For the anthropological cinema created by the MacDougalls does not involve entry into a dark mysterious place where transformation occurs through the disruption of mind and body. Instead they create a space for the exercise of critical reason. Audiences are not expected to surrender their rationality, their cognitive faculties. Indeed, it is to these very faculties that the MacDougalls' films appeal, since in the darkness of the auditorium the film-makers make their audience work. This work, however, engages the audience largely at the level of thinking rather than feeling. For the anthropological cinema of the MacDougalls' makes its primary appeal to the intellect rather than to the emotions.[4]

The features I have identified as specific to an enlightenment project in anthropology cannot be considered aside from the historical context in which such an enquiry took shape. Although understood to be a way of seeing, expressing personal sensibilities as much as distinctive traditions of anthropology and cinema, the MacDougalls' project has also been significantly influenced by the political circumstances in which they have worked as ethnographers. Hence any interpretation of their work involves an acknowledgement that the MacDougalls embarked on their project in Africa a decade after Jean Rouch produced his celebrated set of films – *Les Maîtres Fous, Jaguar, Moi, Un Noir* and *La Pyramide Humaine*. The situation they found contrasted sharply with the mood of optimism and change which marked the moment of colonial independence some ten years earlier. For, if Rouch's cinema was a response to the creative possibilities unleashed by political emancipation, the ethnographic enquiry pursued by the MacDougalls took shape in a period marked by the consolidation of state power and the rise of new African elites. Specifically, as anthropological film-makers, the MacDougalls confronted social and political problems emerging as part and parcel of the establishment of African nationhood. These problems focused around what was known as the process of 'modernization'. It encompassed questions of development, education, health, national identity and so on. The structural fluidity in which Rouch had flourished as a film-maker during the 1950s had been replaced by political hierarchies built upon opposition and conflict. Moreover, the MacDougalls positioned themselves differently with respect to contemporary African life. They did not seek out the crowded spaces of urban Africa, where identity and community were being actively made and re-made. Instead they located themselves in the wide, open landscapes of pastoralist people. Their commitment was to the documentation of ways of life which were at odds with contemporary definitions of 'progress'.

To Live With Herds

Basil Wright's *Song of Ceylon* was described by a commentator as 'one of the most beautiful films ever made'.[5] Funded by the Empire Marketing Board and produced in 1935 as the experimentalism of the British documentary movement under Grierson reached its peak, Wright sought to weave together different ryhthms, sounds and images into a complex poetic whole. He created a work of striking originality, one distinguished by an extraordinary simplicity and beauty.

More than thirty-five years later, *Song of Ceylon* formed the inspiration for *To Live With Herds*, a subtle, carefully crafted work by David MacDougall made with Jie pastoralists in north-eastern Uganda. This film marked a turning point in the development of anthropological cinema. It influenced a whole generation of film-makers struggling to find new ways of giving expression to anthropological knowledge. Among them, for example, was Melissa Llewelyn-Davies who, with other members of the *Disappearing World* team, attended a screening of *To Live With Herds* organised by Brian Moser: 'I was so overwhelmed by it; and I didn't realise you could just take a camera and listen to what people were saying and put it on the screen and that it would be so thrilling. There was an honesty and seriousness about the whole enterprise. It was an extraordinary thing for me to see'.[6] Although Rouch's work was much admired by those seeking to go beyond conventional literary forms, its style was not obviously compatible with anthropological approaches moulded by the more 'British' models of ethnographic enquiry.[7]

To Live With Herds thus provides an important point of entry into the second attempt considered here to synthesise the separate but related practices of cinema and anthropology. Moreover, this early film stands as a template for the MacDougalls' work as a whole. It raises central questions concerning vision (and voice) as method and metaphysics which have animated their anthropological enquiry for two decades. For, despite their development of different cinematic forms and their exploration of changing cultural contexts, *To Live With Herds* remains the point of anchorage. Indeed *Tempus De Baristas* (1993), David MacDougall's most recent work to date, powerfully reaffirms that fundamental orientation to the world which was given such eloquent expression in the early Jie film.

To Live With Herds: A Dry Season Among the Jie (1971) has five parts or movements. Each part is self-contained, and yet the carefully selected sequences which comprise it set up resonances with the other sections of the film organised under different headings. The MacDougalls construct an argument through the subtle juxtaposition of different cinematic devices – images, text, subtitles and commentary. Thus in spatial terms the film can be conceived as a mosaic, a series of overlapping associations or patterns, where meaning is generated through relationships of correspondence and contrast. Its temporal dimensions mirror this distinctive spatial configuration. The film's linear development through time is crosscut and subverted by other rhythms and movements.

In *To Live With Herds*, the MacDougalls attempt to match form with content, to create a cinematic structure which mirrors their substantive concerns. Their interest, stimulated by Peter Rigby's essay 'Pastoralism and Prejudice', is to explore the life of herding peoples in the context of wider political and economic changes; and thus the open nature of the film text itself mirrors the fluidity of the world in which the Jie live.[8] As the film reveals, the Jie exist precariously at the margins, their integrity and autonomy undercut by conflicting currents of history and contemporary society. For, following independence from British rule, many of the new African governments perceived pastoralists as a problem in their ambitions for nation-building. These groups were mobile; they were difficult to tax; and they were reluctant to engage with the agents of state bureaucracy such as providers of health services and education.

To Live With Herds opens in the heart of a Jie compound. Without any preliminaries, the MacDougalls simply place the spectator there, among people and cattle, immersed in the bustle of everyday activity. But, juxtaposed to this rich texture, constructed through the technique of montage, is a single extended shot in which Logoth, responding to a request from the film-makers, maps the extent of Jie terrain. It is through Logoth then that the MacDougalls establish the film's orientation – the place of the Jie in the world and the fragile relationships which sustain it, relationships which exist in time as well as space, between past and present, between people and natural resources, between the Jie and neighbouring peoples, between herders and the new state apparatus.

From these opening sequences, we can identify the distinctive qualities of the MacDougalls' film-making style. First of all, their approach is characterised by an intimacy rooted in close observation and in amassing the details of daily life. But equally the MacDougalls use extended scenes or encounters to suggest specific dimensions of the argument they seek to articulate. Indeed it might be argued that the film's compelling force lies in just a handful of images. As I have indicated, the early scene with Logoth can be understood as a metaphorical statement of the film's broader concerns. But so too can the extraordinary sequence of the dust storm which sweeps across the landscape at the climax of the film, evoking perhaps more than anything else the MacDougalls' fundamental belief in the Jie's fragile yet tenacious grip on a harsh, shifting terrain.

Progressively, at a whole series of different levels, the MacDougalls build a devastating case which lays bare the casual brutality of national government. Against the quiet dignity of a pastoralist way of life, rooted in its own rhythms and collective practice, stands an unknown, external and coercive power. But the MacDougalls' indictment is all the more effective for their scrupulous observations of the characters who represent this new state order. They show them to be neither cunning nor evil, but simply callow, a bunch of superficial people who have exchanged their humanity for political slogans and bureaucratic procedure.

The MacDougalls' argument then develops through the cumulative force of juxtaposed sequences and associations. The effect is rather like the ripples in a pool of water after a stone has been cast. Gradually the film extends beyond the confines of the Jie compound, moving outwards to encompass bigger worlds of state and market; but in passing through the climax, a series of stark encounters where difference cannot be reconciled except through coercion, the MacDougalls return us to the gentle, unchanging tempo of Jie society. The film unfolds through time, carrying the audience from beginning to end, but its fundamental rhythm is cyclical. This dual movement is suggested by the five chapter titles – 'The balance'; 'Changes'; 'The nation'; 'The value of cattle'; and 'News from home' – which take us from the equilibrium of Jie society through the impact of colonialism, the postcolonial state and the market back to the herders themselves.

The film closes, however, with a re-affirmation of the MacDougalls' belief in the organic unity of a pastoralist way of life. For the ritualised greetings which Logoth finally exchanges with his fellow Jie at the edge of the cattle camps expand and reverberate beyond the life of the film itself. Thus the MacDougalls' formal commitment to the cyclical nature of social life seals the film's substantive rejection of linear notions of progress.

To Live With Herds is a remarkable work. It is distinguished, perhaps above all, by the humanity of its vision, one painstakingly built through the forging of a new intimacy with people. It is also impressive in its achievement of formal perfection. It is here, in the film's construction, that the influence of Basil Wright is most often sought.[9] The use of chapters to structure *To Live With Herds*, for example, certainly brings *Song of Ceylon* to mind; but the connections need to be probed at a number of levels, as David MacDougall's own comments on Wright's film suggest: 'I think it stands out as the only film of its kind in that whole period. I can't think of another that comes anywhere near it in its combination of personal investment and intellect.'[10]

Wright attempted in *Song of Ceylon* to give expression to the distinctive texture of modern life. In so doing, he created a symphonic poem. For he sought not only to uncover the different rhythms of the modern world, but to explore their interconnection through the construction of a complex whole. As the film's title suggests, Wright took a village in Ceylon as his focus; but in celebrating its rhythms of spiritual and material life, he revealed, simultaneously, its existence within an extended world of trade and commerce. Moving effortlessly between inside and outside, past and present, rural and urban, religion and commerce, the village and the world, Wright weaves together overlapping, intersecting and cross-cutting currents. As one critic wrote: '[*Song of Ceylon*] is a very important attempt at creating a picture of an entirely strange life, from the native rather than the foreign point of view, and to express the tempo of that life in the texture of the film itself.'[11] The formal inventiveness of *Song of Ceylon*, the skilful use of the new medium of sound as a counterpoint to visual sequences and text, thus mirrors the complex and fluid world which Wright evokes through the substance of the film itself.

Wright's concern with complexity and movement in his 1935 work may be considered as a continuation of the tradition associated with the European and Soviet film-makers, such as Ruttman, Cavalcanti, Ivens and Vertov. During the 1920s, this group established a new genre, the city symphony. It was uniquely cinematic, and the use of montage represented a profound rejection of conventional forms derived from a literary aesthetic. Taking the city as a focus, these film-makers gave expression to the modernist fascination with speed, movement, machines, structure and process; and, for them, the cinema was an integral part of this new industrial, mechanised world. The camera itself moved as a machine, and as an advanced scientific instrument it could transcend human limitation. Cinema was celebrated as an industrial product, at the site of both production and consumption; the complex social relations embodied in cinema mirrored the characteristic features of the modern age.

But *Song of Ceylon* also marked a new departure in the tradition of the city symphony, not least because its centre was not the city *per se*. Although the film's formal qualities and construction owe much to *Berlin – Symphony of a Great City* (Ruttman), *The Bridge* (Ivens) or *A Man With A Movie Camera* (Vertov), its distinctive feature is the humanism of its vision. For, in important ways, *Song of Ceylon* echoed the poetic humanism most associated with the work of Robert Flaherty. If, on the one hand, the city symphony films were criticised because the people in them were turned into mere cogs in a vast industrial machine, objectified and dehumanised by an omniscient camera eye, the limitations of Flaherty, on the other hand, stemmed from his refusal to address movement or change at all. Wright, however, achieved a new synthesis, fusing the romantic lyricism of Flaherty with the intellectual brilliance of Ruttman.[12]

A number of the key elements which make up this creative synthesis may be discerned in *To Live With Herds*. As David MacDougall himself noted, in *Song of Ceylon* Wright successfully combined the qualities of passion and intellect. So, too, do the MacDougalls in their own work. The means by which such a synthesis, indeed a sort of transfiguration, is achieved demands closer attention. Certainly it is not 'found'; rather it is striven for, constructed through conscious intention and the unconscious processes of intuitive connection.

To Live With Herds is a film rooted in a particular historical moment. The MacDougalls' intention was to question simple notions of progress widely held at the time by both African and European intellectuals; they sought to insert their film into the contemporary debates concerning development and national identity. Although, like most documentary film makers of their generation, the MacDougalls turned away from authoritative, didactic film-making, they did not abdicate from the responsibility to offer a particular interpretation of the world. Thus, despite the simplicity of the images and the seemingly effortless movement of *To Live With Herds*, the audience is left in no doubt that its purpose is to persuade.[13] But to understand how the MacDougalls attempt to establish a certain reading of the film, we need to look more closely at their method. This, in turn, opens up deeper questions concerning the metaphysics which underlie the MacDougalls' exploration of society.

To Live With Herds is recognised as an important example of *observational cinema*, a term coined by Colin Young to describe the new kind of film-making which was being developed by a small group of people working at UCLA in the late 1960s.[14] It is often characterised as involving a fusion of direct cinema techniques with a style of ethnographic fieldwork derived from Malinowski. For emphasis was laid upon detail, paying close attention to what Malinowski in *Argonauts of the Western Pacific* called 'the imponderabilia of actual life'. At a deeper level, however, observational cinema, in many of its key features (not least its fundamentally moral and humanistic orientation) may be understood as the extension of the Italian neo-realist project as envisaged by Zavattini and by Bazin in his call for a 'cinema of "duration"'.[15]

Interestingly, the most prominent members of the UCLA group associated with Young (notably the MacDougalls, Herb Di Gioia and David Hancock) were not professional anthropologists; but they were drawn to the discipline in their attempt to discover ways of exploring previously neglected areas of social life – specifically 'ordinary' people at home and abroad.[16] Like their predecessors in the postwar Italian cinema renaissance and the leading figures of the American direct cinema movement, UCLA film-makers sought to effect a shift in focus, from ideas to life, which demanded the adoption of new technology. The commitment to small working partnerships, light portable equipment and synchronous-sound cameras mirrored the minimalist approach to fieldwork of Malinowskian anthropologists themselves – symbolised, perhaps above all, in the stubborn reliance on nothing more than a notebook as fieldwork equipment.

Crucial to the new kind of cinematic ethnography that the MacDougalls attempted to develop were particular techniques of working. The term 'observation' was used to describe a certain kind of social relationship. It was one premised upon humility or respect, expressive of film-makers' sensitivity towards their subjects. This changed relationship found aesthetic expression in the distinctive camera work, sound recording and editing of the observational film itself.[17]

The remarks made by one of the UCLA film-makers, David Hancock describing the method of working he devised with Di Gioia, offer valuable insight into these dimensions.

We shoot in long takes dealing with specific individuals rather than cultural patterns or analysis. We try to complete an action within a single shot, rather than fragmenting it. Our work is based on an open interaction between us as people (not just film-makers) and the people being filmed. Their perspectives and concerns shape and structure the film rather than our emphasis on a particular topic or analysis of their culture which would distort or over-emphasize, perhaps, the importance of that topic to those people and that culture.[18]

The principle of respecting the integrity of events applies at the editing stage, too, as Hancock's further remarks indicate; but now the film-maker assumes a new responsibility towards his or her subjects.[19]

Despite the new relationships established at the time of filming, the subjects of observational cinema have rarely been active participants in the editing process. Instead the film-maker consolidates his or her role as 'witness', being actively engaged during shooting and editing, and uniquely present at all stages of production. Thus he or she comes to both symbolise and guarantee the film's authenticity. But in becoming a sort of moral guardian, the observational film-maker must mediate between the people in the film and the people who engage with them as spectators. For the practitioners of observational cinema, conceived as 'essentially revelatory rather than illustrative', attempt to establish a different kind of social relationship with their audience as well.[20] Thus spectators are expected be active, not passive; to piece together the small details and clues offered by the film-maker; and to reach their own conclusions on the basis of evidence presented. This process depends, of course, on the 'truth' of the evidence put before an audience by the film-maker. Most important of all, we need to believe that the film-maker has not 'cheated' (like Flaherty, for example).[21] We must be convinced that the film-maker has genuinely 'been there' as Geertz puts it, that they embody the truth of what is presented.[22]

In looking closely at *To Live With Herds*, we can identify a number of different strategies which the MacDougalls employ in their attempt to persuade us of the film's truth. Prominent among these are techniques identified with an observational approach, with its origins in Italian neo-realism as conceived in its late form. Their film is distinguished by its visual and aural detail, its close attention to characters in everyday life and to the nuances of particular social situations or encounters. The intimacy of the film is also created by the focus and intensity of the camera eye (David MacDougall's). It serves as a filter, one which seems anxious not to intrude, but to simply to be there, quietly watching, an expression of the film-maker's sensitivity and deference towards his subjects. And yet the occasional movements of the camera and its changing positions are necessary, in fact, to remind us of MacDougall's presence, to reassure us of the integrity of the vision he is presenting, one intimately tied to his having genuinely been there. Indeed we begin to feel that we have been there, too. For the intense realism of *To Live With Herds* effects the sense of a direct encounter with another world, the world of the Jie.

The MacDougalls, like Malinowski in many ways, seek to persuade their audience of the film's authenticity by means of a layering of rich, descriptive detail. But, unlike the author of *Argonauts*, endlessly distracted in the course of his rambling, picaresque narrative, the MacDougalls never allow their attention to wander. The classicism of their cinematic vision is strikingly reminiscent of the luminosity of an Evans-Pritchard monograph. *To Live With Herds* is a model of economy, a text whose power surely derives as much from the intensity of its focus, its discipline and restraint, as from its concrete detail. Thus, if the reader of *Argonauts* is carried along by Malinowski's sheer exuburance and by his dense, vivid prose, the MacDougalls engage the viewer in a very different way. There is an ordered simplicity to the film's surface detail, in sharp contrast with the messiness of Malinowski's account of Trobriand life. The film's appearance disguises the complexity of its underlying structure. This raises the problematic status of the work itself. Is it indeed an example of 'observational cinema'?

The film is constructed through an unusual combination of the two tendencies in cinema, montage and deep-focus, identified by the critic, André Bazin, as polar opposites. *To Live With Herds* is marked by its dense, extended scenes in which 'meaning arises in due course from relationships disclosing themselves within this field, and the film-maker's participation is that of originator and observer of the natural development of these relationships within their own block of time. His job is not creating new meaning, but [as Bazin expresses it] "framing the fleeting crystallisation of a reality of whose environing presence one is ceaselessly aware"'.[23] And yet the juxtapositions of these extended scenes depends upon the principle of montage, 'the creation of a sense or meaning not objectively contained in the images themselves but derived exclusively from their juxtaposition'.[24] By interweaving cinematic techniques in this way, the film-makers seek to move their audience affectively at the same time as they engage with it at the level of ideas.

It seems paradoxical, given many of its key features (not least its elaborate formal construction), to describe *To Live With Herds* as an example of observational cinema. It is hardly a 'found' film. Certainly, I find it difficult to agree with Colin Young when he writes: 'After seeing David and Judith MacDougall's *To Live With Herds*, you get very impatient with films that don't let you see.'[25] Here he refers to one of the central features of the new approach, namely that 'observational' films *reveal* rather than illustrate, enabling the audience to embark on its own journey of discovery. But this seems at odds with *To Live With Herds*, where a powerful argument, albeit a personal and not an anonymous, disembodied one, drives everything we encounter in the film. Indeed one might suggest that the MacDougalls' argument is all the more effective for their use of observational techniques in the service of older didactic purposes. *To Live With Herds* may present itself as a film which 'shows'; but it is, in important ways, one which 'tells'. David MacDougall's comment on the work of Basil Wright may be said to describe equally their own approach in *To Live With Herds*: '*Song of Ceylon* was . . . a style of synthesis, a style that used images to develop an argument or impression'.[26] The irony, however, lies in the fact that this statement was made in the context of an essay which established Wright's kind of synthetic documentary as the opposite of the new observational style which the MacDougalls, among others, claimed to be pioneering.

I want to suggest, however, that the description of *To Live With Herds* as a work of observational cinema refers more accurately to its meta-physics than to its methods. For, above all, what is striking about the MacDougalls' film is its conception of people in the world. The clarity and integrity of the film's vision is one predicated on a notion of presence, that there is something 'out there' (called perhaps 'culture' or 'society' or 'humanity'). I take observation then to mean a particular stance toward reality, that it implies a *seeing deeply into*, penetrating beyond the superficiality of surface appearance to encounter the 'real', the authentic, that which is whole and universal. Thus, although *To Live With Herds* is highly specific (rooted in a certain time and place), the MacDougalls see deeply into that moment in modern society and come up with a compelling vision of humanity as a whole. It is through the film's intense realism, one painstakingly constructed through a close observation of the intimate details of a remote society, that the MacDougalls are simultaneously able to evoke a universal symbol.

Moreover, in attempting through an observational approach to reinvent a kind of primitive cinema based on showing, what Gunning calls 'a cinema of attractions', the MacDougalls seek to enable us, the viewers, to 'recognise' the Jie. It is an attempt to forge a relationship which reaches beyond cultural difference to a deeper level of shared humanity.[27]

The Jie are the still point in a turning world; and the idea of the postcolonial state as a transient phenomenon is even more compelling today than it was twenty-five years ago. This image is sealed unforgettably in the sequence of the dust storm. The MacDougalls construct the argument of *To Live With Herds* through a number of key oppositions contrasting the stability of Jie society with the turbulent history of the twentieth century. The film is founded upon distinctions – between inside and outside, depth and surface, presence and absence and cyclical versus linear time. Ironically then, while the film-makers seek to foster an encounter across cultural difference, their anthropological cinema, in fact, rests upon a series of categories and divisions. But, as we will discover, the relationships between these categories begin to shift in the course of the MacDougalls' subsequent work.

Turkana Conversations

Political difficulties in Uganda, following the rise of Idi Amin, prevented the MacDougalls from continuing to develop their anthropological research with the Jie. They were forced to shift contexts, moving their work to neighbouring pastoralist groups in Kenya – first to the Boran and later to the Turkana. Although their substantive focus remained the same – herding peoples who defied the categories of the colonial and postcolonial state – the MacDougalls now sought to develop a different film-making approach, one which they hoped would reveal pastoralist society in new ways. It became known as *participatory cinema*. I will suggest, however, that this new approach could not be fully realised by the MacDougalls in an East African situation. The innovations that they made at the level of practice were not matched by changes in what I have called their metaphysical orientation.

From first viewing we are aware of the change that the films which make up the Turkana trilogy represent. By comparison with the intense focus and complex formal structure of *To Live With Herds*, *Turkana Conversations* seems extraordinarily slack, even meandering, as we move around with the film-makers trying to find our bearings inside a strange Turkana world. It is not immediately obvious that the trilogy is united by a single animating idea. Thus, in an important sense, the films appear to be more genuinely exploratory or revelatory than the earlier Jie work.

The MacDougalls' original intention was to make a series of ten short films with the Turkana in which individuals would offer their own perspectives on a particular story. Out of these distinctive parts or perspectives several longer films would be assembled. The film-makers quickly discovered that such a plan was too complex, but they retained the central idea which underlay it – that is, Turkana society was imagined as a construction. It was to be approached as something emergent, provisional and contested rather than as a fixed or objectified structure in the Durkheimian sense.

From the material the MacDougalls shot in Kenya during 1973–74, they edited three films: *Lorang's Way*; *A Wife Among Wives*; and *The Wedding Camels*. The first focuses on a particular character, Lorang ('A Turkana Man' as the subtitle explains); the second is organised around an idea (marriage); while the third documents the course of an event (a wedding). Progressively, then, the different films take us into Turkana society, from our initial encounter with Lorang through domestic life to an immersion in the full complexity of a contested social reality. Moreover, the relationships embodied in this ethnographic encounter also subtly change. In *Lorang's Way* the MacDougalls present their audience with evidence as a basis for knowledge; in *A Wife Among Wives* they confess to difficulties in finding out what is happening; in *The Wedding Camels* they do not even pretend to know what is happening. Increasingly Turkana society is revealed as in flux. The films explore the shifting relationships between ideals and reality, between what ought to happen and what actually happens, and they expose the processes by which society is actively made and re-made. The films emerge as a network of complex relationships, existing not just among the Turkana themselves, but also between the Turkana, the film-makers and the audience.

In beginning the Turkana trilogy, the MacDougalls employ devices which were effective in their earlier film, *To Live With Herds*. *Lorang's Way* opens in the midst of a howling dust storm. Caught up in the turbulent forces of nature, we watch people and animals as they struggle to move across a harsh windswept terrain. But counterposed to this violent eruption is a man's strong and steady voice, banishing the wind and reaffirming the Turkana's place in the landscape. Thus, as in the Jie film, the dust storm is an important symbol of the tenacity of pastoralist people in the face of change; but, this time, it has other resonances.

Lorang, a Turkana elder who was once a soldier, is the figure through whom we begin to explore the parameters of pastoralist life. This, the first film in the trilogy, presents the audience with different kinds of evidence, elicited by the film-makers through questions, eavesdropping and observation. Although our understanding is only partial and provisional, we begin to piece together a picture of Lorang – to learn what matters to him, what he believes and how he acts.

The tripartite structure of the film – 'Making Up For Lost Time'; 'Preserving the Household'; and 'Setting His Limits' – indicates the contours of the biography which the MacDougalls seek to expose. Moreover, as the title *Lorang's Way* suggests, the central character has a keen sense of himself as an active agent in both history and society. Thus the opening scene of the dust storm, while expressive of the film-makers' vision of pastoralist peoples in the modern world, also symbolises something quite specific – namely, Lorang's personal struggle to find his own life, to overcome his years of exile and to re-establish himself as a Turkana man. This fractured and unknown past, which we glimpse through the fragments of an incomplete story, is juxtaposed in the first part of the film with the integrity of Lorang's present circumstances. Now we follow him as he moves with ease and authority through his homestead, indicating both the extent and limits of his world. Taking the example of Logoth in *To Live With Herds*, the MacDougalls again use this activity of spatial mapping as a metaphor for the trilogy as a whole. It serves to anchor the films in a metaphysics of presence (people in the landscape) and to place us, initially through Lorang, in a certain relationship to Turkana society.

But, in making Lorang the point of entry, we immediately encounter a world which is moulded by individual agency as much as it is embedded in underlying principles of social structure. Lorang's way, as we begin to discover, is built upon his successful negotiation of a whole series of complex relationships, and these relationships exist in time as well as in space. The film-makers attempt to expose different facets of Lorang's character through the encounters with wives, sons and elders which make up everyday Turkana life, but equally important is his attempt to reconcile past and present. It becomes clear that Lorang has chosen to reject the values and rewards offered by the wider society; but his experiences in exile are inseparable from his contemporary perspective. They are central to Lorang's sense of his place in the world.

There is a radical shift of perspective in *A Wife Among Wives*, the second part of the Turkana trilogy. The film-makers now seek to expose different dimensions of pastoralist society through the lives of a number of its women; and, as the subtitle 'Notes on Turkana marriage' suggests, the organising theme is the question of marriage. Moreover, instead of a neatly edited view of social life anchored in a particular character or event with different chapters or sections, the film-makers pursue an idea; they present a single text comprising 'notes' or jottings fashioned from an assembly of different kinds of material – conversations, questions, impressions, rumours and snippets of information.

A Wife Among Wives is perhaps the most intriguing part of the trilogy, not least because the opening sequences seem to promise a certain kind of film which is not, in fact, realised. It begins by focusing on strategies of fieldwork, foregrounding the apparatus (for example notebooks and cameras) and the relationships involved in the making of the film itself. Most striking are the discussions which the MacDougalls hold with a number of Turkana women about what should be the focus of the film. These exchanges culminate in one of the women filming the film-makers with a Super 8 camera; her footage is edited together with the material shot by the MacDougalls of her filming. But what is equally striking is how quickly these reflexive sequences are brushed aside, as the film-makers return to a more conventional way of working and establish their own subject of enquiry. As David MacDougall himself has commented: 'I see those passages at the beginning of *A Wife Among Wives* as more emblematic of our relationships with people and a kind of communion or commonality that we felt.'[28]

This second film then is driven by questions posed by the film-makers. But their attempt to understand the meaning of marriage in a pastoralist society becomes a metaphor for the anthropological task itself. For a Turkana wedding, like fieldwork, is a long, complex process. It is full of obstacles, and unexpected twists and turns; the knowledge of the participants is partial and provisional; and the outcome is always uncertain. Thus, in contrast to the presentation of evidence which characterised *Lorang's Way*, the difficulties involved in acquiring the evidence itself become the driving force behind *A Wife Among Wives*. This is most fully developed in the subsequent film, *The Wedding Camels*, which David MacDougall has described as the 'centrepiece' of the trilogy: 'It was the film in which we made the greatest effort to try to create a sense of indeterminacy about knowledge, about the situation that one finds oneself in in the field, trying to make sense of complex events, and not necessarily being able to do it. The film is more than anything about the acquisition of knowledge, rather than about a wedding.'[29]

The Wedding Camels focuses on an event, the marriage of Lorang's daughter, Akai, to his friend and age-mate, Kongu; the film follows the difficult, protracted negotiations which surround its successful completion. Already the MacDougalls had decided that marriage was a key moment in Turkana society, the point of intersection for relationships of kinship, economics, politics and ritual. But in charting the course of a particular marriage, they raise more fully questions implicit in the other parts of the trilogy, namely questions of individual subjectivity and social structure, fieldwork and ethnography, participation and observation. For it is what the documentary film-makers associated with the direct cinema movement call a crisis situation (the equivalent of Van Gennep's notion of liminality) which throws such issues into sharp focus.[30]

The discrepancy between what should happen and what actually does happen lies at the heart of *The Wedding Camels*. By exploring the different perspectives and changing positions of key participants (including their own), the film-makers reveal Turkana society as contested, as an arena of competing interests. The film develops through time as a narrative with successive chapters – 'Preparations'; 'The Problem of Bridewealth'; 'The Wedding Ox'; 'Departures' – but it also extends laterally. Indeed, its forward movement is constantly undermined by other currents which delay, and threaten to subvert, the moment of resolution. Thus again the MacDougalls seek to weave two kinds of time, linear and cyclical, into the text of their film. In *To Live With Herds*, a notion of progress represented by historical time was rejected in favour of the cyclical or organic rhythms of pastoralist life. On this occasion, however, it is linearity which symbolises order in the face of conflicting, chaotic forces.

The Wedding Camels captures a liminal phase in people's experience of Turkana society. Moreover, the MacDougalls attempt to recreate such a moment in and through the film itself. Their intention is that the viewer's experience should mirror that of the participants in the event; thus, the film is not so much about Turkana marriage as it is an exploration of knowledge – 'about what one can and cannot know'.[31] At the core of *The Wedding Camels* is an acknowledgement of active human agency. The viewer is a participant along with the film-makers and their Turkana subjects in the production of meaning. This notion of the open-endedness of meaning, evoked through what Bill Nichols calls the film's 'modernist strategies', represents an important change in the MacDougalls' anthropological perspective. It raises new methodological and metaphysical questions.[32]

The films of the Turkana trilogy are much discussed as examples of a new kind of film-making – participatory cinema.[33] This approach evolved out of the earlier observational style and consequently retains many of its characteristic features, such as close attention to the details of social life, intimate camera work, the use of synchronous sound and subtitles, and a respect for the natural integrity of events. The innovation which participatory cinema represents, however, lay in a focusing of the filmic encounter itself. Thus a film is no longer just a disembodied product, a film *about* something; rather, it is now acknowledged to be a process. It is an expression of the different social relationships negotiated through the ethnographic encounter itself.

For the MacDougalls, innovations in film-making style were prompted by their own awareness of the limitations of an observational approach. These crystallised in a notion of what David MacDougall calls the 'privileged camera style'.[34] By this he meant a disembodied camera eye, one which transcends the limitations of human vision and perspective, taking up a position anywhere within a scene. Such a camera was, of course, the great innovation of D.W. Griffith, whose development of a distinctive cinematic language broke with the early 'primitive' cinema of Lumière; but, as the MacDougalls discovered, behind this aesthetic lay important questions of power. A camera which could be anywhere within a scene was not 'human'. It became an eye of surveillance, spying on and objectifying human subjects. By contrast to the observational style of their earlier Jie film, the MacDougalls began to develop in the Turkana trilogy an 'unprivileged style'. This essentially involved 'humanising' the camera. There was an acknowledgement of film's subjective qualities, and the text itself was to reveal that 'film-makers are human, fallible, rooted in physical space and society, governed by chance, limited in perception'.[35]

Central to the new style of film-making was the notion of conversation. For the move from observational to participatory cinema involved a shift away from vision and towards voice. Conversation signalled informality, spontaneity and open-ended interaction. Film-makers, their subjects and audiences were now engaged in dialogue; but it was not just about an exchange of information between the different parties.[36] Conversation initiated a process through which original knowledge could be generated. But in making this change in their practice, the MacDougalls may again be considered to be turning away from the distinctive aesthetic of cinema after Griffith. As James Agee noted, in his much quoted remarks on Griffith: 'For the first time the movies had a man who realized that while a theatre audience listened, a movie audience watched. "Above all . . . I am trying to make you see", Griffith said.'[37] Thus, if *To Live With Herds* was distinctively cinematic, the Turkana trilogy was, by contrast, explicitly theatrical in its conception. The participatory approach developed by the MacDougalls began to modify the original cinematic premises of their anthropological enquiry. The distinctively Italian neorealist or Bazinian perspective gave way to a film-making style which owed more to Robert Drew and the 'live action' television documentary. Moreover, if the first film echoed an ethnographic vision and style associated with Malinowski and Radcliffe-Brown, the MacDougalls' subsequent East African work brought them much closer to the social theatre model of Max Gluckman and the Manchester ethnographers.

There are a number of interesting parallels between the work carried out with Kenyan pastoralists by the MacDougalls and the kind of anthropological enquiry pioneered by Gluckman and his colleagues. For instance, at the level of method there are echoes of the extended case study in the Turkana trilogy, examples of the dialectic between principles and practice, ideas and reality which we may readily associate with Victor Turner, among others.[38] The MacDougalls, like those working within the Manchester school, also focused upon crisis, using points of conflict to expose the more general dynamics of social life. Their shift of allegiance from the orthodoxy of British structural-functionalism towards the more eclectic approaches associated with Max Gluckman enabled them to express new ideas about both subjectivity and society.

The development of participatory cinema, as we have seen, involved important changes in ethnographic technique. Such innovations, however, are inseparable from shifts of emphasis in what I have called 'the metaphysics' or way of seeing at the heart of the MacDougalls' work. For although their anthropological enquiry remains anchored in the problem of knowledge, there are a number of interesting changes in notions of culture, society and the individual from those animating their earlier Jie work.

To Live With Herds was predicated on the integrity of pastoralist life. Against the backdrop of a wider, changing society, Jie culture was evoked as an organic whole with its own dynamic and rhythms, its members bound harmoniously together by a Durkheimian consensus. The MacDougalls created an authentic, idealised Jie world in which they sought to locate fundamental human values. The symbolic power of such a vision, however, derives from its precariousness, from the very threat posed to its existence. *To Live With Herds* is, of course, an expression of anthropology's classic salvage paradigm.[39]

The vision, or more strictly speaking *the voice*, articulated through the films of the Turkana trilogy is markedly different. For the conception of society as akin to theatre reveals it as emergent, contested and shaped by the activities of real, living people. The MacDougalls now open up the relationship between structure and agency so often elided in anthropological work. Furthermore, in shifting from vision to voice, the MacDougalls exchange a metaphysics of presence (the idea of seeing deeply into a pre-existent reality 'out there', people within landscape) for the evocation of absence (the notion that, in speaking, people call forth something new and potentially unrecognisable). But in opening up Turkana life as an arena of contestation, the MacDougalls simultaneously insulate it from the wider society. Thus, if *To Live With Herds* celebrates Jie integrity in an unstable world, the Turkana trilogy exposes internal flux within an unchanging landscape separated from the currents of modern history.

The MacDougalls' failure to incorporate broader currents of society and history into the ethnographic present of their Turkana trilogy limits, I believe, their development of a genuinely new form of anthropological cinema. Although in a number of significant ways their later East African work constitutes a break up or critical exposure of fieldwork-based ethnography's conventional categories, in other ways it remains stubbornly wedded to the classic paradigm. This is not least because the Turkana trilogy privileges the rationality of intellectual enquiry in contrast with the chaos, indeed *cacophony*, of people's voices.[40] For, despite the MacDougalls' attempt to initiate a conversation through their Turkana films, there is in fact only interaction (a rather one-sided exchange) and not *participation*.

Colin Young's remarks, describing the reflexive sequences at the beginning of *A Wife Among Wives* as 'two cultures looking at each other', are particularly telling. He draws attention to the MacDougalls' belief, implicit in the films themselves, that there are different and separate cultures. At one level this means their abandonment of a vision of shared humanity – the spectator now confronts difference or the obstacles inherent in cultural relativism. At another level, the MacDougalls continue to reify notions of culture or society. Thus a number of key assumptions at play in the Turkana trilogy are, in significant ways, at odds with the new method that the film-makers are seeking to develop. Vision (culture as object, knowledge) and voice (culture as performance, politics) are in contradiction. This contradiction inhibits the development of a genuinely 'participatory cinema'. A radical shift of context enabled the MacDougalls to realise more fully their notion of a collaborative anthropology pursued within the context of documentary film-making.

The Australian Aboriginal films

During the late 1970s the MacDougalls began to collaborate with the Australian Institute of Aboriginal Studies, becoming resident film-makers among Aboriginal communities in the Aurukun area of northern Queensland. Unlike the East African pastoralists, who had shown little interest in the MacDougalls' film-making activities, Australia's native peoples were highly aware of the political significance of media engagement. Already film had been used by the institute as a medium for what David MacDougall described as 'salvage anthropology'; but, as he pointed out, interest was moving away 'from reconstruction of pre-contact situations towards an examination of the realities of contemporary Aboriginal experience'.[41]

From the outset, the MacDougalls confronted a complex political situation in which they were active participants. No longer interested outsiders, they were now implicated as never before in what they sought to represent. As Fred Myers notes: 'The Aurukun films are related to the complex process of the Aboriginal community there struggling to maintain and transmit its autonomy, culture and land. Not only do the films represent this process, but quite obviously – and intentionally – they are part of it.'[42] These conditions not only shaped the MacDougalls' particular methods of working; they also throw into sharp relief certain key concepts which anchor their anthropological practice.

The Aurukun film project developed out of conversations which the MacDougalls had with members of the Aboriginal community. Central to the collaboration, however, was the idea that the film's mandate should clearly come from the subjects themselves and not from the filmmakers. Thus, unlike the East African films which were driven by an intellectual agenda originating outside the society, the MacDougalls allowed their practice here to be shaped by the interests and concerns of the people for whom they now worked. Although this subordination of interests was a fundamental premise of their Australian work, the MacDougalls nevertheless retained a sense of their own distinctive concerns in the development of Aboriginal projects. From the beginning, then, the Aurukun films brought together different people whose agendas were not necessarily identical. These relationships, evolving and changing in the course of the collaboration, form the substance of the films; but the meaning of these encounters resonated beyond the immediate context. For the negotiation of relationships within any particular film may be taken as symbolic of the dynamics at work in modern society as a whole.

The conditions under which the MacDougalls worked in Australia led to a significant extension of the methodological innovations which they had begun to pursue through their anthropological work with the Turkana pastoralists. Specifically, they sought to create a new and expanded form of participatory cinema. The shift away from the primacy of vision towards a privileging of voice was now taken much further. Conversation, for example, formed the original point of departure for the Aurukun project. It became a central organising principle of the MacDougalls' Aboriginal films. But, unlike the Turkana trilogy, conversation was not about dialogue or exchange – that is, what David MacDougall calls 'a transmission of prior knowledge'. Instead, as he explains it, the film-makers attempted to create conditions 'in which new knowledge can take us by surprise.'[43]

The changes in technique which the MacDougalls explored within the Australian context were importantly linked to the modification of their 'metaphysic' or worldview. This movement may be understood as a response to the situation which they now confronted. From the outset the question of native people in Australia could not be simply represented as a problem of isolated groups struggling to preserve a notion of cultural integrity. History and national politics were not something external to Aboriginal life, as suggested by the MacDougalls' East African work. They were at the very heart of it.

The Aurukun films, which include *Familiar Places*, *The House-Opening*, *Three Horsemen* and *Take-Over*, powerfully evoke the complex and fluid relationships which constitute the contemporary Aboriginal situation – relationships between past and present, landscape and settlement, humans and spirits, Aboriginal people and white settlers, Aboriginal communities and anthropologists, as well as relationships between and within Aboriginal communities themselves. The MacDougalls sought to give voice to people, allowing people to tell their own stories, to name experience, such that members of the Aboriginal community could assert, challenge or redefine relationships with the world on their own terms. But the different acts of speaking – soliloquy, conversation, speeches, debate, argument – reveal the complexity of the social relationships which make up this contemporary world.

Conversation is the central motif of *Familiar Places* (1980). It brings together a number of participants (an anthropologist, Peter Sutton; different generations of an Aboriginal family – Jack Spear, Angus Namponen, his wife Chrissie and their children; and the MacDougalls) whose interests converge in the activity of mapping the landscape. Their agendas overlap, but they are neither identical nor coterminous. This distinctive configuration is neatly symbolised in the film's foregrounding of the different technologies – camera, tape-recorder, transistor radio, memory, eyesight – which the participants use.[44] It is a striking expression of the fact that each individual, not least the children, has a different relationship to the world which the film seeks to evoke.

The MacDougalls, as we have already noted, used a similar mapping device in their earlier East African work to indicate a distinctive pastoralist orientation towards the world. But what was then more of a preliminary to the film's substantive concerns now constitutes the very film itself. Moreover, there is no longer any assumption of a unitary culture existing 'out there', articulated by a single person as its representative (Logoth, for example). Culture is now presented as fluid and constructed. The landscape, once conceived by the MacDougalls as the locus of culture and identity, becomes the focal site of contestation.

The MacDougalls attempt to match the formal qualities of *Familiar Places* with their intellectual concerns. Conversation is about the mapping of a social landscape, the establishment of different relationships and networks. And, like the physical activity which the film documents, culture as conversation is open-ended and unfinished. Although the opening sequences of *Familiar Places* establish that the terms of the collaboration will be defined by the film's Aboriginal subjects, we are also aware that acts of speaking to, speaking with and speaking about are crosscut by the necessity to speak *through*. The anthropologist and the film-makers are important conduits for Aboriginal messages. For it is through them that the film's native subjects initiate conversation with a wider audience. *Familiar Places* then is not just about creating a site for discussion; it is also about projection, the assertion of certain definitions of the world to other Aboriginal communities, to white Australia and beyond.

Take-Over, a later film in the MacDougalls' Aboriginal series, sees the anthropologists expand their notion of contemporary life as constituted by means of different speech acts. The context is a highly charged political struggle in which members of the Aurukun community organise to resist the unilateral decision made by the Queensland government to take over the administration of the Aboriginal area from the United Church. The film dramatically documents the unfolding battle.[45] Building to an extraordinary climax in which the Aboriginal community lives in hourly expectation of invasion from state government officials, it exposes the conflicting forces at the heart of contemporary Australia. For the Aurukun community's battle for self-determination draws together agents of the church, the state government, the federal government, the media, white sympathisers and Aboriginal people. This eclectic alliance of different constituencies finds expression through the polyphonic form of the created text. It evokes the complexity of the discourse which is created in and through the film as an integral part of the political process itself.

The power of *Take-Over* stems from the intensity of its focus. It illuminates a particular moment in modern history. In this way the film resonates with the MacDougalls' first work, *To Live With Herds*. For again, the central axis is the relationship between people at the margins and centralised bureaucratic power. There is now, however, a crucial difference. The Aboriginal people of Aurukun, unlike the Jie pastoral-ists, are not so easily fobbed off by minor government officials; rather, as the film exposes, they become the focus of political discussion at the highest level of Australian society.

By describing *Take-Over* as 'polyphonic', I want to draw attention to the centrality of voice, functioning as both the film's method and metaphysic. For this film is the perhaps most verbal (and least visual) of all the work which the MacDougalls have carried out as film-makers. From their ingenious use of a transistor radio to document the succes-sive stages in the development of the political struggle to their emphasis upon the different verbal strategies (argument, discussion, speeches, bureaucratic orders), the film-makers suggest a world constructed through speech. The fundamental nature of this struggle is exposed early on, specifically in the sequence which features Mr Porter, the state government representative, addressing the people of Aurukun. Porter refuses to permit the MacDougalls to film inside the meeting, allowing them only to record the sound of different voices (predominantly his own). He can be heard but not seen. Thus, like the people of Aurukun themselves, we are forced to listen to the disembodied voice of bureau-cracy seeking to impose a political reality; but it is one, as the film progressively reveals, which calls forth a response, a chorus of human voices which contest and challenge such authoritative definitions of contemporary reality.

The decisive shift from vision to voice in the MacDougalls' Australian work is linked to their recognition that cultural or political realities are not pre-existent but must be evoked as emergent. David MacDougall's camera, once critical in asserting presence, the situation of people in the world, is now secondary. It is sound, symbolised by the centrality of the transistor radio, which is primary, activating the relationship between presence and absence, spanning as it does disjunctions of time and space.

Take-Over raises, however, perhaps more sharply than the other Aurukun films, the problematic status of voice. Just who is speaking for whom? For the question of representation, far from being resolved by innovations in ethnographic techniques, is now posed even more acutely – as David MacDougall himself has subsequently acknowledged.[46] Indeed, we may discern in the film an implicit recognition by the MacDougalls of their own predicament. It is prefigured in the fate of Mr Viner, the Federal Minister for Aboriginal Affairs, caught between bureaucratic politics and the demands of the Aurukun people. He is a mediator, working in a rapidly changing situation which eventually renders the services of such figures unnecessary. The film-makers, too, discover that what is achieved at the level of individual practice is undermined by a broader political reality.

The MacDougalls' involvement in Aboriginal politics was motivated by their commitment to an expansive democratic project. This engagement is a concrete example of the new kind of anthropology which is much more written about than actively pursued.[47] The MacDougalls' participation in a brief, but formative moment in Australia's modern history overturned a number of established relationships at the centre of scientific ethnography and implicit in much of their previous work – namely, conventional hierarchies of intellectuals and people, ideas and life, order and chaos, observation and participation, vision and voice, metaphysics and method. But, in the course of their Aurukun collaboration, the MacDougalls came up against the limitations of democracy itself – or, at least, democracy as they conceived it or were able to conceive it in a particular historical situation.

David MacDougall's view was that the kind of participatory politics in which he and the Aurukun had been engaged confused rather than clarified issues of representation. Specifically, it denied individual agency and authorship. Part of the problem here stems from the machinery of bureaucratic politics which appropriates the democratic ideal and subverts it, turning it into a series of rhetorical slogans. But, equally, the film-makers themselves are trapped within a certain kind of intellectualism. They conceive the alternative to authority as a self-sacrificing kind of service, rather than a Rouchian 'adventure', an open-ended partnership in which new, unimagined forms are invented through the collaboration itself. In the end, the categories defining the MacDougalls' world – self and other, individual and society, particular and universal – resist the changes set in train by their own innovative practice.

At the beginning of the 1990s, a decade after the Aurukun project, the MacDougalls made two films. The first, *Photo Wallahs* (1991), was a joint collaboration; the second, *Tempus de Baristas* (*Time of the Barmen*) (1993), was credited to David MacDougall alone. These films, set in the Himalayas and Sardinia respectively, are a curious pair. For, in an important sense, they return the MacDougalls to the place where they began their project of anthropological cinema some two decades earlier. Certainly both films represent the return to a preoccupation with vision rather than voice, with what David MacDougall calls 'visual ways of knowing'. The animating vision, while remaining a predominantly enlightenment one, a way of seeing predicated upon the problem of knowledge, is now tempered by the release of romantic sensibilities. There is an explicit concern with experience, embodiment, subjectivity, intuition, 'the quick' – indeed with the transcendent.[48]

Running throughout the MacDougalls' work, beginning with *To Live With Herds* (1971), is a strong undercurrent of romanticism. Their investigations of contemporary social realities have always been tinged with a sense of nostalgia, even yearning. Until the 1990s such sensibilities were largely held in check by a particular kind of intellectualism enclosing each film and linking one to another through the exercise of critical reflexivity which defines the MacDougalls' enterprise as a whole. Now, with the late work, the romanticism of their anthropology is given fuller expression.[49] Hence, although *Photo Wallahs* and *Tempus de Baristas* appear at first sight to be very different films (in their location, subject matter and formal qualities), they are linked through their expression of profound romantic longing.

Photo Wallahs, subtitled 'An encounter with photography in Mussourie, a North Indian hill station', involved another radical shift of context for the film-makers. After twenty years of working first in East Africa and later in Australia, David and Judith MacDougall now moved the focus of their ethnographic enquiry to India. This change of location also involved a significant new configuration of people and landscape. For the wide, open plains across which pastoralist and aboriginal peoples moved was replaced by the different levels of a steeply sloping Himalayan terrain – the landscape itself signalling the centrality of hierarchy to the MacDougalls' investigation of photography practice. Hierarchy, both social and aesthetic, lies at the heart of *Photo Wallahs*.[50]

Photo Wallahs is organised around a single idea – photography. It is explored through the rich visual texture of Indian life; and, presented in a form resembling a series of still photographs, the film's meaning, like that of the photograph itself, remains open-ended and indeterminate. But it is a film and not a photographic album. *Photo Wallahs* unfolds through time as much as it remains anchored in space. Hence it is important to ask what relationship is established between movement and stillness, cinema and photography within the piece itself. The film is both subtle and complex. It is a form of ethnographic enquiry, pursued not conventionally by means of language but primarily through a series of associations and resonances evoked by the juxtaposition of visual images.[51] As such, there is a remarkable synthesis of content and form. The film's substantive concerns, focused within a particular cultural location, resonate with its aesthetics such that an unusual reflexive dynamic is established. *Photo Wallahs* brings an anthropological perspective to bear upon the medium of photography and a photographic perspective toward anthropological questions, promising a new kind of visual anthropology founded upon what Pinney characterises as 'the other's figural yearnings as a subject of the film's own figural representation'.[52] But it is more than this. The status of anthropological knowledge is also raised as a problem by the particular aesthetics of such a project. What kind of epistemological questions are posed when ethnography is pursued by means of photographic techniques and technologies?

The place chosen by the MacDougalls as the site for their exploration of Indian photographic practice is an interesting one. Mussourie exists as a relic from another age. It is a former hill station from the days of the British Raj, now functioning as a popular vacation and honeymoon destination for Indians who seek relief from the heat of the plains. The particular synthesis of photography and cinema achieved in *Photo Wallahs* perfectly expresses these different historical moments. For the film's forward movement is perpetually thwarted by its recursive turns.[53] The garish images of modern Hindi film and bazaar video games disrupt the silence and mystery of the fading black-and-white photographs which evoke another age. The inherent logic of the film narrative expresses the shift from the old to the new, but its internal rhythms of association draw attention to the slow dwindling of human qualities. Despite their documentation of photography's endless reinvention, the vitality and ingenuity of contemporary practice, the filmmakers cannot disguise the sense of loss that pervades the work as a whole. *Photo Wallahs* is a deeply nostalgic film. It is a lament for the past, for art, beauty, truth, skill, craft, patience and dedication as represented by the tradition of black-and-white photography.

Photo Wallahs appears to mark a new stage in the development of the MacDougalls' anthropological cinema. It is almost as if, having exhausted the intellectualism of their project launched at the end of the 1960s, they now attempt to recover an anthropology built upon different premises; and, in so doing, their very first film re-emerges as the critical point of anchorage. For, of all the films in the MacDougall corpus, *Photo Wallahs* and *Tempus De Baristas* most powerfully evoke *To Live With Herds*. If *Photo Wallahs* mirrors the Jie film in being an exercise in the cinematic exploration of ideas, then *Tempus De Baristas*, made two years later, returns David MacDougall to the foundational questions of people and place.[54]

Tempus De Baristas, as its title indicates, is a film about time. It is explored at a number of levels within the work, from the time of shepherds, of barmen and of the ethnographer himself, to an exploration of the different kinds of time contained within the film medium itself.[55] But equally, *Tempus De Baristas* is a film about knowledge. What do people know and how do they know it? In taking up once more the question at the centre of his work, David MacDougall now makes manifest the isolation, loss and yearning which lurks within all his other films. The film-maker's own desire for re-integration becomes projected, in the classic Italian neo-realist style, as the embedding of people within landscape. The film's 'photogenic effects' (as Guynn writes of *Song of Ceylon*) effect a transformative movement at the core of the work. It is no longer ethnography. It becomes a redemptive experience.[56]

Watching *Tempus De Baristas*, I found myself recalling the reflexive sequences which mark the beginning of *A Wife Among Wives*, the second film in the MacDougalls' Turkana trilogy. For here the extent of the ethnographers' library in the field is startlingly revealed. It always seemed to be an expression of the intellectual burden their project carried. Now, in the closing image of *Tempus De Baristas*, MacDougall frames a Sardinian shepherd, alone with his thoughts, contemplating the landscape from a high mountain peak. The quiet celebration of that single moment of peace and harmony seems to come from a place deep within the film. It is as if the director can finally allow himself to imagine himself free from the intellectual weight of his own personal history.

8 The anthropological television of Melissa Llewelyn-Davies

Anthropologists as modern intellectuals have not successfully entered the arena of public debate. Unlike their academic counterparts in history, literature or cultural studies, they are rarely sought out for their observations on modern society. If acknowledged at all, anthropologists are imagined as an esoteric group of people associated with the study of strange peoples and customs. This is an image that has been fostered by the discipline itself, not least because the consolidation of scientific ethnography as a discrete arena of academic enquiry depended upon a claim to expert knowledge and specialised practice.

There are, of course, a number of significant exceptions. Margaret Mead was a national figure in the United States, and Claude Lévi-Strauss has long enjoyed the acknowledgement that is accorded to French intellectuals. But the dangers of public recognition and the suspicion of 'popularisation' remain strongly linked in the minds of many academic anthropologists. Certainly in Britain, the media profile of anthropologists has been much more modest than that of their French or American colleagues. During the 1950s people like Evans-Pritchard and others gave radio talks on topics such as Azande witch-craft, but it was the *succès de scandale* of Edmund Leach's 1967 Reith Lectures, *A Runaway World?*, which most effectively reminded a public audience of anthropology's potential to offer a critical perspective on the contemporary world.[1]

The discipline's 'acute problems of public image and visibility', as one writer put it, have now become a matter of discussion among anthropologists.[2] There is an acknowledgement that anthropologists, like everyone else, have a responsibility to address major issues of war, ethnic conflict, genocide, environmental destruction, scientific innovation, religious fundamentalism, human rights, ethics and so on. The concern about how anthropology might engage with the late twentieth-century world is, however, inseparable from the radical rethinking of methods and practices at the centre of the discipline. For, over more than a decade, there has been a sustained critique of scientific ethnography, the paradigm around which modern anthropology was consolidated; and with it, there has been a loss of confidence in many established ideas and practices. This moment of critical reflection in the discipline has been a creative one. It has stimulated experimentation in ideas, methods and forms of communication, linking today's work with the innovative spirit of enquiry which marked anthropology's modernist birth at the turn of the century.

The renewal of anthropology as a project of late modernity is importantly dependent upon the discipline forging new links with society and upon finding ways of locating what has become a narrow and specialised academic practice within a broader context of politics and change. Although the writing of literary texts remains the dominant form by which anthropological work finds expression, there is growing interest in other media forms whose features encompass the movement and complexity of the contemporary world. Television, like cinema, offers itself as an interesting site in which a new kind of ethnography might be explored. Its power and ubiquity, however, have long made intellectuals uneasy. Anthropologists, too, have shared this wariness and suspicion, remaining largely aloof from engagement with television's presence in the worlds they seek to investigate and rejecting, almost by instinct, its potential as a medium of ethnographic communication.[3]

Despite general scepticism within the profession, there have been a number of attempts to bring together anthropology and television. Many of these collaborations have been forged within the context of British broadcasting, the most notable being Granada Television's *Disappearing World* series which was launched in 1971. The BBC has also commissioned programmes marked by an explictly anthropological orientation – for example, those transmitted in the *Worlds Apart* and, more recently, in the *Under The Sun* series.[4] The interest in making such programmes emerged during the 1970s and early 1980s, when anthropology's professional confidence was high and the paradigm of scientific ethnography still held sway. Although the beginnings of a self-critique were manifest, there was still a widespread assumption of academic expertise built upon the mastery of a body of 'objective knowledge', and there was confidence in the 'scientific' techniques of ethnographic enquiry which transformed personal observations into theoretical pronouncements.

Given these circumstances, it is not surprising that the early experiments in collaborative working were fraught with difficulty as anthropologists and programme-makers struggled to discover common ground. At its simplest, the problem was characterised by the academics as involving a conflict between their grasp of the detail and complexity of ethnographic realities, and the drive for simplicity which they accorded to the television producers. Revealingly, David Turton, a long-term collaborator with Leslie Woodhead in the *Disappearing World* series, presented the tension as one between 'ideas' and 'storytelling'. We know now, of course, that anthropologists tell stories, too.[5]

The crux of the problem is, in fact, exposed in the expression most often used to describe these collaborations. For 'anthropology on television', when referring to a self-identifying series legitimated by the presence of a professional anthropologist, usually involves the delivery of 'expert' knowledge to an anonymous audience without any serious interrogation of either the conditions under which such knowledge has been generated or the means by which it was being communicated. Anthropological television, I suggest, is a different enterprise. It involves neither the popularisation of specialist knowledge, nor the uneasy grafting of an academic style onto a cultural form irrespective of its own particular features. Rather, it emerges from the development of a critical perspective toward established ideas and conventions in both television and anthropology. Anthropological television means an active engagement with genres unique to television as the means to expose ethnographic assumptions about, for example, the nature of social reality or conceptions of subjectivity. Conversely, it also involves the use of anthropological ideas and techniques in interpretating how television operates as a mode of cultural representation in the contemporary world.[6]

The work of Melissa Llewelyn-Davies presents an interesting case study in the emergence of anthropological television. My approach to understanding her project mirrors the one which I pursued with respect to the anthropological cinema of Jean Rouch, and David and Judith MacDougall. In the case of these film-makers, I drew attention to how certain features of cinema (not just those of film as a medium, but of cinema as a social site) came to be fused with particular interpretations of the anthropological task such that a new form was generated. Here my concern is to explore the ways in which Llewelyn-Davies has drawn upon television's distinctive qualities as the means to extend and transform her ethnographic work.

Llewelyn-Davies is most well known for the cycle of films she has made over a period of almost twenty years with the Maasai people, pastoralists who live in an area called Loita which straddles the Kenyan–Tanzanian border. The early films, *Masai Women* (1974) and *Masai Manhood* (1975), were transmitted as part of Granada Television's *Disappearing World* series. A decade later, she made *The Women's Olamal* (1984) and *Diary of a Maasai Village* (1984) for the BBC. Llewelyn-Davies's most recent film in this cycle to date, *Memories and*

Dreams, was broadcast in 1993 as part of BBC2's documentary series, *Fine Cut*. It is significant that apart from publishing a handful of academic articles, television, and not the academy, has been the site in which Llewelyn-Davies has pursued her anthropological interests.[7]

The Maasai film cycle forms the focus for my exploration of anthropological television. Two features distinguish this body of Llewelyn-Davies' work. First of all, there is a remarkable intellectual consistency to it. From the beginning of her television career, Llewelyn-Davies has explored ethnographic questions by means of a self-consciously articulated feminist perspective. Gender forms the central axis through which she interprets the dynamic of Maasai society. Secondly, and connected to this particular orientation, there is an unusual degree of formal experimentation marking the film cycle as a whole. Thus, although at the heart of each film lies the qestion of women and the reproduction of Maasai society, Llewelyn-Davies has continually recast it through her experimentation with television forms.

The interpretation of Llewelyn-Davies' work which I offer takes the substantive concerns of the Maasai films as a point of departure. But my discussion of the particular questions concerning gender and social life is inseparable from an exploration of the changing formal features which characterise the film cycle as a whole. One of my primary intentions in highlighting Llewelyn-Davies' innovative use of genres distinctive to television (soap opera, for example) is to raise questions about anthropology itself. Hence the emphasis of my approach will be placed not upon the development of an anthropological perspective towards television as a cultural form. Instead, I will be seeking to ask how engagement with television poses questions about the nature and scope of anthropological enquiry. For Llewelyn-Davies' Masaai film cycle, as it unfolded over two decades, was marked by a number of interesting changes in the focus and method of anthropological investigation. If it was originally a project with enlightenment features (holistic and knowledge-based), it subsequently changed from being marked by a 'visualist' bias (that is, society conceived as an object to be observed and described) toward a discursive form of ethnographic engagement. This shift from vision toward voice, however, is marked by a distinctive feminist sensibility which renders Llewelyn-Davies' approach different from the kind of conversational style developed by the MacDougalls during the 1980s. Llewelyn-Davies once described her fieldwork technique as about 'chatting'. As a method and orientation toward the world, it reveals a new kind of anthropological encounter built around the intimate, the informal, the fostering of human connection in a context of what Lila Abu-Lughod calls 'dailiness'.[8] For although

Llewelyn-Davies pursues her anthropological work by means of an image-based technology, it is in fact television's particular hierarchy of vision and voice, its privileging of sound over image, which facilitates her development as an ethnographer who 'speaks nearby'. Such a stance, as E. Ann Kaplan explains, 'evokes the body. It evokes an ethnographer whose presence is noted, who listens and speaks, but does not assume knowledge of the other'.[9]

The early Maasai films

The first Maasai films, *Masai Women* and *Masai Manhood*, were made for *Disappearing World*, Granada Television's series of anthropological documentaries. The series, launched in 1971, reflects the distinctive culture of broadcasting associated with Granada and its chairman Denis Forman; but it also evokes the broader context of postwar television programme-making and professional anthropology. The period after 1945 was, as we have seen, one in which documentary was redefined due to changes taking place elsewhere in society. Challenges to established interpretations of fiction and reality, ways of working, and innovations in film-making technology were all part and parcel of a new landscape dominated by television. Although cinema remained an important site, not least because documentary approaches played a significant role in the renaissance of fiction film, documentary itself depended upon television for its creative renewal. In becoming a television genre, however, it was transformed. The 'cinematic essay' (what Corner describes as 'impressionism put to promotional ends') never entirely disappeared; but, on the whole, documentary for television became a form of 'expanded reportage'. Its origins were in journalism rather than in notions of art or education.[10]

From the beginning, television developed in particular aesthetic, social and institutional directions which clearly marked it off from cinema. Its small screen and domestic location change the conventional hierarchy of image and sound existing within cinema, and its characteristic 'flow' offers the world as ever-present to be apprehended by means of distracted attention – that is, by a series of glances – as distinct from the tightly focused attention of the cinematic gaze. Television is routine, familiar, mundane. Constituted from segments, its loose organisation and repetitive rhythms defy the linearity and narrative closure of cinema. Moreover, as a private activity, television viewing is not about entering a special site, a physical, psychological and social limbo in order to surrender to experience; rather it is about consciously engaging with the world from the security of one's everyday surroundings.[11]

Despite the rise of new documentary forms expressive of television's distinctive attributes, specifically its 'live' quality which gives the sense of relaying action as it happens, the older Griersonian style continued to exert a significant influence upon programme-makers.[12] This was especially true in Britain. Here a number of prominent figures in the commercial and public sectors of postwar broadcasting regarded television as a creative medium for the communication of ideas. There was an interest in the creative renewal of the documentary as a means by which the contemporary world might be known. But, in following Grierson, there was also an acknowledgement by the emerging generation of television documentarists that such knowledge must be linked to the equally important notion of citizenship. Its extension was to be fostered through a process of mutual recognition or empathy.

Granada Television, under its chairman, Denis Forman, developed during the 1950s and 1960s into an important location for innovative programme-making. From early in his career, Forman was interested in engaging audiences with new subject matter and committed to experimentation through the formal qualities of the medium itself. His response to Brian Moser's passionate dedication to the plight of indigenous peoples was a characteristic one. Forman offered to commission a number of programmes which posed questions about globalisation and native peoples to British television viewers. The resulting series, *Disappearing World*, was distinguished by its anthropological agenda harnessed to an established documentary form. It involved the grafting of Radcliffe-Brown's structural-functionalism onto a Griersonian conception of the documentary project.

If the early work of Llewelyn-Davies was moulded by the particular television context in which the *Disappearing World* series was located, influences originating in the British school of anthropology were equally important. The paradigm of scientific ethnography with its distinctive object (primitive society), method (fieldwork) and theory (structural-functionalism) around which the academic discipline had been consolidated, was central to the intellectual culture in which Llewelyn-Davies was trained. There was a marked Durkheimian orientation toward topics of anthropological investigation, expressed through an interest in questions of social order, rules, norms, kinship, and political and judicial structure. The analytical emphasis was focused upon action socially conceived within a largely synchronic framework. Questions of history and consciousness, however, were largely outside the normal scope of anthropological enquiry.

Although Llewelyn-Davies' anthropological interests were initially shaped by the paradigm of scientific ethnography, they were subsequently transformed by the development of critical perspectives within the discipline. For, by the late 1960s, a number of challenges to the scientism of Radcliffe-Brown's approach were emerging. In particular, the women's movement became an important source for a wide-ranging critique of the substance, method and forms of anthropological work. Feminism exercised a profound influence upon all aspects of Llewelyn-Davies' Maasai work.[13]

Masai Women

Masai Women opens Llewelyn-Davies' film cycle. It was transmitted in 1974 as the eleventh programme in the *Disappearing World* series.[14] Certainly the film (and its companion, *Masai Manhood*) reflects the conventions of the series to which it belonged; but, in significant ways, it may be understood to represent a move away from the type of salvage anthropology which had formed the early inspiration behind the *Disappearing World* project. For *Masai Women* (and *Masai Manhood*) is not about a fragile society whose internal coherence and reproduction is under threat from more powerful forces at work in the world. Instead, Llewelyn-Davies sets out to subvert such a conception, focusing upon the internal mechanisms of social reproduction which underpin the strength, confidence and integrity of Maasai society.

Masai Women was closely tied to Llewelyn-Davies' original ethnographic research in East Africa. Moreover, in its concerns and methods, the film reveals the particular feminist paradigm through which questions concerning power, gender and wealth were refracted during the 1970s. Llewelyn-Davies investigates the roles of women in a pastoral society where cattle are the basis of wealth, and where a man's wealth is measured not just by his herds, but by the numbers of his dependants, wives and daughters-in-law, who look after the cattle but have no rights in them. This is explained in an introductory commentary by Llewelyn-Davies herself, establishing the context for the division she makes between the world of women and the world of men. As the film's title reveals, it is *about* Maasai women; but it is also the film-maker's intention, if only partially realised, that the film be *by* women. Thus its perspective is explicitly partial – it sets out to present to the viewer the world of women as they experience and describe it to a woman anthropologist.

Masai Women is structured around the major transitions which mark a woman's life. These are circumcision, marriage and motherhood. In the first part of the film, Llewelyn-Davies explores the question of the transition from girlhood to maturity and marriage. It is marked by the

Maasai with a ceremony of circumcision, after which a young woman makes the journey from her father's house to the village of her new husband. Using interviews and commentary, Llewelyn-Davies provides the contextual information which informs what we actually see. Most strikingly what we do *not* see is the circumcision itself; rather Llewelyn-Davies, in shifting to the next moment of female transition, makes the arrival of a new wife at her husband's village the dramatic climax of the film. Here she is met by a hostile and abusive crowd of women, who dance around her, shouting ritualised insults and reducing her to tears. Later we follow the new wife's incorporation into the village, receiving the blessings of the *laibon*, her father-in-law, and assuming control over her own small herd of cattle. As a married woman she is now expected to increase her husband's wealth through the production of children and to manage her husband's cattle until her sons assume control after their period in the forest as warriors, or *moran*.

The second part of the film is concerned with the next stage in a woman's life, motherhood. Llewelyn-Davies seeks to give focus to its meaning through the preparations for the dramatic spectacle which marks the end of warriorhood for young Maasai men. It is a time of celebration for those women who have succeeded in producing children. It marks the reaching of maturity of their sons, and the details of the ritual preparations of these proud warriors which the film reveals must then be seen as if through the eyes of their mothers.

With hindsight Llewelyn-Davies has confessed to feeling that perhaps the warriors occupy too large and colourful a place in a film about women, admitting that, like all film-makers, she became carried away by the visual splendour of the occasion.[15] It is true that it is often difficult in these latter scenes to remember that we should be watching the warriors with a mother's eye (and with the eyes of the childless women, too). But in another sense the *moran*'s ritual preparations work effectively both to conclude the film and to provide the link to its sequel, *Masai Manhood*. The ritual marks the completeness of a woman's life, achieved at the moment when she sees her son enter elderhood and take charge of the herds which she has held in trust until his social maturity. Thus while the film's climax emphasises separation, the liminal moment in a woman's life as she passes from her father's village to that of her husband, the scenes from the warriorhood ritual stress integration, bringing together mothers and sons with Maasai elders to celebrate a successful transition.

Masai Women is organised around an idea, around what it means to be a woman in Maasai society. The centrality of gender to the substance and form of the film, and the particular way in which Llewelyn-Davies articulates her analytical perspective, reveal much about the dominant concerns of the women's movement during the early 1970s. Specifically, there was an interest in 'real women'. Much attention was focused upon making women present through the reclaiming of experience. Challenges to the conventional images and status of women in society were to be mobilised by means of women sharing and validating their experiences with other women. Many of the issues debated within the women's movement were filtered through academic anthropology, crystallising into a new research field with its own particular intellectual concerns and techniques of enquiry. It was known as the 'anthropology of women'.[16]

It is clear that Llewelyn-Davies' ethnographic concerns were heavily influenced by the 'anthropology of women' orientation within the discipline. For although *Masai Women* was an exploration of traditional anthropological questions about kinship, property and power, the film's focus represented the introduction of a new subject matter into established areas of anthropological enquiry.[17] Moreover, by investigating the world of women, Llewelyn-Davies was also contributing to a broader project which was concerned with the cross-cultural documentation of women's lives. The documentation process itself was built upon self-conscious methodological innovation. Central were the development of informal, non-hierarchical working methods. Knowledge was to be generated through a process of sharing and empathy; and collaboration was predicated upon sameness, the assumption of a universal category 'woman'.

At one level it is possible to interpret *Masai Women* as the expression of a particular feminist sensibility. This is evident despite the fact that Llewelyn-Davies was constrained by the position (anthropologist/researcher) she occupied within a larger television production team and by the conventions of the series as a whole. For example, the film is marked by the fluidity and intimacy of its camera work. It is, in places, strongly reminiscent of the style pursued by David and Judith MacDougall in their early film, *To Live With Herds*. The intimacy evoked by the film's particular aesthetic depends a great deal, too, upon the distinctive presence of Llewelyn-Davies herself within the work. As the narrator she is the mediating figure between the unknown world of her subjects and the domestic familiarity of her television audience. But it is her interpretation of such an established television role that critically establishes the distinctively feminist orientation which runs throughout her Maasai ethnography. The approach Llewelyn-Davies fosters is one in which anthropological understanding emerges from an exchange of confidences founded upon trust and respect.

At another level, however, any critical appraisal of *Masai Women* inevitably exposes the limitations of the approach which Llewelyn-Davies was pursuing during the mid-1970s. The radical possibilities opened up with the development of a feminist perspective were checked by the premises upon which *Disappearing World* was based. Certainly Faye Ginsburg is correct to remind us of the important innovations in television documentary that *Disappearing World* represented (for example subtitling, small crews and conversational styles).[18] Nevertheless, its constituent programmes were essentially the expression of older ideas in both anthropology and documentary. Both forms of social enquiry were already changing. On the one hand, television documentary was developing in new directions, moving away from the older top-down style epitomised by the 'cinematic essay' towards more popular forms. On the other hand, academic anthropology was characterised by the growing challenge to its central paradigm, scientific ethnography, around which the discipline had been consolidated in the universities.

Hence despite the television location of her early Maasai work, it is important to recognise that Llewelyn-Davies' approach remained predominantly within the older, more literary style of documentary. It belonged to a genre marked by exposition or 'telling', rather than one of 'showing' and revealing, features which were identified with the adoption of a *vérité* stance toward social life. Indeed *Masai Women* might be said to exemplify the kind of 'word-logic show' that had been so decisively repudiated by Robert Drew and the new documentary film-makers working in America.[19] For it is, inescapably, a film constructed around an idea originating in the head of the anthropologist. Events and people are recruited to illustrate the unfolding of what is largely an academic argument about gender and power. The images, sound and narration are unified in pursuit of an abstract thesis anchored in the expertise of the anthropologist herself. Llewelyn-Davies' commentary serves to guide almost everything encountered on the screen, rendering viewers passive in the face of specialist knowledge. The overwhelming experience is of images merely serving as the passive counterpart to the spoken narrative. Subtitling is only selectively used, employed most frequently to translate statements about social norms rather than informal conversation. Furthermore, the interviews with certain key women express what might be called the 'official' story concerning their lives; as such, they serve to underline the normative orientation of *Masai Women* as a whole.[20] The film's academic thesis functions to absorb all details into a single coherent argument about how gender structures Maasai society, rather than exposing how it operates in day-to-day life. This perspective is symbolised in the final statement which one of the mothers offers to Llewelyn-Davies. She explains the myth which legitimates women's subordinate place in Maasai society. Closing the film in this way serves to underline its fundamentally Durkheimian stance toward ethnographic realities.

Although *Masai Women* is unusual in presenting an explicitly gendered perspective and allowing women themselves to speak directly to Llewelyn-Davies about the roles and conventions which structure their lives, the emphasis of the film is upon women telling us how things *should* be. There is very little indication of women as individual subjects. The film reveals little of what they think or feel or, moreover, what kind of activities constitute their day-to-day lives. But what people say and what they actually do is, of course, often at variance. The slippages between the ideal and the actual offer interesting and revealing insights into social life. There are indications of such slippages within the early film, *Masai Women*; but it is in her later television work that Llewelyn-Davies begins to subject such areas to ethnographic investigation.

The films made a decade after *Masai Women* were marked by a shift away from the normative stance of Llewelyn-Davies' initial approach. What we might term the 'visualist' paradigm of her early work, namely the Radcliffe-Brownian assumption that society exists as an object to be observed and described rather than imagined as constituted through the actions of individual subjects, was steadily eroded.[21] The use of a predominantly structural-functional framework to interpret Maasai ethnography is replaced by a more fractured and problematic conception of the nature of social reality. Inseparable, however, from the important changes in Llewelyn-Davies' anthropological perspective is the question of ethnographic form itself. For, in seeking to open up the complexity of contemporary Maasai life, Llewelyn-Davies breaks with the Griersonian model of documentary exposition. Increasingly she begins to experiment with features unique to television. They are central to the expression of new ethnographic understandings.

The Women's Olamal

In the opening scene of *The Women's Olamal*, a Maasai woman in conversation with Llewelyn-Davies, states: 'Women have nothing of their own. Only men own livestock.' Llewelyn-Davies then asks: 'Women have nothing at all?' The reply comes: 'A woman has her cowhides, her scouring stick, her axe – that's all. Your husband gives you cattle to look after, but they're not really yours – or only in a way. Your husband can't reallocate them to his other wives but he can give them all away to another man. You can't stop him. He's the owner.' The narrative of the film, made ten years after *Masai Women*, reveals that questions of gender and power in Maasai society are considerably more fraught and contested than such an establishing statement implies. *The Women's Olamal* charts an extraordinary battle between the women and Maasai elders. It builds to a dramatic climax which lays bare fundamental tensions in the society and appears to threaten the foundations of social harmony.

The potential for conflict between men and women was, in fact, signalled much earlier in Llewelyn-Davies' engagement with the Maasai. She intriguingly places the question of female resistance to control exerted by Maasai elders at the centre of *Masai Women*. She suggests that the harmony of gender relations is disrupted by the practice of married women taking lovers. Young brides, married to old men, subvert the hierarchy of power by illicitly conducting affairs with the *moran*, Maasai warriors.[22] This implicit struggle forms an important thread in the complex sequence of events which leads up to the performance of the *olamal* ritual. Significantly, as the film reveals, the ritual itself, the different preliminary stages and the battle between men and women lie outside everyday village life.

The Women's Olamal is concerned with the preparations for a fertility ceremony performed every four years by the Maasai. It is the most important ritual occasion for women. The film, like *Masai Women*, is explicitly partial in its perspective. The exploration of questions about reproduction and power at the heart of Maasai society are again anchored in Llewelyn-Davies' documentation of female experience. Using a handful of statements from key subjects, the opening sequences of the film establish the centrality of the *olamal* ceremony to women; but at every stage, from the beginning to the end of the entire ritual process, the film exposes the necessity of men's active collaboration. Although women themselves take the initiative for the ceremony, forming *olamal* groups and organising the preliminary tasks, their actions are ultimately dependent upon persuading Maasai elders to conduct the Blessing ceremony. *The Women's Olamal* documents the complexity of negotiations conducted between men and women to bring about such an outcome. For, in most years of its performance, there is conflict and uncertainty surrounding the ceremony; and such struggle, often bitter and protracted, is an integral part of the ritual's efficacy.

The film is structured by the sequence of events which unfold as the women, having begun to mobilise and to lobby the men for the ceremony, confront a serious obstacle to their plans. An unresolved dispute in a neighbouring village threatens the progress of these preparations; the Maasai elders will not agree to conduct the ceremony while a claim for compensation is outstanding. Once the conflict is established in this way, the film follows closely the women's changing political strategies, from the discussions conducted among themselves, ranging between public oratory and huddled whisperings, to the moment of emotional explosion. It exposes the increasingly charged exchanges the women have with the Maasai elders. As with Llewelyn-Davies' earlier film, the climax of *The Women's Olamal* is the point of maximum dislocation. The men continue to resist the women's demands. The women respond by breaking down and weeping. Finally, the threat of a curse arising from the women's anger forces the elders to concede. They agree to perform the fertility blessing. Thereafter the tension of the film subsides. The remaining sequences, while documenting the ceremony itself, also reveal the progressive integration of social division as women once more take up their conventional position in Maasai society.

Unlike *Masai Women*, the film emerges from the unfolding actions and events of particular human subjects. It is not constructed by means of an abstract argument about gender relations; rather Llewelyn-Davies seeks to expose the dynamics of Maasai society as acted out within an area of ritual space. The techniques used by the ethnographer to document the drama surrounding the ceremony are an expression of a new perspective toward Maasai society. The feminist sensibility which infused Llewelyn-Davies' earlier ethnographic approach remains, but *The Women's Olamal* goes beyond the limitations of the initial 'anthropology of women' paradigm which framed her work. Now the interpretation of women's lives is considerably more nuanced and ambiguous than that suggested by *Masai Women*. Assumptions about the nature of female subordination and the notion of shared experiences between women are exposed, too, as problematic within the film itself.

The Women's Olamal presents a critical dynamic of Maasai society through a series of dramatic events. In shifting from structure to process in this way, Llewelyn-Davies renders the question of gender problematic. Integral to this shift is Llewelyn-Davies' abandonment of the older, static documentary form and her experimentation with one of television's defining characteristics, what John Fiske calls its 'now-ness': 'Film presents itself as a record of what *has* happened, television presents itself as a relay of what *is* happening.'[23]

The Women's Olamal appears to be live television. It presents events as they happen; and, as such, the participants in the ritual are no longer remote people of another time and place. Their actions are immediate and contemporary. With the minimum of explanation, Llewelyn-Davies allows the drama to unfold as if it were occurring in real time. She adopts an observational stance toward the representation of reality, the camera quietly watching and listening from a place close to the action.

The anthropologist and the viewer are also positioned as witnesses. By relinquishing the role she adopted in *Masai Women* as an expert, Llewelyn-Davies now reveals the limitations of her own ethnographic understanding. Hence the film is as much about the effort to make sense of a complex and highly charged situation as it is a document of the events themselves.[24]

Llewelyn-Davies' approach in *The Women's Olamal* clearly owes much to documentary techniques pioneered by Robert Drew and Richard Leacock. It reveals also the influence of work by David and Judith MacDougall – specifically their adaptation of direct cinema methods to explore situations of ethnographic complexity.[25] The use of such techniques by Llewelyn-Davies, however, may be understood as an expression of the gendered perspective which anchors her work. Thus, in place of active, male heroes facing crisis situations, Llewelyn-Davies uses the methods of direct cinema to trace the mobilisation of women as a collective force. Moreover, she locates the dramatic focus of the film in a moment of female resistance expressed as an outburst of collective emotion. Experimenting with ethnographic technique in this way represents an extension of Llewelyn-Davies' earlier commitment to documenting women's lives. For the different stance toward reality implied in this new approach – that is, the situating of subjective action within social landscape – opens up the question of female experience beyond the confines of the normative statements presented in *Masai Women*. *The Women's Olamal* reveals the performative nature of gender. It is not simply ascribed. It is acted out within particular contexts; and as the *olamal* ritual suggests, the issues about gender are not merely structural matters. Intense emotion is involved, too.

The Women's Olamal represents an abandonment of the static essay form of documentary television harnessed to a Radcliffe-Brownian style of scientific ethnography. This shift from ideas to life, from an abstract conception of Maasai society towards its empirical documentation, poses anew questions of 'evidential representation' – that is, the status of ethnographic evidence yielded by direct cinema methods.[26] *The Women's Olamal* appears to be a film which is 'found', emerging from the events and personalities without self-conscious manipulation. And yet, as Llewelyn-Davies herself notes, what appears to be spontaneous also contains elements of premeditation and contrivance.[27] The documentation of the emotional drama and intense struggle between men and women which is offered by *The Women's Olamal* seems to yield new insight into Maasai social dynamics, but the division between what is 'real' and what is 'acted', between what is truth and what artifice, remains, not least within the aesthetics of film itself, ambiguous.

Although Llewelyn-Davies exposes Maasai society in a moment of crisis, when social relationships appear to be stretched almost to breaking point, and she demands from her audience a more active, interpretive role, the film ultimately reaffirms the conventional order. The use of features associated with classic drama are the means by which a fluid, contradictory reality is integrated and rendered meaningful. Significantly, the film has closure. It concludes with the performance of the *olamal* ceremony, uniting the different participants in a ritual celebration of social cohesion which serves, simultaneously, to reinstate the conventional hierarchy of men and women. *Diary of a Maasai Village*, a series of five films made a year later, contains no such conventional closure. For Llewelyn-Davies now situates the Maasai people in a broader world. She evokes the spatial and temporal extension of contemporary pastoralist life through a further experimentation with ethnographic form.

Diary of a Maasai village

Describing the five films as akin to a diary, Llewelyn-Davies attempts to express the distinctive texture and rhythm of day-to-day Maasai life. 'We have made them as a diary and have not organised the material into a particular story or argument. Instead we hope that a collection of episodes in the life of the village will describe a moment in its history', she explains in a short statement which prefaces the individual films. At the same time, Llewelyn-Davies' use of such a genre draws attention to important aspects of fieldwork itself. Until recently, the writing of notebooks, diaries and journals remained a critical but hidden part of fieldwork activity. With her *Diary* series, however, Llewelyn-Davies makes central one of the forms through which ethnographic work is carried out, highlighting the essentially *ad hoc*, idiosyncratic nature of fieldwork enquiry. Hence, as with *The Women's Olamal*, the films are about issues of anthropological epistemology and method as much as they are an exploration of Maasai experience within postcolonial Africa.

At other times, Llewelyn-Davies refers to the *Diary* as a kind of documentary soap opera.[28] In this respect, her adaptation of an established television form represents a bold attempt to discover new ways to express new kinds of ethnographic understanding. By imagining the film series as both diary and soap opera, Llewelyn-Davies draws upon the open, unfinished characteristics shared by such aesthetic forms to express her particular perspective upon pastoralist life. Her concern is to avoid any reductive framing of Maasai ethnography. Specifically, she rejects a developmental paradigm which posits a single, progressive movement by means of the simple opposition between tradition and modernity. Instead the *Diary* films evoke the continuities and changes which simultaneously shape contemporary Maasai existence. Hence through the harnessing of certain qualities inherent to television as a medium – that is its 'flow', its episodic, discontinuous, repetitive movement – Llewelyn-Davies underlines her rejection of any straightforwardly linear narrative of modernization. There is, however, a curious irony in Llewelyn-Davies' use of a diary/soap opera approach to ethnographic exploration. Both are strongly feminised forms; but, in contrast to the predominant emphasis of her previous Maasai work, the *Diary* series takes the experience of men as its starting point.

The *Diary* series is assembled from the day-to-day events of village life. Over a period of several weeks, people come and go, men exchange news and gossip, cattle fall sick, there are births, disputes, problems with the authorities, ceremonies of divination and healing, and so on. Life as orderly and predictable, symbolised above all in the performance of Maasai rituals marking circumcision and marriage, is constantly cross-cut by unexpected, spontaneous events. Although ultimately Llewelyn-Davies uses a single narrative thread to connect the different parts of the series – namely, the unfolding drama which surrounds the arrest and imprisonment of a village man, Rarenko, in Nairobi on charges of cattle theft and the attempts by his relatives to secure his release – other events and movements always threaten to subvert the sense of forward momentum. Each film is distinguished, then, by a subtle interplay of rhythms generated from the interweaving of diverse narrative strands.

The *Diary* explores different perspectives, different voices and different locations; but, as its title suggests, it remains primarily anchored in the world of the village. Hence, despite her interest in exploring the experience of men, Llewelyn-Davies is inevitably drawn back into familiar areas of enquiry. For, as the films reveal, it is men who move. Women remain with children and cattle in the village, while men try to mediate the different, and often contradictory, relationships which constitute Maasai life. The mosaic structure of the series evokes the complexity of the world with which the Maasai engage, a world characterised by the simultaneity and interconnectedness of events in time and space.

The picture of contemporary life that Llewelyn-Davies expresses through the *Diary* is mirrored by the synthetic style of the individual films themselves. They are neither didactic nor observational; rather, they contain an eclectic mixture of conversation, eavesdropping, observation and participation. It is, however, the conception of the series as a soap opera which is perhaps most unusual. Critics frequently refer to the soap opera as a form expressive of television's distinctive features.[29] For its aesthetic qualities, and the nature of the relationship established with audiences, distinguish it as an important example of television's pre-eminent form, the serial; and, as such, a number of critical features serve to distinguish it from genres of literature or cinema. Soap operas are marked by their open structure. The loose, fragmented character of the text is made up of multiple story lines in which key personalities and their relationships (as opposed to events and plots) are central. Moreover, the dynamic of the work tends toward the cyclical rather than toward any single linear movement, and there is a lack of equilibrium or narrative closure.

The formal qualities which distinguish the television serial also make for a different kind of relationship with television audiences. In the case of the soap opera, it is their informality and predominantly oral character which invites the active participation of viewers in the negotiation of textual meaning. Hence viewers may establish for themselves a direct engagement, a sort of conversation, with the world of the soap opera, or, as John Fiske explains: 'The orality of television is not just a spoken version of a literate culture: its textual forms, not just its "spokenness," are oral, and, more significantly, it is *treated* as oral culture by many of its viewers. They enter into a "dialogue" with it, they gossip about it, they shift and shape its meanings and pleasures.'[30]

The Masaai *Diary* films contain many classic features associated with the genre of the television serial, especially the soap opera. It is Llewelyn-Davies' attempt to use the latter in the context of documentary situations which is unusual. A decade before the rise of the now ubiquitous docu-soap, Llewelyn-Davies recognised the potential of such a hybrid form; and, in the *Diary* films, she seeks to develop it as the means to interest television audiences in the everyday lives of East African pastoralists. The nature of the ethnographic encounter now made possible is significantly different from the kinds of engagement established in Llewelyn-Davies' earlier work. By taking account of the particular gendered features inherent in soap opera, we can begin to unravel the links in her work between changes in forms of ethnographic communication and shifts in methodological and theoretical orientation.

Melissa Llewelyn-Davies' experimentation with television soap opera may be understood as an extension of her feminist approach toward Maasai life. In a general sense, it reveals a certain self-consciousness about forms of representation; and, as such, it may be linked to critical debates in feminism which began to challenge the assumptions built into the early 'add women and stir' paradigm.[31] For, as Llewelyn-Davies had discovered in the course of her own work with Maasai women, questions of gender were more complex than could be encompassed within a conventional explanatory or normative approach. In *The Women's Olamal*, her use of dramatic narrative to explore ethnographic realities reflects the development of an approach which is not predicated on the self-evident nature of certain anthropological categories. It focuses instead upon the ritualised context in which they are made. The innovation in ethnographic form which Llewlyn-Davies now pursues through the *Diary* series is not merely an attempt to express the changing circumstances of Maasai people in a postcolonial world. It is also expresses a different conception of the anthropological task itself.

The gendered qualities of the soap opera become the means by which Llewelyn-Davies pursues a new kind of feminist ethnography. Drawing upon its conventionally 'feminised' features (the soap opera's orality, its personalisation, its foregrounding of relationships and character, its rhythm), she is able to make central the inter-subjective nature of ethnographic work. The *Diary* series evokes a complex web of relationships, not just ones mediated by the Maasai themselves but those which include the ethnographer and the television viewer, too. Moreover, the formal features of soap opera effect a certain *kind* of inter-subjective exchange. They bring about, as Tania Modleski notes, a 'connection to, rather than separateness from, others'. It facilitates the experience of 'nearness', the establishment of social relations through processes of intimacy and extension rather than through (cinematic) identification.[32]

The unfolding of the Maasai film cycle over a period of almost twenty years increasingly exposes the presence of Llewelyn-Davies within the ethnographic landscape. Television, the site in which her work is located, has played a significant role in shaping her distinctive sensibilities as an anthropological film-maker. For, following Fiske, we may acknowledge that it is television's pre-eminently oral rather than literate or cinematic character that has functioned to ground her anthropological work ever more closely in everyday practice, rather than in a body of abstract, disembodied knowledge.[33] This gradual movement toward a position resembling what Trinh calls to 'speak nearby' is most fully realised in *Memories and Dreams*, a film made by Llewelyn-Davies almost twenty years after her first engagement with Maasai people.[34]

At the centre of the *Diary* series lies the question of change. Llewelyn-Davies establishes at the outset her concern to explore contemporary life as comprised by both stability and movement. The complex relationship she posits between tradition and modernity becomes manifest in the formal tension of the films themselves, that is, in the tension between the open-ended texture of the series and the impetus toward narrative closure. Eventually, Llewelyn-Davies accedes to the latter, using Raren-ko's story as the thread which unifies the different parts of the *Diary*. The resolution of his case provides the series with a certain formal completion; and, in so doing, it confirms a broader movement implied in the film sequence from crisis to resolution, from the unpredictable world of an unknown city to familiar rituals which reaffirm village life. Hence, by the final episode, we are once again engaged with matters of marriage, cattle and social reproduction. Although our understanding is considerably changed, there remains in the *Diary* (as in *Masai Women*) an underlying, if increasingly tenuous, vision of Maasai social integrity.

Memories and Dreams

The approach Llewelyn-Davies develops in the *Diary* films explores change in terms of spatial relationships. *Memories and Dreams* (1993), her latest work, is also built around the centrality of this issue to contemporary Maasai experience. Here, however, Llewelyn-Davies explores change and continuity within a temporal framework. Ironically, she finds herself confronting anthropology's deeply rooted salvage paradigm, which she had resisted in her original *Disappearing World* films. Returning to Maasai-land in 1992, she is forced to address the decline of a pastoralist way of life. By posing this question, not as a matter of principle but as the outcome of her twenty-year engagement with the Maasai people, Llewelyn-Davies also raises a number of ethical issues which were problematic within her earlier ethnographic work.[35]

Memories and Dreams begins with a group of Maasai men and women gathered around a small television monitor, watching themselves in Llewelyn-Davies' earlier films. The contrast between then and now is the film's central theme; Llewelyn-Davies sets out to discover, as she puts it, 'whether people are happy with the way things have turned out'. But, as its title indicates, the film also strays beneath the surface, opening up previously unexcavated areas of Maasai experience. This development is anticipated by Llewelyn-Davies' films of the mid-1980s. *The Women's Olamal* and *Diary* series evoke a more complex and turbulent world than could be expressed within the normative vision of *Masai Women* (or *Masai Manhood*). Now the more nebulous regions of dream, memory, individual aspiration, fear, anxiety and disappointment are opened up to exploration. Llewelyn-Davies' interest in these areas is the logical outcome of the growing reflexivity of her ethnographic style as a whole. For the different phases of her Maasai work are marked by a progressive subversion of the conventional object of enquiry (society) as questions of subjectivity and experience increasingly come to the fore.

Memories and Dreams has no conventional anthropological or dramatic narrative as such; rather, it is a montage of episodes and conversations, with moments from the past (footage from previous films) juxtaposed with scenes from contemporary life. Its texture is constituted by means of association and resonance.[36] The disjunctions of time are used to striking effect, undermining any attempt to develop a single perspective on changing Maasai society. Nevertheless the film remains anchored in the lives of women. It addresses again the central and enduring questions of marriage, circumcision and reproduction; but, in opening up a space in which confidences are shared, the film makes possible the expression of emotion and feeling hitherto obscured by the more public presentation of gender identities. It also does more than this. It reveals the distinctive kind of interpersonal exchange which lies at the heart of Llewelyn-Davies' work. For two decades, television has functioned as the site in which Maasai fieldwork encounters and relationships have been mediated. Now the process of mediation itself is a central theme of *Memories and Dreams*. Extracts from earlier films serve as the point of departure for reflection and discussion.

Memories and Dreams is marked by the distinctive feminist sensibility which runs throughout Llewelyn-Davies' anthropological work. In the midst of cultural change, she reaffirms the centrality of women's knowledge and experience to the creative renewal of Maasai identity, but the ethnographic perspective she offers is no longer predicated upon an uncritical acceptance of certain cultural practices. Significantly, Llewelyn-Davies returns to themes which were present, though not fully explored, within her early work. Most notably, she no longer seeks to elide the question of wife-beating or female circumcision, now approaching such contentious areas from a position of what she calls 'solidarity' rather than 'sympathy'.[37] Hence she elicits from women their views about marriage and their relationships with co-wives. They express to her a strong sense of community between themselves, a sort of sisterhood and a resignation to the beatings of their husband. But suddenly the film shifts perspective, cutting to Loise, one of the co-wives, who has left their husband and the village in order to find her own life. She makes a powerful and eloquent statement of her independence, forcing us to reconsider the village women and their acceptance of customary practice. And yet Loise's fate is double-edged, and prefigured in all the other Maasai films. She failed to bear children. We see her scratching out a living with her new husband on the edges of a small town, and we remember both the community and security of village life and the curse of barren women.

The question of female circumcision is perhaps the most revealing of changes in Llewelyn-Davies' conception of a feminist ethnography. *Memories and Dreams* follows Kunina, a young Maasai girl, as she prepares to undergo a ceremony of circumcision in preparation for her marriage. Llewelyn-Davies makes use of sound she recorded at the time of *Masai Women*, but failed to include in the early film because of political sensitivities in the women's movement surrounding the question of female circumcision. Now, in *Memories and Dreams*, she juxtaposes the screams of the 1974 girl with contemporary statements by Maasai women about the happiness of Kunina's initiation.

Memories and Dreams is an elegy, a film of poignancy and unusual personal intimacy. 'I kind of made that film with my eyes closed', Llewelyn-Davies explains.[38] It moves effortlessly, creating a place for the sharing of experiences between people whose lives are deeply intertwined despite disruptions of time and space. As with most films about change, and peoples' perceptions of change, there is always a sense of loss as the sense of a social integrity weakens, traditions are discarded and confidence ebbs in the face of a fluid, uncertain world. But Llewelyn-Davies' latest film raises more complex questions. For we are conscious that the destruction of a way of life is not just a result of forces external to the Maasai village, as documented by familar shots of Maasai wearing European clothes and using cheap mass-produced utensils. The forces are internal, too – the rethinking by individuals of traditions held central to a way of life. For this reason the figure of Loise remains an unsettling one in the film as a whole.

Towards a new anthropological television

Some twenty years after the launch of the *Disappearing World* series, David Turton, himself a veteran television anthropologist, addressed the question 'Anthropology on Television: What Next?'. This phrase is suggestive of the old practice of trying to harness 'expert' knowledge to a popular medium. It involves not just a failure to acknowledge television's unique qualities, but also, in many cases, it results in anthropologists actually working *against* them to produce both bad television and bad anthropology. But, as Turton acknowledges in his lecture, the discipline of anthropology has undergone a transformation since the beginning of the Granada Television series in 1971: 'whereas twenty years ago "anthropological knowledge" was treated as a fairly unproblematic category, the examination of it has now become a major – perhaps *the* major – preoccupation of anthropologists' (original emphasis). Central to such a transformation has been the erosion of confidence in the notion of anthropology as a source of objective knowledge about the world, and an increasing recognition that ethnographic understanding involves a process, and that it is mediated through inter-subjective exchange.[39]

The changes occurring in contemporary anthropology, specifically this shift from professional confidence to intellectual doubt as the conventional object of enquiry gives way to more fluid notions of engagement and understanding, may be traced in Llewelyn-Davies' work. Through a critical analysis of her Maasai film cycle, my intention has been to highlight its unusual degree of formal innovation. This continuous process of experimentation must be considered as the expression of fundamental changes in her conception of the anthropological task. One of the distinctive aspects of Llewelyn-Davies' approach, however, is its gendered qualities. The refraction of her changing ethnographic concerns through the prism of feminism makes Llewelyn-Davies a critical figure in the creation of a different kind of anthropology. It is based upon dailiness, inter-personal exchange and informality – the fundamental groundedness of ethnographic practice. It is a feminist anthropology.[40]

We have become so used to denigrating television as a medium that it is hard to remember that it was once widely believed to hold enormous creative possibilities. But for the documentary film-makers and dramatists of the 1960s (people like Denis Mitchell or Richard Leacock and, of course, Dennis Potter), television offered a new sort of challenge; working for a broad public audience stimulated individuals to innovate in both form and content. Llewelyn-Davies has to be considered as an important figure in this tradition, since her anthropological approach has not just introduced new subject matter to established television programmes, but her way of working has challenged established formal conventions. We see a transition from her early attempts to graft anthropology onto television (throwing into sharp relief the fundamental contradiction between a popular form and a professional discipline), to the later experiments, exemplified by *Diary of A Maasai Village* and *Memories and Dreams*, which exploit television's distinctive genres for the generation of new kinds of ethnographic understanding. In short, Llewelyn-Davies has transformed the archaic and limited conception of 'anthropology on television' into something new, a genuinely *anthropological television*.[41]

It is my belief that the experimental impulse of Llewelyn-Davies' Maasai film cycle stems from the location of her anthropological work within a public space. By placing herself in a liminal position, outside the academy but making anthropological television for a lay audience, she has, I believe, been more open to changes coming from society, not least from feminist politics. Her project, while public, is not about 'popularising' anthropology. It is driven by a profound respect for her audience, and by her desire to engage them. By setting herself the enormously difficult task of doing this, rather than addressing a restricted circle of academics, Llewelyn-Davies has been forced to innovate in ways that have changed her conception of the audience, the subjects of her films, herself as an ethnographer and the nature of anthropological knowledge itself.

Epilogue

The Ethnographer's Eye is conceived as a manifesto. It seeks to establish a new agenda for visual anthropology. My interest is not in arguing for its legitimacy as a subdiscipline with its own specialist interests and methods; rather I suggest that vision is central to modern anthropology whether explicitly foregrounded or not. For an exploration of anthropology's ways of seeing opens up the questions concerning knowledge, technique and form at the heart of the anthropological project itself.

In arguing for the dissolution of boundaries around the subdiscipline, I follow other commentators such as Faye Ginsburg and David MacDougall in proposing the reintegration of a visual perspective into ethnographic work.[1] But, as both MacDougall and Lucien Taylor have noted, the pursuit of such a strategy is made difficult by the suspicion and defensiveness which exists on both sides of the divide. On the one hand, anthropologists committed to language and writing have long sought to establish anthropology as the pursuit of a particular kind of knowledge built upon the marginalisation, containment and sometimes downright suppression of the visual. On the other hand, many 'visual' anthropologists have sought legitimation by turning away from an engagement with the mainstream textual tradition at the same time as transposing its concerns by means of the attempt to 'linguify' film.[2] This curious paradox is, of course, hopelessly self-limiting. MacDougall suggests that 'visual anthropology may need to define itself not at all in terms of written anthropology but as an alternative to it, as a quite different way of knowing related phenomena'. His proposal is not made with the intention of reifying difference as the basis for separation, but instead drawing upon the difference to investigate epistemological assumptions at the heart of anthropological work.[3]

The pressing questions as to what might constitute a new visual anthropology are given interesting focus if considered alongside other potentially subversive perspectives which have emerged within anthropology. Among the most notable of these is the case of feminist anthropology. Its development as a critical perspective was predicated upon resistance to containment and subdisciplinary confinement (as about women). Henrietta Moore's vision of a genuinely feminist anthropology is not concerned, as she puts it, with '"adding" women into the discipline, but is instead about confronting the conceptual and analytical inadequacies of disciplinary theory'.[4] Likewise, the potential of a new visual anthropology lies not merely in the recognition of what is different in pursuing questions of ethnographic knowledge and understanding through an interrogation of vision. It depends, too, on the reflexive use of such insights to expose critically other ways that we, as anthropologists, engage with the world.

The mood of self-consciousness which characterises anthropology today suggests possibilities for a reintegration of the visual into the field. Questions about the substance, epistemology, techniques and forms of ethnographic enquiry have been subject to a radical rethinking over the course of the last decade. Ironically, however, this moment of reflection and experimentation has coincided with a period in which anthropology has been subject to unprecedented pressure for bureaucratic conformity as a university discipline. The growing puritanism of academic life, accompanied by the narrow specialisation and reification of archaic literary forms, runs counter to the open, eclectic spirit which marked an earlier anthropology. But it is important to remember that much to the exasperation (and admiration) of more established intellectuals, anthropologists have been remarkably resistant to established categories of knowledge and forms of enquiry. A new engagement with the question of vision, and its different forms and manifestations, offers a valuable starting point for the renewal of a project more creatively engaged with the world in which we live.

Notes

PREFACE

1 Faye Ginsburg 'Institutionalizing the unruly: charting a future for visual anthropology', *Ethnos* 63:2, 1998, pp. 173–201.
2 A number of essays touch upon these questions, for example Colin Young 'Observational cinema' in P. Hockings (ed.) *Principles of Visual Anthropology* (2nd edn, The Hague: Mouton de Gruyter, 1995), pp. 99–113; Marcus Banks 'Which films are the ethnographic films?' in P. Crawford and D. Turton (eds.) *Film as Ethnography* (Manchester University Press, 1992), pp. 116–29; and Peter Loizos 'First exits from observational realism: narrative experiments in recent ethnographic film', in M. Banks and H. Morphy (eds.) *Rethinking Visual Anthropology* (Yale University Press, 1997), pp. 81–104. Such questions, however, are pursued with characteristic rigour and insight by David MacDougall in a number of essays which make up his collected volume, *Transcultural Cinema* (Princeton University Press, 1998). Many of his interests and concerns, as will become evident, overlap with my own.
3 Seamus Heaney 'Feeling into words' in *Preoccupations* (London: Faber, 1980), p. 47.
4 Despite anthropology's recent reflexive turn, the role of belief within ethnographic practice is yet to be addressed.

INTRODUCTION

1 Eliot Weinberger 'The camera people' in L. Taylor (ed.) *Visualizing Theory: Selected Essays from V.A.R. 1990–1994* (London: Routledge, 1994), pp. 3–4.
2 Anna Grimshaw and Keith Hart *Anthropology and the Crisis of the Intellectuals* (Cambridge: Prickly Pear Press, 1993). Anthropologists working within other subdisciplines also express anxieties about marginalisation and a lack of legitimation. See, for example, Henrietta Moore's discussion of these issues with respect to feminist anthropology, *Feminism and Anthropology* (Cambridge: Polity Press, 1988). See also Joan Vincent's investigation of the changing nature of 'political anthropology', *Anthropology and Politics: Visions, Traditions and Trends* (Tuscon and London: University of Arizona Press, 1990).

3 Paul Hockings (ed.) *Principles of Visual Anthropology* (The Hague: Mouton, 1975) p. ix.
4 Marcus Banks and Howard Morphy 'Introduction', *Rethinking Visual Anthropology* (New Haven and London: Yale University Press, 1997), p. 5.
5 Margaret Mead 'Visual anthropology in a discipline of words', in Paul Hockings (ed.) *Principles*, pp. 3–10. For example, Howard Morphy 'The Interpretation of Ritual: reflections from film on anthropological practice', *Man* NS 29:1, 1994, pp. 117–46; and George Marcus 'The modernist sensibility in recent ethnographic writing and the cinematic metaphor of montage', in L.Taylor (ed.) *Visualizing Theory*, pp. 37–53. David MacDougall's discussion of visual anthropology's status overlaps in many places with my own analysis, see his *Transcultural Cinema* (Princeton, N.J.: Princeton University Press, 1998).
6 Indeed it is the sheer predictability of academic writing which often repels many students. The problem stems partly from features inherent to the written form itself. For, as David MacDougall notes, the expository text with its 'declarative linking of ideas' does not offer much scope for independent discovery. He suggests that films, by contrast, call forth more 'exploratory' or 'imaginative' responses. See his essay 'Visual anthropology and ways of knowing', in *Transcultural Cinema*, pp. 61–92.
7 David MacDougall's reflections on these issues offer unusual insight, see, in particular, 'The fate of the cinema subject' and 'Whose story is it?', in MacDougall *Transcultural Cinema*, pp. 150–64.
8 It is what Ginsburg celebrates as visual anthropology's eclecticism which makes this possible. But the strong counter-current, the desire for professional acceptance of the subdiscipline, always threatens to circumscribe such a creative space. See Faye Ginsburg 'Institutionalizing the unruly: charting a future for visual anthropology', *Ethnos* 63:2, 1998, pp. 173–201.
9 For example see various contributors to E. Edwards (ed.) *Anthropology and Photography 1860–1920* (New Haven and London: Yale University Press, 1992).
10 The volume *Writing Culture: The Poetics and Politics of Ethnography*, edited James Clifford and George Marcus (Berkeley: University of California Press, 1986) was a key text in precipitating anthropology's moment of self-consciousness. Since its publication, many others have addressed the questions of how anthropologists write.
11 A glance at other schools, however, reveals a slightly different situation than that found in Britain. In the case of American and French anthropology, for example the work associated with Boas and Mead or Griaule and Rouch, visual techniques and technologies form a distinctive and integral part of modern practice. Moreover, the intellectual contexts in which particular 'national' schools began to emerge in the early decades of the last century were also significantly different. For example, in the case of French anthropology, the work of Griaule and Rouch cannot be understood without reference to the poetry, art, cinema and music of the Parisian avant-garde. Their anthropology absorbed, rather than excluded in the name of science, a whole range of influences and experiments. Although the so-called British school, after Malinowski, defined the teamwork-based fieldwork model as

'archaic', the bureaucratic pressures to which academic anthropology is now subject in Britain has resulted in the re-emergence of this model. The revival of multi-skilled projects is an important context for contemporary experimentation with different technologies and methodologies.

12 For instance the work of Pierre Bourdieu, especially *An Outline of a Theory of Practice* (Cambridge University Press, 1977) and Tim Ingold's various writing, including 'Tool-use, sociality and intelligence' in K.R. Gibson and T. Ingold (eds.) *Tools, Language and Cognition in Human Evolution* (Cambridge University Press, 1993), pp. 429–45, and 'Situating action V: the history and evolution of bodily skills', *Ecological Psychology* 8:2, 1996, pp. 171–87.

13 Techno-phobia, with its origins in a repudiation of industrial civilization, remains a stubborn feature of anthropological life.

14 James Clifford 'On ethnographic authority', in *The Predicament of Culture: Twentieth-Century Ethnography, Literature, and Art* (Cambridge, Mass.: Harvard University Press, 1988).

15 Lucien Taylor 'Iconophobia: how anthropology lost it at the movies', *Transition* 69, 1996, pp. 64–88. It is also a point made by MacDougall in *Transcultural Cinema*. For a recent outburst of 'iconophobia' see Bill Watson's contribution to the 1997 Manchester debate organised around the motion: 'In anthropology images can never have the last say', published in P. Wade (ed.) *In Anthropology Images Can Never Have the Last Say* (Manchester: Group for Debates in Anthropological Theory, 1998), pp. 6–14.

16 Andrew Graham-Dixon *A History of British Art* (London: BBC Books, 1996) p. 36; and Jack Goody *The Domestication of the Savage Mind* (Cambridge University Press, 1976).

17 Martin Jay *Downcast Eyes: The Denigration of Vision in Twentieth-Century French Thought* (Berkeley: University of California Press, 1993). There has been an explosion of writing about the status of vision within Western discourse: see, for example, S. Melville and B. Readings (eds.) *Vision and Textuality* (London: Macmillan, 1995); D.M. Levin (ed.) *Modernity and the Hegemony of Vision* (Berkeley: University of California Press, 1993); C. Jenks (ed.) *Visual Culture* (London and New York: Routledge, 1995).

18 This paradox lies at the heart of Malinowski's own identity as a fieldworker. He was an active photographer in the field at the same time as he was a key figure in marginalising visual technologies from his model of enquiry. See Elizabeth Edwards 'Introduction', in E. Edwards (ed.) *Anthropology and Photography*, pp. 3–17; and Terence Wright 'The fieldwork photographs of Jenness and Malinowski and the beginnings of modern anthropology', *Journal of the Anthropological Society of Oxford* 22:1, 1991, pp. 41–58. See also Michael Young *Malinowski's Kiriwina: Fieldwork Photography 1915–1918* (University of Chicago Press, 1998).

There are a number of ironies here. 'Going to see for yourself' coincided with the rise of language as the primary 'way of knowing'. But although language became the dominant form, it too was not in itself interrogated.

19 Johannes Fabian *Time and the Other: How Anthropology Makes Its Object* (New York: Columbia University Press, 1983). David Howes (ed.) *The Varieties of Sensory Experience* (Toronto: University of Toronto Press, 1991);

Michael Jackson *Paths Toward A Clearing: Radical Empiricism and Ethnographic Enquiry* (Bloomington: Indiana University Press, 1981); Linda Jonsen 'Visualism and ambiguity in visual anthropology', in P. Crawford (ed.) *The Nordic Eye* (Højbjerg, Denmark: Intervention Press, 1993), pp. 63–72; Paul Stoller *The Taste of Ethnographic Things* (Philadelphia: University of Pennsylvania Press, 1989)

20 Fabian *Time and the Other*, p. 67.

21 Trinh T. Minh-ha 'Reassemblage' in *Framer Framed* (New York: Routledge, 1992), p. 96. See also, for example, Vincent Crapanzano *Tuhami: Portrait of a Moroccan* (University of Chicago Press, 1980); Kevin Dwyer *Moroccan Dialogues* (Baltimore: Johns Hopkins University Press, 1982); and Marjorie Shostak *Nisa* (Cambridge, Mass.: Harvard University Press, 1981). See also James Clifford's essay 'Introduction: partial truths' in J. Clifford and G. Marcus (eds.) *Writing Culture*, pp. 1–26.

22 Paul Stoller has been a key figure in this development, conceiving of a sensuous approach not as the basis of a new field (for example, David Howes (ed.) *Sensuous Experience*); but as the means for expanding existing conceptions of anthropological knowledge. See especially Stoller *The Taste of Ethnographic Things* and *Sensuous Scholarship* (Philadelphia: University of Pennyslvania Press, 1997). Michael Jackson's work, *Paths Toward a Clearing*, is also important.

23 Stoller *Ethnographic Things*, p. 8.

24 Fabian's argument is strongly reminiscent of Laura Mulvey's interrogation of the male gaze, see her classic essay 'Visual pleasure and narrative cinema', *Screen* 16:3, 1975, pp. 6–18. Mulvey's totalising critique has, in turn, been subject to interrogation in a manner suggestive of how as anthropologists we might develop and refine Fabian's approach. Judith Okely (personal communication) develops a critique of Fabian's work from a different perspective. Drawing on ethnographic research in Normandy, she pursues questions of vision and knowledge through an exploration of landscape. Her distinction between 'looking' and 'seeing' resonates with the different ways of seeing I explore in this book.

Observation has been extensively discussed within the context of debates about gender and science; see particularly Evelyn Fox Keller *Reflections on Gender and Science* (New Haven and London: Yale University Press, 1985). The issues explored with respect to scientific activity are highly pertinent to anthropological work.

25 Martin Jay *Downcast Eyes*.

26 Holdsworth uses this concept to explore the transformation of nineteenth-century anthropology into its modern form. Holdsworth 'The Revolution in Anthropoogy: A Comparative Analysis of the Metaphysics of E.B. Tylor and Bronislaw Malinowski', unpublished D.Phil thesis, Oxford, 1993.

27 George Steiner *Tolstoy or Dostoevsky* (London: Faber, 1959), p. 6. Steiner's approach owes much to the late nineteenth-century philosophical orientation of Dilthey and his notion of the *weltannschauung*.

In following more of a philosophical than a textual approach, my concerns in this book lie closer to those of William Rothman *Documentary Film Classics* (Cambridge University Press, 1996), rather than those of Bill

Nichols *Ideology and the Image: Social Representation in the Cinema and Other Media* (Bloomington: Indiana University Press, 1981), or Brian Winston *Claiming the Real: the documentary film revisited* (London: British Film Institute, 1995). Adopting the perspective of 'worldview' also means that my concern is with the question of authorship, rather than that of spectatorship or readership. The creative act of engagement by audiences in transforming the meaning of ethnographic work is an important issue, but it lies beyond the scope of this work.

28 Steiner *Tolstoy or Dostoevsky*, p. 234.
29 Herbert Read *A Concise History of Modern Painting* (London: Thames and Hudson, 1991), p. 12.
30 David Parkin 'Comparison as a search for continuity', in L. Holy (ed.) *Comparative Anthropology* (Oxford: Blackwell, 1987), pp. 53–80; and Elizabeth Edwards 'Beyond the boundary', in M. Banks and H. Morphy (eds.) *Rethinking Visual Anthropology* (New Haven and London: Yale University Press, 1997).
31 For the purposes of my argument, I will deal with the three key figures as ideal types rather than as complex historical subjects. Hence I will be emphasising the differences between their anthropological visions, rather than exploring the coexistence of ways of seeing within any single project.
32 Eisenstein 'The cinematographic principle and the ideogram', in *Film Form* (New York: Harcourt Brace, 1949), p. 38.
33 Marcus in Taylor *Visualizing Theory*, p. 39.
34 See Ilisa Barbash and Lucien Taylor *Cross-Cultural Filmmaking* (Berkeley: University of California Press, 1997), p. 375; and Elizabeth Mermin 'Being where? Experiencing narratives of ethnographic film', *Visual Anthropology Review* 13:1, Spring 1997, pp. 40–51.

1 THE MODERNIST MOMENT AND AFTER, 1895–1945

1 John Grierson 'The course of realism' in F. Hardy (ed.) *Grierson on Documentary* (London: Faber, 1979), p. 70.
2 Original emphasis. Quoted by Ian Dunlop in 'Ethnographic film-making in Australia: the first seventy years 1889–1968', *Studies in Visual Communication* 9:1, 1983, pp. 11–18. For a detailed discussion of early anthropology and film, see Alison Griffiths 'Knowledge and visuality in turn of the century anthropology: the early ethnographic cinema of Alfred Cort Haddon and Walter Baldwin Spencer', *Visual Anthropology Review* 1996/97, 12:2, 1996/7, pp. 18–43, and her forthcoming book *The Origins of Ethnographic Film* (New York: Columbia University Press). Her analysis of the Torres Straits film overlaps significantly with my own. Baldwin Spencer's use of visual technologies in the field is discussed by Arthur Cantrill 'The 1901 cinematography of Walter Baldwin Spencer', *Cantrill's Film Notes* 37/38, 1982, pp. 26–42.
3 Stephen Kern *The Culture of Time and Space: 1880–1918* (Cambridge, Mass.: Harvard University Press) pp. 1–2.
4 Alan Bullock and Malcolm Bradbury 'The cultural and intellectual climate

of modernism' in Bullock and Bradbury (eds.) *Modernism 1890–1930* (Harmondsworth, Middlesex: Penguin Books, 1976), p. 57.

5 For example, Roy Armes *A Critical History of British Cinema* (London: Secker and Warburg, 1978); David Robinson *World Cinema: A Short History* (London: Eyre Methuen, 1978).

6 Marshall Deutelbaum 'Structural patterning in the Lumière film', *Wide-Angle* 3:1, 1979, pp. 28–37.

7 Dai Vaughan 'Let there be Lumière', in T. Elaeassar (ed.) *Early Cinema: Space, Frame, Narrative* (London: British Film Institute, 1990), pp. 63–7. This feature, spontaneity, was much exploited by later practitioners of direct cinema and *cinéma vérité*.

8 Tom Gunning 'The cinema of attractions – early film, its spectator and the avant-garde', in Elaessar (ed.) *Early Cinema*, pp. 56–62.

9 Gunning, 'The cinema of attractions' p. 59.

10 Haddon in his 'Introduction' to *Reports of the Cambridge Anthropological Expedition to Torres Straits*, Vol. I (Cambridge, 1901).

11 The six volumes covered general ethnography, physiology and psychology, linguistics, arts and crafts, magic and religion. For an important appraisal of the Torres Straits expedition, see Anita Herle and Sandra Rouse (eds.) *Cambridge and the Torres Strait: Centenary Essays on the 1898 Anthropological Expedition* (Cambridge University Press, 1998). The editors missed a valuable opportunity to invite a historian of cinema to assess the significance of the moving film generated during Haddon's expedition. Alison Griffiths' forthcoming book, *The Origins of Ethnographic Film*, represents the beginning of a serious analysis of early ethnographic film within the context of cinema's development at the turn of the century. Elizabeth Edwards' important essay 'Performing science: still photography and the Torres Strait Expedition' explores the centrality of the question of vision to Haddon's fieldwork project, in Herle and Rouse (eds.) *Cambridge and the Torres Straits*, pp. 106–35.

12 See James Urry '*Notes and Queries on Anthropology* and the development of field methods in British anthropology 1870–1920', *Proceedings of the Royal Anthropological Institute* 1972, pp. 45–57; and George Stocking (ed.) *Observers Observed* (Madison: University of Wisconsin Press, 1983).

13 Clifford Geertz *Works and Lives* (Cambridge: Polity Press, 1988).

14 Simon Schaffer *From Physics to Anthropology – and Back Again* (Cambridge: Prickly Pear Press, 1994).

15 Henrika Kuklick *The Savage Within: The Social History of British Anthropology 1885–1945* (Cambridge University Press, 1991), p. 142. Kuklick cites Haddon's account book.

16 Lorraine Daston and Peter Galison 'The image of objectivity', *Representations* 40, Fall 1992, pp. 81–128. For an important assessment of the still photography produced in the context of the Torres Straits expedition, see Edwards in Herle and Rouse (eds.), *Cambridge and the Torres Straits*.

17 See Elizabeth Edwards 'The image as anthropological document', *Visual Anthropology* 3, 1990, pp. 235–58; and her edited volume *Anthropology and Photography* (London and New Haven: Yale University Press, 1992). Also Christopher Pinney 'Classification and fantasy in the photographic con-

struction of caste and tribe, *Visual Anthropology* 3, 1990, p. 259; and Griffiths 'Knowledge and visuality'.

18 E.F. Im Thurn 'Anthropological uses of the camera', *Journal of the Anthopological Institute*, 22, pp. 184–203.

19 This is in sharp contrast with the later Malinowskian model in which visual media, if present at all, serve as a passive illustration of the text. The work of Mead and Bateson in Bali during the 1930s was built around the use of different methods and their juxtaposition. See Edwards 'Performing science' in Herle and Rouse, *Cambridge and the Torres Straits*.

20 See also Griffiths 'Knowledge and visuality'.

21 This distinction between showing and telling is critical in the development of postwar anthropological cinema, especially to the observational approach. It raises the important question of the metaphysics of vision versus voice. See the chapter on David and Judith MacDougall in Part II, this volume.

22 In his letter to Baldwin Spencer recommending the purchase of a cinematographe, Haddon also comments: 'I have no doubt your films will pay for the whole apparatus if you care to let them be copied by the trade.' Quoted in Ian Dunlop, 'Ethnographic Film-making in Australia'.

23 Jacob W. Gruber 'Ethnographic salvage and the shaping of anthropology', *American Anthropologist* 172, 1970, pp. 1289–99.

24 John Berger and Jean Mohr *Another Way of Telling* (Cambridge: Granta Books, 1989), p. 128.

25 James Clifford 'On Ethnographic Allegory' in J. Clifford and G. Marcus *Writing Culture* (Berkeley: University of California Press, 1986), p. 115. See also Fatimah Tobing Rony *The Third Eye: Race, Cinema and Spectacle* (Durham, NC and London: Duke University Press, 1996).

26 Original emphases, Berger and Mohr *Another Way*, p. 279.

27 Daston and Galison 'The image of objectivity'.

28 Martin Jay 'Photo-unrealism: the contribution of the camera to the crisis of ocularcentrism', in S. Melville and Bill Readings (eds.) *Vision and Textuality* (London: Macmillan, 1995), pp. 344–5. See also his *Downcast Eyes* (Berkeley: University of California Press, 1993).

29 Jonathan Carey *The Intellectuals and the Masses: Pride and Prejudice among the Literary Intelligentsia, 1880–1939* (London: Faber, 1992).

30 James Agee *Agee on Film* (London: Peter Owen, 1963), p. 397.

31 As we will discover, the question of whether the camera should be human or not becomes central to the development of anthropological cinema. The contrasting projects of Rouch and the MacDougalls reveal different conceptions of how the camera should be used to explore the world. In Rouch's hands it becomes 'magical', while MacDougall's development of what they call 'unprivileged' camera style sets out to humanise it. See Part II.

32 Griffith's camera assistant recalled that at the end of its first screening 'the audience didn't just sit there and applaud, but they stood up and cheered and yelled and stamped feet until Griffith finally made an appearance.' Quoted in Scott Simmon *The Films of D.W. Griffith* (Cambridge University Press, 1993), p. 105.

33 'Film critics often write as if Griffith invented techniques as Edison invented the electric light. But the film techniques which Griffith created are the

result of the extended interests, awareness, needs and sensibilities of modern men [sic]. Our world of the twentieth century is *panoramic*. Contemporary society gives man a sense, on a scale hitherto unknown, of connections, of cause and effect, of the conditions from which an event arises, of other events occurring simultaneously. His world is one of constantly increasing multiplicity of relations between himself, immense mechanical constructions and social organisation of worldwide scope. It is representation of this that demanded the techniques of *flash-back*, *cross-cutting* and a camera of extreme mobility. Along with this panoramic view we are aware today of the depth and complexities of the individual personality as opened up by Freud and others. This finds its most plastic representation in the *close-up*. Modern content demanded a modern technique, not vice versa. What is the content that this technique serves? Ours is an age of war. D. W. Griffith's *The Birth of a Nation* portrays the American Civil War, the first great modern war. Ours is an age of revolution. *The Birth of a Nation* is the first great epic of a modern nation in revolutionary crisis' [original emphases]. C. L. R. James 'Popular art and the cultural tradition' (1954), reprinted in Anna Grimshaw (ed.) *The C.L.R.James Reader* (Oxford: Blackwell, 1992), p. 247.

34 George Marcus 'The modernist sensibility in recent ethnographic writing and the cinematic metaphor of montage', in L. Taylor (ed.) *Visualizing Theory* (New York and London: Routledge, 1994), pp. 37–53. It is interesting that Marcus does not trace the development of montage to Griffith, and that he chooses Eisenstein over Vertov. See also Elizabeth Mermin's essay 'Being where? Experiencing narratives of ethnographic film', *Visual Anthropology Review* 13:1, 1997, pp. 40–51.

35 See Kuklick *The Savage Within*.

36 See Brian Winston *Claiming the Real* (London: British Film Institute, 1995).

37 Anna Grimshaw and Keith Hart *Anthropology and the Crisis of the Intellectuals* (Cambridge: Prickly Pear Press, 1993).

38 For example, Talal Asad (ed.) *Anthropology and the Colonial Encounter* (London: Ithaca Press, 1973); Dell Hymes (ed.) *Reinventing Anthropology* (New York: Random House, 1974); and Edward Said *Orientalism* (London: Routledge, 1978).

2 ANXIOUS VISIONS: RIVERS, CUBISM AND ANTHROPOLOGICAL MODERNISM

1 In Rivers' case the source of unease is his late conversion to diffusionism and advocacy of ideas about cultural history long after they had been discredited. In the case of Griffith, there are two problems: the first stems from the elements of Victorian melodrama which persist in his work; the second from the racial order he celebrated in his controversial film, *The Birth of a Nation*.

2 Especially Ian Langham *The Building of British Social Anthropology: W.H.R. Rivers and his Cambridge Disciples in the Development of Kinship Studies, 1893–1931* (Dordrecht: Reidel, 1981); Richard Slobodin *W.H.R. Rivers* (New York: Columbia University Press, 1978); George Stocking *Observers Observed* (Madison: University of Wisconsin Press, 1983), *The Ethno-*

grapher's Magic (Madison: University of Wisconsin Press, 1992) and *After Tylor: British Social Anthropology 1888–1951* (London: Athlone Press, 1996); and James Urry '*Notes and Queries on Anthropology* and the development of field methods in British anthropology', *Proceedings of the Royal Anthropological Institute*, (London: Royal Anthropological Institute, 1972) pp. 45–57.

3 See Langham *British Social Anthropology*, and Stocking *After Tylor*.

4 Some of these ideas I explored in an earlier essay 'The Eye in the Door: Anthropology, Cinema and the Exploration of Interior Space', in M. Banks and H. Morphy (eds.) *Rethinking Visual Anthropology* (New Haven and London: Yale University Press, 1997), pp. 36–52.

5 Langham, *British Social Anthropology*; Mary Bouquet *Reclaiming English Kinship: Portugese Refractions of British Kinship Theory* (Manchester University Press, 1993) and 'Family trees and their affinities: the visual imperatives of the genealogical diagram', *Man* NS 1996, pp. 43–66.

6 John Berger *Ways of Seeing* (London: BBC, 1972).

7 It forms a central theme of Barker's first novel, *Regeneration*, which takes its title from the famous 1903 Rivers-Head experiment.

8 For example, Michael Jackson *Paths Toward A Clearing* (Indiana University Press, 1981); George Marcus, for example, his essay 'The modernist sensibility in recent ethnographic writing and the cinematic metaphor of montage' in L. Taylor (ed.) *Visualizing Theory* (London and New York: Routledge, 1994), pp. 37–53; and James Clifford *Routes: Travel and Translation in the Late Twentieth Century* (Harvard University Press, 1997).

9 George Bataille *Visions of Excess Selected Writings 1927–1939* (Manchester University Press, 1985). See also Martin Jay *Downcast Eyes* (Berkeley: University of California Press, 1993).

10 Stocking *After Tylor*, p. 112. See Bouquet *Reclaiming English Kinship*; Langham *British Social Anthropology*; Stocking *The Ethnographer's Magic*; Urry, '*Notes and Queries*'.

11 Langham *British Social Anthropology*, p. 70.

12 For a detailed discussion, see Bouquet *Reclaiming English Kinship*.

13 Langham *British Social Anthropology*, p. 72.

14 Bouquet 'Family trees', p. 44. See also Bouquet *Reclaiming English Kinship*.

15 See Berger's classic essay 'The moment of Cubism', reprinted in *The White Bird* (London: Chatto and Windus, 1985), pp. 159–88.

16 Herbert Read *A Concise History of Modern Painting* (London: Thames and Hudson, 1991), p. 182.

17 See 'The Modernist Moment and After, 1895–1945', this volume.

18 John Golding *Cubism: a History and an Analysis* (London: Faber, 1988), p. 51.

19 See Stephen Kern *The Culture of Time and Space 1880–1918* (Cambridge, Mass.: Harvard University Press, 1983); and John Berger *Success and Failure of Picasso* (London: Granta Books, 1992), p. 54.

20 Read *A Concise History*, p. 20.

21 *Ibid.*, pp. 16–17.

22 Especially John Golding *Cubism*, and Stephen Kern *The Culture of Time and Space*.

23 See John Berger 'The moment of Cubism' and *The Success and Failure of Picasso* (London: Granta Books, 1992).

24 Original emphases, Berger 'The moment of Cubism', p. 176.

25 *Ibid.*, p. 178.

26 Langham *British Social Anthropology*; Stocking *After Tylor*.

27 Pat Barker's novelistic rendering of Rivers' life has many parallels with Langham's interpretation.

28 Martin Jay 'The disenchantment of the eye: Surrealism and the crisis of ocularcentrism' in L. Taylor (ed.) *Visualizing Theory* (New York and London: Routledge, 1994), p. 174.

29 C.L.R. James 'Popular art and the cultural tradition', in A. Grimshaw (ed.) *The C.L.R. James Reader* (Oxford: Blackwell, 1992).

30 For important essays on Bateson, see George Marcus 'A Timely Rereading of *Naven*: Gregory Bateson as Oracular Essayist', *Representations* 12, 1985, pp. 66–82; and John Tresch 'Heredity is an open system: Gregory Bateson as descendant and ancestor', *Anthropology Today* 14:6, December 1998, pp. 3–6.

3 THE INNOCENT EYE: FLAHERTY, MALINOWSKI AND THE ROMANTIC QUEST

1 See Pat Barker's trilogy of novels *Regeneration* (1991), *The Eye In The Door* (1993) and *The Ghost Road*, 1995.

2 See Raymond Firth's essay 'Contemporary British social anthropology', *American Anthropologist* 53, 1951, pp. 474–89; George Stocking *After Tylor* (London: Athlone Press, 1996); and Paul Stoller *The Taste of Ethnographic Things* (Philadelphia: University of Pennsylvania Press, 1989).

3 It leads to the problem of 'the self and scientism' which runs through classic ethnography. See Judith Okely's important early essay 'The self and scientism', *Journal of the Anthropological Society of Oxford* 6:3, 1975, pp. 171–85. I draw on Barker's image of the eye in the door to evoke this splitting of the ethnographer's personality, see 'The eye in the door' in M. Banks and H. Morphy (eds.) *Rethinking Visual Anthropology* (New Haven and London: Yale University Press, 1997), pp. 36–52.

4 Quoted in Raymond Firth (ed.) *Man and Culture* (London: Routledge, 1957), p. 6. See also Jonathan Spencer 'Anthropology as a kind of writing', *Man* NS 24, 1990, pp. 145–64.

5 For example Harry Payne 'Malinowski's style', *Proceedings of the American Philosophical Society* 125:6 1981, pp. 416–40; Clifford Geertz *Works and Lives* (Cambridge: Polity Press, 1988); and James Clifford *The Predicament of Culture* (Cambridge, Mass.: Harvard University Press, 1988).

6 See James Clifford's essay 'On ethnogaphic authority', in *The Predicament of Culture*, pp. 21–54.

7 See Jay Ruby's essay ' "The Aggie will come first": the demystification of Robert Flaherty' in J.B. Danzker (ed.) *Robert Flaherty: Photographer/Film-maker* (Vancouver: Vancouver Art Gallery, 1980), pp. 66–73; and Fatimah

Tobing Rony *The Third Eye: Race, Cinema and Ethnographic Spectacle* (Durham, NC, and London: Duke University Press, 1996).

8 Rony *ibid.* and Ruby *ibid.* Also Brian Winston *Claiming the Real* (London: British Film Institute, 1995); and Dai Vaughan 'Complacent rebel: a re-evaluation of the work of Robert Flaherty', *Definition* 1, 1960, pp. 15–25.

9 Paul Rotha *Robert J. Flaherty: A Biography* (Philadelphia: University of Pennsylvania Press, 1983), p. 275.

10 See Martin Jay 'The disenchantment of the eye: Surrealism and the crisis of ocularcentrism', reprinted in L. Taylor (ed.) *Visualizing Theory* (New York and London: Routledge, 1994), pp. 15–38.; and Paul Fussell's classic book *The Great War and Modern Memory* (Oxford University Press, 1975).

11 Winston *Claiming the Real*, p. 8

12 *Ibid.*

13 Vaughan, 'Complacent rebel', p. 15.

14 Malinowski 'Introduction: the subject, method and scope of this inquiry', in *Argonauts of the Western Pacific* (London: Routledge, 1922), p. 25.

15 Despite the many contrasts between the cinema of Griffith and Flaherty, I find it impossible to watch the latter without seeing the former. Each time I view *Nanook of the North*, I see behind it Griffith's 1919 *Broken Blossoms*. It is the way that Flaherty uses close-up and panoramic shots to suggest people in the physical (rather than historical/social) landscape which seems to owe much to Griffith.

16 Robert Flaherty 'Nanook' (1951) reprinted in L. Jacobs (ed.) *The Emergence of Film Art* (New York: Hopkinson and Blake, 1969), p. 221.

17 Added emphases, quoted in Richard Barsam *The Vision of Robert Flaherty* (Bloomington: Indiana University Press, 1988), p. 15.

18 Rotha *Robert J. Flaherty*, p. 284.

19 André Bazin 'The evolution of the language of cinema', in *What Is Cinema?* Vol. I (Berkeley: University of California Press, 1967), p. 27.

20 Dudley Andrew '*Broken Blossoms*: the vulnerable text and the marketing of masochism', in *Film in the Aura of Art* (Princeton University Press, 1984), p. 21. Although Andrew is referring to Griffith's 1919 film, his description is evocative of the dramatic structure Flaherty uses in his film. See also note 15, this chapter

21 Bazin 'Evolution', p. 38. For a fuller discussion of André Bazin, see 'Cinema and anthropology in the postwar world', this volume.

22 The notion of 'non-preconception' is a phrase much used by Frances Flaherty, see her memoir *The Oddyssey of a Film-maker: Robert Flaherty's Story* (Urbana, Ill.: Beta Phi Mu), 1960. John Goldman provides a valuable account of working with Flaherty in Arthur Calder-Marshall's biography *The Innocent Eye* (London: W.H. Allen, 1963), pp. 158–63.

23 Rony *The Third Eye*, p. 101.

24 See John Berger and Jean Mohr *Another Way of Telling* (Cambridge: Granta Books, 1989).

25 See William Rothman's essay on *Nanook of the North* in *Documentary Film Classics* (Cambridge University Press, 1996), pp. 1–20.

26 John Berger *The White Bird* (London: Chatto and Windus, 1985), p. 160.

27 Rony *The Third Eye*, p. 14.

28 See the discussion of neorealism and Bazinian interpretation in 'Cinema and anthropology in the postwar world', this volume; also Rothman's essay on *Nanook* in his *Documentary Film Classics* (Cambridge University Press, 1997), pp. 1–20.

29 For a discussion of different kinds of light, see Martin Jay *Downcast Eyes* (Berkeley: University of California Press, 1993).

30 See Andrew Barry 'Reporting and visualising', in C. Jenks (ed.) *Visual Culture* (London: Routledge, 1995), pp. 42–57; and Lorraine Daston and Peter Galison 'The image of objectivity', *Representations* 40, Fall 1992, pp. 81–128; and Martin Jay *Downcast Eyes*.

31 Simon Schaffer *From Physics to Anthropology – and Back Again* (Cambridge: Prickly Pear Press, 1994).

32 For a fuller discussion of the Torres Straits expedition, see 'The modernist moment and after', this volume.

33 See the work of Paul Stoller, for example *The Taste of Ethnographic Things* (Philadelphia: University of Pennsylvania Press, 1989) and *Sensuous Scholarship* (Philadelphia: University of Pennsylvania Press, 1997), and my essay on the visionary impulse in anthropological understanding 'The end in the beginning: new year at Rizong', in C.W. Watson (ed.) *Being There: Fieldwork in Anthropology* (London: Pluto Press, 1999), pp. 121–40.

34 Geertz *Works and Lives*, pp. 4–5.

35 Anna Grimshaw and Keith Hart *Anthropology and the Crisis of the Intellectuals* (Cambridge: Prickly Pear Press, 1993), p. 15.

36 For example Elizabeth Edwards 'Introduction', in E. Edwards (ed.) *Anthropology and Photography* (New Haven and London: Yale University Press, 1992), pp. 3–17; Terence Wright 'The fieldwork photographs of Jenness and Malinowski and the beginnings of modern anthropology', *Journal of the Anthropological Society of Oxford* 22:1, 1991, pp. 41–58; and Michael Young *Malinowski's Kiriwina: Fieldwork Photography 1915–1918* (University of Chicago Press, 1998).

37 Christopher Pinney 'The parallel histories of anthropology and photography', in E. Edwards (ed.) *Anthropology and Photography*, p. 82.

38 This distinction is also central to the strand of French anthropology associated with Marcel Griaule, see his *Méthode de l'ethnographie* (Paris: Presses Universitaires de France, 1957). For an assessment of Griaule's approach, see James Clifford 'Power and dialogue in ethnography: Marcel Griaule's initiation', in *The Predicament of Culture* (Cambridge, Mass.: Harvard University Press, 1988), pp. 55–91; and Paul Stoller *The Cinematic Griot* (University of Chicago Press, 1992). See also the chapter in Part II, this volume, on the anthropological cinema of Jean Rouch.

39 Geertz *Works and Lives*, p. 77.

40 Grimshaw and Hart *Crisis of the Intellectuals*.

41 See George Marcus 'The modernist sensibility in recent ethnographic writing and the cinematic metaphor of montage', in L. Taylor (ed.) *Visualizing Theory*, pp. 37–53.

42 John Berger *Keeping A Rendezvous* (London: Granta Books, 1992), p. 14.

43 Walter Benjamin 'The work of art in the age of mechanical reproduction', in *Illuminations* (New York: Schocken Books, 1969), pp. 217–51.

4 THE LIGHT OF REASON: JOHN GRIERSON, RADCLIFFE-BROWN AND THE ENLIGHTENMENT PROJECT

1 Edmund Leach *Rethinking Anthropology* (London: Athlone Press, 1961)
2 See Brian Winston *Claiming the Real* (London: British Film Institute, 1995).
3 Antony Gormley *Antony Gormley* (London: Phaidon Press, 1997). See also Martin Jay *Downcast Eyes* (Berkeley: University of California Press, 1993), p. 122.
4 See Fabian's *Time and the Other* (New York: Columbia University Press, 1983). I do not deal here with the gendered implications of Fabian's interpretation of observation as an anthropological technique. But see my essay 'The Ethnographer's Eye: notes on work in progress', *Martor, The Museum of the Romanian Peasant Anthropology Review*, 2, pp. 42–9.
5 See Michel Foucault *Discipline and Punish* (New York: Vintage Books, 1979). *Foucault: A Critical Reader* ed. D. Couzens Hoy (Oxford: Blackwell, 1986) offers a good range of critical reflections on Foucault's work. See especially Martin Jay's essay 'In the empire of the gaze: Foucault and the denigration of vision in twentieth century French thought', pp. 175–204.
6 John Grierson 'Flaherty' (1931) reprinted in (ed.) F. Hardy *Grierson on Documentary* (London: Faber, 1979), p. 32.
7 See Bill Nichols *Ideology and Image: Social Representation in the Cinema and Other Media* (Bloomington: Indiana University Press, 1981) and *Representing Reality: Issues and Concepts in Documentary* (Bloomington: Indiana University Press, 1991); also Winston, *Claiming the Real*.
8 John Carey *The Intellectuals and the Masses* (London: Faber 1992).
9 *Ibid.*, p. 31 and p. 12 respectively.
10 *Ibid.*
11 See Ian Aitkin *Film and Reform: John Grierson and the Documentary Film Movement* (London: Routledge, 1990). See also Paul Swann *The British Documentary Film Movement 1926–1946* (Cambridge University Press, 1989).
12 There are interesting issues here in relation to the rise of the 'docu-soap'. For this new genre, with its marked emphasis on 'ordinary' people in the workplace, might be understood as a reinvention of the Griersonian project even though the docu-soap is widely conceived as an explicit rejection of Griersonian documentary. Unfortunately it is beyond the scope of this work to pursue these questions.
13 John Corner *The Art of Record: A critical introduction to documentary* (Manchester University Press, 1996), p. 63.
14 'Drifters', reprinted in Hardy *Grierson on Documentary*, p. 19.
15 Corner *The Art of Record*.
16 Adam Kuper *Anthropology and Anthropologists: The Modern British School 1922–1972* (London: Routledge, 1983), p. 50.
17 See his essays in Hardy, *Grierson on Documentary*.
18 Winston *Claiming the Real*, p. 39.
19 Raymond Firth 'Contemporary British social anthropology', *American*

Anthropologist 53, 1954, pp. 474–89; and George Stocking *After Tylor* (London: Athlone Press, 1996).

20 Fabian *Time and the Other*.

21 Ian Langham *The Building of Social Anthropology* (Dordrecht: Reidel, 1981), p. 252.

22 Winston *Claiming the Real*.

23 For example *Method in Social Anthropology* ed. M.N. Srinivas (University of Chicago Press, 1958).

24 Stocking *After Tyler*, p. 304.

25 For example, Langham *Social Anthropology* and G. Stocking (ed.) *Functionalism Historicized: Essays on British Social Anthropology* (University of Wisconsin Press, 1984).

26 Mary Bouquet *Reclaiming English Kinship* (Manchester University Press, 1993), p. 61.

27 Harry C. Payne 'Malinowski's style', *Proceedings of the American Philosophical Society* 125:6, December 1981, pp. 416–40.

28 Robert Thornton 'The rhetoric of ethnographic holism', *Cultural Anthropology* 3, 1988, pp. 285–303.

29 Clifford Geertz *Works and Lives* (Cambridge: Polity Press, 1988), pp. 63–6.

30 Fabian *Time and the Other*, p. 107; Geertz *ibid.*, p. 68.

31 Anna Grimshaw and Keith Hart *Anthropology and the Crisis of the Intellectuals* (Cambridge: Prickly Pear Press, 1993).

32 Fabian *Time and the Other*, p. 104.

33 Grimshaw and Hart, *ibid.*

34 See, for example, Henrika Kuklick *The Savage Within* (Cambridge University Press, 1991) and Winston *Claiming the Real*.

35 Winston, *Claiming the Real*.

36 Winston *ibid.*, p. 53.

5 CINEMA AND ANTHROPOLOGY IN THE POSTWAR WORLD

1 Peter Bondanella's writings form a key source on Rossellini and Italian neo-realist cinema, especially *Italian Cinema: From Neorealism to the Present* (New York: Frederick Ungar, 1983) and *The Films of Roberto Rosssellini* (Cambridge University Press, 1993). See also Peter Brunette *Roberto Rossellini* (Oxford University Press, 1987); and Millicent Marcus *Italian Film in the Light of Neorealism* (Princeton, N.J.: Princeton University Press, 1986).

2 Dudley Andrew *André Bazin* (New York: Columbia University Press, 1990), p. 21.

3 *Ibid.*, p. 109.

4 David MacDougall makes a similar point in arguing for the distinctiveness of visual ways of knowing, see *Transcultural Cinema* (Princeton, N.J.: Princeton University Press, 1998), p. 70.

5 The major films considered to constitute Italian neo-realism include: Rossellini's 'The War Trilogy' – *Roma Citta Aperta/Rome, Open City* (1945), *Paisa/Paisan* (1946) and *Allemania Anno Zero/Germany Year Zero* (1947); *Obsession*

(1942, Visconti); *La Terra Trema/The Earth Trembles* (1948, Visconti); *Sciuscia/Shoeshine* (1946, De Sica); *Ladri de Biciclette/The Bicycle Thief* (1948, De Sica) and *Umberto D* (1951, De Sica).

6 Quoted in Bondanella *Italian Cinema*, p. 32.

7 See, in particular, his essays collected as *What Is Cinema?* Vol. I and Vol. II (Berkeley and London: University of California Press, 1967 and 1971). See also Andrew, *André Bazin*.

8 The classic features associated with realism, according to Williams, are social extension, the situation of action in the present and the secular nature of action. See 'A lecture on realism', *Screen* 18:1, Spring 1977, 61–74.

9 Bondanella, *Italian Cinema*, p. 34.

10 Bazin, *What Is Cinema?* Vol. II, p. 21.

11 Marcus, *Italian Film*, p. 72.

12 Bazin, *What Is Cinema?* Vol. II, p. 33.

13 Quoted in Dudley Andrew, *André Bazin*, p. 120. See also MacDougall's essay 'Visual anthropology and ways of knowing', *Transcultural Cinema*, pp. 61–92.

14 Bazin, *What Is Cinema?* Vol. II, p. 76 and p. 81. The kind of cinema envisaged by Bazin was more fully explored by Cesare Zavattini in his essay 'Some ideas on the cinema' (1953), reprinted in R. Dyer McCann (ed.) *Film: A Montage of Theories* (New York: E.P. Dutton and Co, 1966), pp. 216–28.

15 See Louis Marcorelles *Living Cinema: New Directions in Contemporary Film-making* (New York and Washington: Praeger, 1973), pp. 43–4. Other useful references to the British Free Cinema may be found in Richard Barsam *Non Fiction Film: A Critical History* (Bloomington: Indiana University Press, 1992).

16 The movement between the genres of documentary and fiction film was usually in one direction; and it was reflected in the trajectory of film-makers themselves. Most began their careers in documentary, using it as a training ground for their later work in fiction film – for example Rossellini himself, Antonioini, and Fellini.

17 I follow conventional usage in employing the term '*cinéma vérité*' to refer to the new approach associated with French film-makers, especially Jean Rouch; and the term 'direct cinema' to refer to the approach identified with American film-makers associated with Robert Drew.

18 For example, Barsam, *Nonfiction Film*. It is an explanation often slipped into accounts without any interrogation of the assumptions that are contained within such a technologically determined perspective. Mick Eaton is an important exception, see his essay 'The production of cinematic reality', in Eaton (ed.) *Anthropology-Reality-Cinema: The Films of Jean Rouch* (London: British Film Institute, 1979).

19 Reprinted in Bill Nichols *Movies and Methods* Vol. I (Berkeley: University of California Press, 1971), pp. 224–37.

20 The contrast in the origins of their critical cinematic perspective (Rouch's emerging from life, Truffaut's emerging from ideas/criticism) finds expression in the contrast between innocence and wit of films made by the former and the knowingness and irony of the New Wave auteurs.

21 Rouch quoted by Eaton, *Anthropology-Reality-Cinema*, p. 57.
22 As Bluem observes, documentary had suffered along with other kinds of film in the period after World War II when cinema audiences collapsed. Television was important in rescuing documentary; it served as an especially appropriate site for this kind of non-fiction film-making. From the beginning of its development as a distinctive form, documentarians conceived of their project as one with an explicit social purpose. Television now provided the mass audience it had always sought. See William Bluem *Documentary in American Television* (New York: Hastings House, 1965). Other important sources on direct cinema include Barsam, *Nonfiction Film*; Steven Mamber *Cinema Verite in America* (Cambridge, Mass.: MIT Press, 1974); and P.J. O'Connell *Robert Drew and the Development of Cinéma Vérité in America* (Carbondale and Edwardsville: Southern Illinois University Press, 1992).
23 Elia Kazan in particular – *On The Waterfront* (1954) is a classic example.
24 He continues 'I have to find a story that's actually happening with its own structure, its own dynamic. I seek people driven by their own forces – forces so strong that they can forget about me – and capture this action as it happens. I want to edit it, but not for information, not for size or weight, or time or space, but for feeling and character and a dramatic development of the story', Robert Drew in Bleum, *Documentary in American Television*, pp. 258–9. Drew was primarily a producer. He took responsibility for raising the finance and negotiating transmission, while those around him were the film-makers proper. They were multi-skilled, functioning variously as camera operators, sound recordists and editors.
25 As Leacock's own remarks reveal. Commenting on an early film he made: '*Jazz Dance* [1954] gave me a taste of freedom. I will never forget the sheer joy of shooting that night, the exhilaration of a small, utterly mobile camera in my hands, whirling, spinning, creating', unpublished memoir written in 1992, reprinted in K. MacDonald and M. Cousins (eds.) *Imagining Reality*: *The Faber Book of Documentary* (London: Faber and Faber, 1996), p. 252. See also James Blue 'One man's truth: interview with Richard Leacock', *Film Comment* 3:2, 1965, 15–23; O'Connell, *Robert Drew*.
26 As MacDonald and Cousins point out, there is a certain irony in the freedom from established documentary conventions that the direct film-makers proclaimed and the speed with which they codified their own rules. See MacDonald and Cousins, *Imagining Reality*, p. 250.
27 See particularly Bazin, *What Is Cinema?* Vol. II, and Zavattini's essay 'Some ideas on the cinema'. Marcorelles describes Leacock's vision as an 'American vision', 'his films are the expression of society in perpetual motion' in 'The Leacock experiment', reprinted in J. Hillier (ed.) *Cahiers du Cinéma – 1960s* (Cambridge, Mass.: Harvard University Press, 1986), p. 266. For a more detailed critique of certain cultural and gendered assumptions built into direct cinema approach, see Mamber, *Cinema Verite*.
28 Bazin quoted in Andrew, *André Bazin*, p. 122.
29 *Ibid.*, p. 109.
30 Rouch's project is a radical one, challenging established conventions including the nature of reality itself. Direct cinema, with its emphasis upon

information and reform, is much more of a liberal project. It is predicated upon a certain belief in the objective existence of reality.

31 The direct cinema of Robert Drew was marked by a renewed commitment to artifice in the form of devices deriving from fiction film, most notably drama, crisis, character and narrative.

32 George Stocking *After Tylor* (London: Athlone Press, 1996), p. xv.

33 See James Clifford's classic essay 'On ethnographic authority', in *The Predicament of Culture* (Cambridge, Mass.: Harvard University Press, 1988), pp. 21–54.

34 The ideas developed here owe much to my collaboration with Keith Hart. Earlier versions of this argument may be found in Anna Grimshaw and Keith Hart *Anthropology and the Crisis of the Intellectuals* (Cambridge: Prickly Pear Press, 1993) and 'The rise and fall of scientific ethnography', in A. Ahmed and C. Shore (eds.) *The Future of Anthropology* (London: Athlone Press, 1995), pp. 46–64.

35 Among the useful sources on different national traditions are – Nicole Belmont *Arnold Van Gennep* (University of Chicago Press, 1979); James Clifford *The Predicament of Culture* (Cambridge, Mass.: Harvard University Press, 1988); Stanley Diamond *Anthropology: Ancestors and Heirs* (The Hague: Mouton, 1980); Maurice Freedman *Main Trends in Social and Cultural Anthropology* (New York: Holmes and Meier, 1979); Tomas Gerholm and Ulf Hannerz 'The shaping of national anthropologies', *Ethnos* 47, 1982, 5–35; A. Gupta and J. Ferguson (eds.) *Anthropological Locations: Boundaries and Grounds of a Field Science* (Berkeley: University of California Press, 1997); Adam Kuper *Anthropology and Anthropologists* (London: Routledge and Kegan Paul, 1983); Sherry Ortner 'Theory in anthropology since the sixties', *Comparative Studies in Society and History* 26, 1984, pp. 126–66; A.I. Richards 'African Systems of Thought: An Anglo-French Dialogue', *Man* NS 2, 1967, pp. 286–98; George Stocking 'Paradigmatic traditions in the history of anthropology', in R.C. Olby *et al. Companion to the History of Modern Science* (New York and London: Routledge, 1990), pp. 712–27; Bob Scholte 'Epistemic paradigms: some problems in cross-cultural research on social anthropological history and theory', *American Anthropologist* 68, Oct 1966, pp. 1192–1201; Joan Vincent *Anthropology and Politics* (Tuscon: University of Arizona Press, 1990).

Of course the differences between these national traditions are important and interesting. I am, however, simplifying these complexities in favour of a more general argument about the context in which visual anthropology was shaped as a subdiscipline.

36 There are no more stories of 'conversion' to anthropology like Haddon's recruitment of Bateson in the course of a train journey from London to Cambridge. See Jack Goody's account of the development of the so-called 'British' school, *The Expansive Moment: The Rise of Social Anthropology in Britain and Africa 1918–1970* (Cambridge University Press, 1995).

37 See David Pace's study, *Claude Levi-Strauss: The Bearer of Ashes* (London: Routledge, 1983). Central to Pace's understanding of Lévi-Strauss's career is the dialectical relationship between the roles of philosopher and academic, social commentator and scientist. Juxtaposing the French anthropologist

with his contemporaries, Sartre, Camus and de Beauvoir, he notes that Lévi-Strauss was not to be found on the barricades but in his laboratory. Pace, nevertheless, reminds us that *Tristes Tropiques* reveals a different side to the detached theoretician. The book stands as an interesting marker in the transition from the older speculative style of anthropology to the newer scientific enterprise. Published in 1955, it reveals the dialectical poles of Lévi-Strauss's own career.

38 Vincent, *Anthropology and Politics*. See also Jane Collier's essay 'The waxing and waning of "subfields" in North American sociocultural anthropology', in Gupta and Ferguson (eds.) *Anthropological Locations*, pp. 117–30. David MacDougall develops a perspective similar to that of Vincent, arguing not for the recognition of visual anthropology as a specialist subfield. He suggests that visual anthropology should develop as the critical counterpoint to the ideas and methods of textual anthropology, 'The visual in anthropology', in M. Banks and H. Morphy (eds.) *Rethinking Visual Anthropology* (New Haven and London: Yale University Press, 1997), pp. 276–94, and his collected essays *Transcultural Cinema*. See also Faye Ginsburg 'Institutionalizing the unruly: charting a future for visual anthropology', *Ethnos* 63:2, 1998, pp. 173–201.

39 Of course, visual anthropology exists as an important strand within the French tradition. Given the personalities of its leading figures, Marcel Griaule and Jean Rouch, it is difficult to describe their work as constituting a subdiscipline in the conventional sense of the term. See chapter 6, this volume, on Jean Rouch.

40 Gregory Bateson and Margeret Mead *Balinese Character: A Photographic Analysis* (New York Academy of Sciences, 1942), p. xi. A fuller discussion of this work may be found in Ira Jacknis 'Margaret Mead and Gregory Bateson in Bali: their use of photography and film', *Cultural Anthropology* 3:2, pp. 160–77. Also Andrew Lakoff 'Freezing time: Margaret Mead's diagnostic photography', *Visual Anthropology Review* 12:1, Spring 1996, pp. 1–18.

41 For example Bateson's analysis of a German propaganda film 'Cultural and thematic analysis of fiction films', *Transactions of the New York Academy of Sciences* 1943; and 'An analysis of the Nazi film "Hitlerjunge Quex"', *Studies in Visual Communication* 6:3, 1980, pp. 20–55. See also Faye Ginsburg, 'Institutionalizing the unruly'; and Sol Worth 'Margaret Mead and the shift from "Visual Anthropology" to the "Anthropology of Visual Communication"', *Studies in Visual Communication* 6:1, 1980, pp. 15–22.

42 Seven films were eventually released. The series, *Character Formation in Different Cultures*, comprised – *Bathing Babies*; *Three Cultures*; *Karba's First Years*; *First Days in the Life of a New Guinea Baby*; *Trance and Dance in Bali* (all released in 1951); followed by *A Balinese Family* (1952) and *Childhood Rivalry in Bali and New Guinea* (1953). Given Mead's predilection for instruction and simplification, the edited films reveal little of the subtlety of the original project.

43 The writings of Karl Heider reveals this most starkly. There is a preoccupation with classificatory features as the means to assert distinctiveness of ethnographic film from its rival forms and thereby to lay claim to academic

respectability, see *Ethnographic Film* (Austin: University of Texas Press, 1976). As Taylor notes, too, there is often an attempt to 'linguify' film, 'Iconophobia: how anthropology lost it at the movies', *Transition* 69, 1996, pp. 64–88. See also J. Rollwagen (ed.) *Anthropological Filmmaking* (Chur, Switzerland: Harwood Academic Press, 1988); Jay Ruby 'Is an ethnographic film a filmic ethnography?', *Studies in the Anthropology of Visual Communication* 2:2, pp. 104–11, and 'Exposing yourself: reflexivity, film and anthropology', *Semiotica*, 3, 1980, pp. 153–79.

44 Brian Winston *Claiming The Real* (London: British Film Institute, 1995), pp. 175–78. Rachel Moore, referring to Asch's work as carried out 'under the auspices of a most pernicious positivism', also articulates a critique of the assumptions underlying *The Ax Fight*. See 'Marketing alterity', in (ed.) L. Taylor *Visualizing Theory* (New York and London: Routledge, 1994), pp. 126–39. Other writers have sought to rehabilitate Asch, claiming that *The Ax Fight*, in highlighting the problem of explanation, anticipated anthropology's later epistemological crisis. See Jay Ruby 'Out of sync: the cinema of Tim Asch', *Visual Anthropology Review*, 11:1, 1995, pp. 19–35; and Dan Marks 'Ethnography and ethnographic film: from Flaherty to Asch and after', *American Anthropologist* 97:2, 1995, pp. 339–47.

Ruby quotes Asch extensively; with the benefit of hindsight, the filmmaker reveals his own reservations about the 'simplistic, straightjacketed, one-sided explanation' advanced in *The Ax Fight*. Asch claims that as the project unfolded he increasingly began to doubt the assumptions underpinning his enterprise – he had, as he put it, 'the suspicion of the whole field beginning to fall apart before my very eyes', Ruby 'Out of sync', p. 28.

45 Among the early critiques were Tal Asad (ed.) *Anthropology and the Colonial Encounter* (London: Ithaca Press, 1973); and Dell Hymes *Reinventing Anthropology* (New York: Pantheon Books, 1972). Later challenges are most strongly associated with J. Clifford and G. Marcus (eds.) *Writing Culture* (Berkeley: University of California Press, 1986) and George Marcus and Michael Fischer *Anthropology as Cultural Critique* (Chicago University Press, 1986). See also Richard Fox (ed.) *Recapturing Anthropology: Working in the Present* (Santa Fe, New Mexico: School of American Research Press, 1992).

6 THE ANTHROPOLOGICAL CINEMA OF JEAN ROUCH

1 Quoted in Paul Hammond *The Shadow and Its Shadow: Surrealist Writings on Cinema* (Edinburgh: Polygon, 1991), pp. 18–19.

2 Paul Stoller *The Cinematic Griot: The Ethnography of Jean Rouch* (Chicago University Press, 1992), p. 151.

3 Martin Jay *Downcast Eyes* (Berkeley: University of California Press, 1993).

4 There is always a problem with Rouch's own explanations and a temptation to take him at his word. This involves following his refusal to operate through conventional intellectual categories, celebrating his originality rather than subjecting it to scrutiny. There are some notable exceptions, for instance Mick Eaton 'The production of cinematic reality', in Eaton (ed.) *Anthropology-Reality-Cinema* (London: British Film Institute, 1979).

5 Jay, *Downcast Eyes*, p. 69.
6 Hammond, following Ocatvio Paz, *The Shadow*, p. 2. There is a vast literature on surrealism; but in terms of my interests here I refer the reader to Victor Burgin (ed.) *Thinking Photography* (London: MacMillan, 1982); Octavio Paz *Children of the Mire: Modern Poetry from Romanticism to the Avant-Garde* (Cambridge, Mass.: Harvard University Press, 1991); and Maurice Nadeau's classic study *A History of Surrealism* (Harmondsworth: Penguin Books, 1978).
7 Jean Rouch 'The camera and man', in Paul Hockings (ed.) *The Principles of Visual Anthropology* (The Hague: Mouton, 1975), p. 89.
8 Paul Stoller's critical writings have been important in bringing Rouch to the attention of contemporary anthropologists, especially those working within the Anglo-American tradition. See, in particular, Stoller *The Cinematic Griot* and *Sensuous Scholarship* (Philadelphia: University of Pennsylvania Press, 1997). Indeed Stoller himself builds upon Rouch's approach to advocate a new kind of anthropological engagement which he variously calls 'radical empiricism' (1992) and 'sensuous scholarship' (1997). A number of other attempts to establish a more experientially-based project strongly resonate with a Rouchian vision of anthropology. The work of Michael Jackson immediately springs to mind – especially his *Paths Toward A Clearing* (Bloomington: Indiana University Press, 1981) and *Minima Ethnographica: Intersubjectivity and the Anthropological Project* (Chicago University Press, 1998). See also Richard Shweder (ed.) *Thinking Through Cultures: Expeditions in Cultural Psychology* (Cambridge, Mass.: Harvard University Press, 1991) and Unni Wikan 'Beyond words: the power of resonance' in P. Palsson (ed.) *Beyond Boundaries: Understanding, Translation and Anthropological Discourse* (Oxford: Berg, 1993), pp. 184–209.
9 The question of what influences have shaped Rouch's project is a vexing one. On the one hand, there is a strong temptation to try and find an appropriate category by which his work may be explained as, say, a form of surrealist, sensuous or shamanistic anthropology. On the other hand, it is tempting to present Rouch as unique, an unusual, idiosyncratic personality whose trajectory cannot be grounded either within the traditions of anthropology or cinema. Certainly he is a beguiling figure, one who instinctively resists the constraints of academic convention. Stoller, *The Cinematic Griot*, provides some important biographical information about Rouch's early life; and James Clifford's essays 'Power and dialogue in ethnography: Marcel Griaule's initiation' and 'On ethnographic surrealism', in *The Predicament of Culture* (Cambridge, Mass.: Harvard University Press, 1988) pp. 55–91 and pp. 117–51, are invaluable in establishing the anthropological setting out of which Rouch's work emerged. But it is perhaps Rouch's own remarks which offer the greatest insight into the context of his intellectual formation: 'in the thirties, "anthropology" per se did not exist. All the people who were in some way "artists" or "anthropologists", well they were philosophers; they were thinkers, they were writers, they were poets, they were architects, they were film-makers, they were members of only one very wide group. It was, in fact, *l'avant-garde*. They were exchanging their experiments, and Paris was a strange kind of workshop where there

was a sharing of all these experiments', quoted in Jeanette DeBouzek 'The "Ethnographic Surrealism" of Jean Rouch', *Visual Anthropology* 2:3 and 4, 1989, p. 302.

In highlighting the unusual character of the historical conditions in which his work developed, I follow the approach of C.L.R. James. For example, James considered the outburst of creativity by Caribbean writers, poets, musicians and cricketers such as Vidia Naipaul, Wilson Harris, George Lamming, Derek Walcott, Mighty Sparrow and Garfield Sobers during the late 1950s and 1960s to be inseparable from the general context of independence politics. The struggle by artists to innovate, to push beyond limits of a colonial language and European aesthetic forms was, in his view, mirrored by the popular movement of peoples across Asia, Africa and the Caribbean which challenged the political structures of colonial rule. Moreover, James pointed out that in these unusual situations a new relationship is forged between artist and audience, a direct unmediated connection which generates a new creative force. Improvisation then emerges as the form which embodies a direct connection between artist and audience. See *The C.L.R. James Reader* ed. Anna Grimshaw (Oxford: Blackwell, 1992). Rouch's openness to his immediate audience, to his African subjects, may be seen in a similar way. He himself likens it to jazz: 'a masterpiece is created when this inspiration of the observer is in unison with the collective inspiration of what he is observing. But this is so rare, it demands such a connivance, that I can only compare it to those exceptional moments in a jam session between Duke Ellington's piano and Louis Armstrong's trumpet', 'Conversation between Jean Rouch and Professor Enrico Fulchignoni', *Visual Anthropology* 2, 1989, p. 299.

What I am *not* saying, then, is that Rouch's work should be interpreted as any straightforward reflection of a particular moment in West African history. Indeed Rouch himself is deeply hostile to the conventional rhetoric of revolutionary politics. Rather I want to suggest that he was working in conditions of extreme fluidity, an instability which resonated through all levels of social life from subjective experiences to structures of political power. Rouch's pushing against the limits of cinematic and anthropological forms is part and parcel of a more general climate in which fundamental challenges were being posed to the established structures of contemporary life. It is in such a complex, unstable world that the artist is able to see deeply, to become a visionary, a sort of prophet or shaman, a seer, who charts a journey through unknown territory, crosses boundaries, reveals worlds which are not yet known to us (as Rouch says in *Les Maîtres Fous*). This is the point of fusion of Flaherty and Vertov – Rouch's acknowledged ancestors. Rouch brings together the innocent/visionary eye of Flaherty with Vertov's refusal to accept the world as it presents itself. Steven Feld's essay 'Themes in the cinema of Jean Rouch', *Visual Anthropology* 2, 1989, pp. 223–49 is a particularly valuable source.

10 One of the most striking early sequences in the film is made up of shots of the different jobs carried out by migrant workers, showing the sheer variety of the work they did. Rouch lists twelve: stevedores, smugglers, carriers,

grass boys, mosquito killers, cattle boys, traders, bottle sellers, tin boys, timber sellers, gutter boys and gold miners.

11 I use the term 'montage' not in the strictly Eisensteinian sense but to refer to a kind of episodic construction, rather than a developmental or progressive narrative. Nevertheless, I am suggesting that there is a connection between the site of the film, the city and this kind of formal assembly. Eisenstein was, of course, the great theoretician and practitioner of montage; but he readily acknowledged his debt to Griffith. See his classic essay 'Dickens, Griffith and the film today', in *Film Form: Essays in Film Theory* (New York: Harcourt, 1949), pp. 195–255. Here Eisenstein portrays Griffith's development of montage as intimately connected to the urban context of America.

12 Indeed Rouch enhances the contrasts between the two aspects of lived reality. For our first glimpse of the Hauka in trance is of dark figures moving against a night sky, while the ceremony which *Les Maîtres Fous* documents is actually held during daylight hours. See also n. 29.

13 Stoller claims that a screening of *Les Maîtres Fous* provokes vomiting in at least one of his students. Stoller *Cinematic Griot*, p. 158.

14 This is a view echoed by a leading contemporary film maker, Martin Scorcese, in his *Personal Journey Through American Movies*, Channel Four Television, May 1995. To these effects we might also add the difficulties in obtaining prints of Rouch's work; and as a consequence screenings acquire a certain aura. For example, Peter Loizos in his book *Innovation in Ethnographic Film: From Innocence to Self-Consciousness, 1955–1985* (Manchester University Press, 1993) describes an almost thirty-year wait to see *Moi, Un Noir*. Moreover, as other commentators have pointed out, for example Eaton (ed.) *Anthropology-Reality-Cinema* the audience's experience of Rouch's films is often mediated through the presence of the Grand Master himself at public screenings. Stoller, in *Sensuous Scholarship*, argues that the transformative properties of Rouch's cinema represent an extension of the Theatre of Cruelty conceived during the 1930s by Antonin Artaud: 'in a cinema of cruelty the film-maker's goal is not to recount per se, but to present an array of unsettling images that seek to transform the audience pyschologically and politically', p. 120. I agree with Stoller that much may be gained by exploring the points of connection between the projects pursued by Artaud and Rouch (more with respect to *Les Maîtres Fous* than the other films). Nevertheless, it is important also to recognise that, despite significant resonances, their work is ultimately driven by very different impulses. The spirit of Rouch's cinema sharply contrasts, I believe, with that of Artaud's theatre. In understanding the nature of this difference I follow Susan Sontag: 'The Surrealists are connoisseurs of joy, freedom, pleasure. Artaud is a connoisseur of despair and moral struggle'. 'Introduction', *Antonin Artaud: Selected Writings* (New York: Farrar, Strauss and Giroux, 1976), p. xxviii. For me, Rouch's project lies much closer to the creative spirit Sontag identifies with Breton and his Surrealist associates. His anthropological cinema, excepting perhaps *Les Maîtres Fous*, has none of the anguish and urgency characteristic of Artaud, whose cinema explodes from

the extremities of his own tortured relationship between mind, body and langauge. Artaud sets out his manifesto in *The Theater and Its Double* ([1938] New York: Grove Press, 1981).

15 Rouch concurs: 'I no longer care for that ending', he says during an interview with Dan Georgakas, Udayan Gupta and Judy Janda 'The politics of visual anthropology' *Cinéaste* 8:4, 1978, pp. 17–24. Rouch blames it on the impromptu nature of the commentary.

16 This is the only time in the narration that Rouch's English translation 'falters'. It occurs at the moment when he cuts to scenes of the Hauka in possession. Is this 'chance', an accident? See also C.L.R. James's thesis concerning the centrality of Africans to modernity, *The Black Jacobins: Toussaint L'Ouverture and the San Domingo Revolution* (London: Allison and Busby, 1980).

17 Eaton 'The production of cinematic reality' in *Anthropology-Reality-Cinema*.

18 *Ibid.*, p. 5.

19 Clifford 'Power and dialogue in ethnography', pp. 81–2.

20 *Ibid.*, p. 60.

21 A number of other features of Griaulian anthropology noted by Clifford resonate with aspects of Rouch's practice – for example, Griaule's distrust of speech: 'Of all the possible avenues to hidden truths the least reliable was speech – what informants actually said in response to questions. This was due not merely to conscious lying and resistance to inquiry; it followed from dramatistic assumptions that were a leitmotif of his work. For Griaule every informant's self-presentation (along with that of the ethnographer) was a dramatization, a putting forward of certain truths and a holding back of others. In penetrating these conscious or unconscious disguises, the field-worker had to exploit whatever advantages, whatever sources of power, whatever knowledge not based on interlocution he or she could acquire', *ibid.*, pp. 67–8. The problem of words runs through Rouch's cinema, nowhere more starkly than in *Chronique d'un été*. See note 25 below.

22 Lucien Taylor 'A Conversation with Jean Rouch', *Visual Anthropology Review*, 7:1, Spring 1991, pp. 92–102.

23 See above 'Cinema and anthropology in the postwar world'. Rouch made a number of short films before *Les Maîtres Fous*. See Eaton, *Anthropology-Reality-Cinema* and Stoller, *The Cinematic Griot*. Rouch's use of a camera in the field, as Stoller notes, owes much to the example of his teacher, Griaule, whose commitment to different technologies within the context of extensive, team-based fieldwork echoed the American and British models of the turn of the century. As we have seen, within the Anglo-American tradition, the team-based approach quickly disappeared and with it the self-conscious interrogation of techniques and technologies. See Part I.

The visual aesthetics of Rouch's work, how he uses the camera, reveal the distinctive way of seeing underlying his work. For his films are not distinguished by the kind of *mise-en-scène* that characterises the anthropological cinema of David and Judith MacDougall. The latter, with its roots in Italian neorealist cinema, foregrounds the relationship between people and landscape, expressing a conception of human subjectivity that is anchored in social context. The camera, in order to see simultaneously both figure and ground, must remain at a distance. Despite the commitment to a new human intimacy, the problem of distance is inherent within observational cinema.

Rouch's camera is not fascinated by people in landscape; rather its focus is upon people who endlessly disrupt such a relationship. For migrants move, their subjectivities are not defined and confined by context. Hence Rouch's camera is always close. See also chapter 7 on the work of David and Judith MacDougall.

24 DeBouzek suggests that Rouch's narration shares important features with the practice of automatic writing developed by surrealist poets such as Breton and Eluard. She cites Rouch's own description of the possession he undergoes which allows his unconscious to shape the commentary. Hence it is improvised, not planned; and it is done without a script. See her essay 'The "Ethnographic Surrealism" of Jean Rouch'. Significantly, though, *Jaguar*'s sound and images are edited together so as to suggest their synchronicity. Thus Rouch re-creates a coherent present with each screening of the film. For another interesting analysis of the use of sound in *Les Maîtres Fous*, see Diane Scheinman 'The "Dialogic Imagination" of Jean Rouch', in B. K. Grant and J. Sloniowski (eds.) *Documenting the Documentary* (Detroit: Wayne State University Press, 1997), pp. 188–203.

25 The recurrent problem of language in Rouch's cinema is a reflection of a more general preoccupation shared by many French artists, film-makers and poets. For example, it stands at the centre of Artaud's work. He was determined to break the stranglehold of language within theatre. 'To break through language in order to touch life is to create or recreate the theatre', Artaud writes in *The Theatre and Its Double*, p. 13. See Jacques Derrida's two commentaries on Artaud 'The theater of cruelty and the closure of representation' and 'La parole soufflée', in *Writing and Difference* (University of Chicago Press, 1978) pp. 232–50 and pp. 169–95, respectively. For the surrealist poets, too, the necessity of transcending the limitations of language was central. Within French cinema it became a critical issue because the coming of the talkies ended the brilliant, inventive era of the silent film. It led to the rise of a more narrative-based, 'story-telling' kind of cinema which grounded spectators more effectively in reality than the freer, experimental aesthetic of the silent film. See Roy Armes *French Cinema* (London: Secker and Warburg, 1985) and Alan Williams *Republic of Images: A History of French Filmmaking* (Cambridge, Mass.: Harvard University Press, 1992).

26 Original emphasis.

27 Taylor 'A conversation with Jean Rouch', p. 101

28 It is the visceral force unleashed at the centre of Rouch's cinema that leads Stoller *Sensuous Scholarship* to use Artaud's term 'cruelty' to characterise it. Artaud himself writes: 'I employ "cruelty" in the sense of an appetite for life, a cosmic rigor and implacable necessity, in the gnostic sense of a living whirlwind that devours the darkness, in the sense of that pain apart from whose ineluctable necessity life could not continue; good is desired, it is the consequence of an act; evil is permanent.' *The Theatre and Its Double*, p. 102.

29 This explains the apparent anomaly of the *Les Maîtres Fous*' opening section, when a Hauka ceremony of strange, dark figures, silhouetted against a night sky, is intercut with life in the city. The ceremony which the film documents takes place in daylight. See also William Rothman's essay on Rouch in his book *Documentary Film Classics* (Cambridge University Press, 1996), p. 70

30 Rothman, *Documentary Film Classics*, p. 103; and Stoller, *Sensuous Scholarship*, p. 130.

31 Stoller, *The Cinematic Griot*, p. 137.

32 It is important to understand that Rouch's camera takes on many of the characteristics of his migrant subjects. Indeed, according to Colin Young and A. Martin Zweibeck, Rouch himself admits that 'he prefers to use a spring-wound camera so that he is compelled to keep on the move, always changing to another angle, with no chance to fall asleep at the tripod. This gives his films an abrupt, rhythmic cadence', 'Going out to the subject' *Film Quarterly* 13:2, 1959, p. 42.

33 Eisenstein, *Dickens, Griffith and the Film Today*.

34 Both Eaton, *Anthropology-Reality-Cinema* and Stoller, *The Cinematic Griot* note that the migrations from Niger to the Gold Coast ceased after independence. Although this may be disputed, since national governments have never been able to control successfully the movement of people, Rouch sets up symbolic opposition between movement and fixity. Rouch highlights the boundaries and bureaucratic rationality embodied in African nationhood. These questions are at the centre of the MacDougalls' films made a decade later in Uganda and Kenya.

35 Despite the films' focus on migrants, it is not the specifics of migration that Rouch concerns himself with here. His primary interest is in showing that people move, their range of movement, and their ability to attach themselves to whatever niche they find in cities.

36 Michele Richman 'Anthropology and modernism in France: from Durkheim to the *College de sociologie*', in M. Manganaro (ed.) *Modernist Anthropology* (Princeton, N.J.: Princeton University Press, 1990), p. 184. See also Stoller, *The Cinematic Griot*.

37 See also Stoller, *Sensuous Scholarship*.

38 Loizos, *Innovation in Ethnographic Film*, p. 50.

39 There is an extensive literature dealing with the nature of Rouch and Morin's collaboration and their attempt to develop a *cinéma vérité* – see Edgar Morin's own account in 'Chronicle of a Film' *Studies in Visual Communication* 11:1, 1985, pp. 4–29; also Feld's essay, 'Themes in the cinema of Jean Rouch'; Eaton, *Anthropology-Reality-Cinema*; and Peter Loizos *Innovation in Ethnographic Film*; and various interviews, especially Georgakas *et al.*, *The Politics of Visual Anthropology*.

40 In an early review of the film, Fereydoun Hoveya noted that despite an apparent concern with characters such as Marceline, the film is really about Rouch and Morin. Moreover, he notes the lack of collaboration between these two central characters, suggesting that the film really belongs to Rouch. See '*Cinéma Vérité*, or Fantastic Realism', in J. Hillier (ed.) *Cahiers du Cinéma 1960s* (Cambridge, Mass.: Harvard University Press, 1986),

pp. 248–63. Louis Marcorelles, too, observes Rouch's wit, describing as 'devilish' his setting up of Morin in the film, *Living Cinema* (New York: Praeger, 1973), p. 35. Certainly the more I watch *Chronique*, the more I am aware of the fundamentally different agendas of Rouch and Morin. Unwittingly, it seems, Morin falls repeatedly into the traps which Rouch enjoys setting for academics.

41 Rothman *Documentary Film Classics*, p. 72.

42 Rothman describes Rouch as 'fugitive and elusive'; his agenda subverts that of Morin, *ibid.* p. 86. See also n. 38 above.

43 It was a 'chance' occurrence that I was reading Melville and writing about Rouch at the same time. The coincidence, to follow Rouch, has opened up creative avenues of critical exploration.

44 'Introduction' to Herman Melville *The Confidence Man* (Oxford University Press, 1989), p. xxii.

45 *Ibid.*, p. xxvii.

46 Roland Barthes *Image-Music-Text* (London: Fontana, 1977); and *The Pleasure of the Text* (London: Jonathan Cape, 1975).

47 Luck or chance play an interesting role in many of the postwar films (*The Bicycle Thieves* or *O Dreamland*); but unlike the characters of the Italian neo-realist or British Free Cinema films, Rouch's players usually win.

48 Barthes *The Pleasure of the Text*. Although a number of contemporary writers (see n. 8 above) have been concerned to explore the possibilities of sensuous and embodied anthropological knowledge, there remains a reluctance to indulge in the wit, irony and playful subversiveness that gives Rouch's work such character. Academic anthropology has yet to find its sense of humour.

49 Rothman *Documentary Film Classics*, p. 99.

50 *Ibid.*

51 Rouch takes this notion further in a subsequent film, *Toutou et Bitti*. When his film-making activity precipitates an occasion of possession, 'the camera is perfectly integrated with the pro-filmic event', Eaton *Anthropology-Reality-Cinema* p. 23.

52 Rothman *Documentary Film Classics*, p. 70.

7 THE ANTHROPOLOGICAL CINEMA OF DAVID AND JUDITH MACDOUGALL

1 The kind of working partnership developed by the MacDougalls is discussed in Ilisa Barbash and Lucien Taylor 'Reframing ethnographic film: a "conversation with David MacDougall and Judith MacDougall" ', *American Anthropologist* 98:2, 1996, pp. 371–87; and also in A. Grimshaw and N. Papastergiadis (eds.) *Conversations with Anthropological Filmmakers* (Cambridge: Prickly Pear Press, 1995). Given the unusually close and long-standing nature of their collaboration, the question of authorship is especially complex in relation to the MacDougalls. Central, too, is the issue of gender. The technical division of labour between the husband and wife

partnership mirrors the conventional hierarchy of camera/sound operation; and yet, the shifting relationship established between vision and voice over the course of their twenty-year work complicates the issue in interesting ways. Unfortunately, a detailed consideration of the gendered dimensions of the MacDougalls' anthropological cinema is not possible here.

It is of some interest that the MacDougalls have recently taken to working in different partnerships. Moreover, David MacDougall has begun to address the problem of authorship within his critical writing – for example, 'Whose story is it?' in *Visual Anthropology Review* 7:2 (1991) reprinted in MacDougall, *Transcultural Cinema*, pp. 150–77; and '*Photo Wallahs*: an encounter with photography' in *Visual Anthropology Review* 8:2, 1992, pp. 96–100. An expanded discussion focused upon the notion of reflexivity is to be found in his collected essays, *Trancultural Cinema* (Princeton, N.J.: Princeton University Press, 1998). See also n. 2.

The case of the MacDougalls' anthropological cinema is further complicated by the fact that David MacDougall is both the spokesman for the partnership (the 'conversation' with Barbash and Taylor stands as a notable exception) as well as being an important commentator on more general questions concerning vision, knowledge and technique within anthropological enquiry. The latter concerns are explored most fully in MacDougall *Transcultural Cinema*.

2 There is certainly a strong undercurrent of romanticism within the Mac-Dougalls' work; but, in designating their enquiry as predominantly the expression of an enlightenment vision, I am seeking to expose the differences between them and Jean Rouch. Hence I will be emphasising contrasts rather than similarities in the interest of my general argument.

3 George Steiner's use of the term 'worldview' evokes the holistic quality of the stance, that is, its eclectic mixture of beliefs, ideas, fantasies and desires. Steiner *Tolstoy or Dostoevsky* (London: Faber, 1980), p. iii.

4 I am aware that in drawing attention to certain hierarchies of mind and body, knowledge and sensibility in the work of the MacDougalls, I am going against a certain self-presentation. But, in proposing the development of a critical perspective toward the MacDougalls' project – that is exploring it in terms which are not necessarily their own – I follow David MacDougall's own lead and utilise the distinction he proposes between 'self' or 'external reflexivity' and 'deep reflexivity', *Transcultural Cinema*, pp. 85–91. The latter, he explains, 'requires us to read the position of the author in the very construction of the work, whatever the external explanations may be', p. 89.

My concern in this essay is with the anthropological cinema of the MacDougalls as represented by the films themselves. The interpretation I offer does not treat the written corpus as 'explanations' of the films, but rather as a parallel discourse which itself must be critically approached. There is, I believe, within both the MacDougalls' films and texts, an intriguing dissonance between what is striven for and what is actually realised. For the resonances of the work, to follow David MacDougall once more, open up other possibilities and suggest all kinds of discoveries which lie beyond the scope of self-conscious authorial intention, p. 70.

James Clifford uses the term 'ethnographic allegory' to describe a similiar phenomenon in mainstream anthropology's written texts, where subtexts, lying beyond the author's conscious control, may be identified within the main narrative. See 'On ethnographic allegory' in J. Clifford and G. Marcus (eds.) *Writing Culture* (Berkeley: University of California Press, 1986), pp. 98–121. See also Johannes Fabian *Time and the Other* (New York: Columbia University Press, 1983).

5 Colin Young 'Observational cinema', in P. Hockings (ed.) *Principles of Visual Anthropology* (The Hague: Mouton, 1975), p. 70. See also William Guynn 'The art of national projection: Basil Wright's "Song of Ceylon"', in B. Grant and J. Sloniowski (eds.) *Documenting the Documentary* (Detroit: Wayne State University Press, 1998), pp. 83–98.

6 A. Grimshaw (ed.) *Conversations with Anthropological Filmmakers: Melissa Llewelyn-Davies* (Cambridge: Prickly Pear Press, 1995), pp. 41–2.

7 See Part I, 'Visualizing Anthropology'.

8 Peter Rigby 'Pastoralism and prejudice: ideology and rural development in East Africa', in R. J. Apthorpe and P. Rigby (eds.) *Society and Social Change in Eastern Africa* (Kampala: Makerere Institute for Social Research).

9 See, for example, Peter Loizos *Innovation in Ethnographic Film* (Manchester University Press, 1993).

10 A. Grimshaw and N. Papastergiadis (eds.) *Conversations with Anthropological Filmmakers: David MacDougall*, p. 17.

11 Marie Seton 'Basil Wright's "*Song of Ceylon*"', in L. Jacobs (ed.) *The Documentary Tradition* (New York: Norton, 1979), p. 103.

12 For a similar interpretation see Guynn, 'The art of national projection'.

13 On the persuasiveness of realism, see Clifford Geertz *Works and Lives* (Cambridge: Polity Press, 1988).

14 Young 'Observational cinema'.

15 See André Bazin's essay 'De Sica: Metteur en Scène' in *What is Cinema?* Vol. II (Berkeley: University of California Press, 1971), p. 76. Also Zavattini's key essay 'Some ideas on the cinema' in R. Dyer MacCann (ed.) *Film: A Montage of Theories* (New York: E.P. Dutton, 1966), pp. 216–28. A more detailed account of Italian neorealism and its late phase may be found in chapter 5, this volume. See also Marcus Banks 'Which films are the ethnographic films?', in P. Crawford and D. Turton (eds.) *Film As Ethnography* (Manchester University Press, 1992), pp. 116–29.

16 For example, Richard Leacock and Robert Drew, both closely identified with the 'direct cinema' movement, were known for their films about powerful people – politicians (e.g. J. F. Kennedy and Hubert Humphrey in *Primary*) and stars (Bob Dylan in *Don't Look Back*, and Jane Fonda in *Jane*); and, for their concern with public dramas and spectacles (*Crisis*, *The Chair*). This scrutiny of prominent figures represented a new departure in the public media. It allowed a broad television audience to see for itself how elected representatives and public figures behaved, and to observe the processes by which political decisions were made. These films are important ethnographic documents, not least because of the unique access to their subjects which the film-makers acquired. For a fuller discussion, see 'Cinema and anthropology in the postwar world', this volume.

17 In significant ways the observational approach to film-making represents a return to the 'primitive cinema' of the early twentieth century. Indeed it shares many features with the first Lumière films. For example, emphasis is placed upon 'showing', rather than 'telling'; the films are made up of scenes (reminiscent of the theatre) in which the spatial and temporal integrity of an event is respected. Hence there is emphasis on capturing a whole action (demolishing a wall, workers leaving the factory), rather than fracturing the scene into different shots from which a new assembly is constituted. Moreover, observational film may be considered as a form of what Gunning has called 'the cinema of attractions'. There is a direct, unmediated relationship created between film subjects and audience. See Tom Gunning 'The cinema of attractions: early film, its spectator and the avant garde', in T. Elaesser (ed.) *Early Cinema – Space, Frame, Narrative* (London: British Film Institute, 1990), pp. 56–62. The effect is to create a space in which what David MacDougall calls 'transcultural' encounters may take place, see *Transcultural Cinema*, pp. 245–78.

Observational cinema has been much caricatured and criticised as a kind of naive realism. See, for example, Peter Loizos 'First exits from observational realism: narrative experiments in recent ethnographic films', in M. Banks and H. Morphy (eds.) *Rethinking Visual Anthropology* (New Haven and London: Yale University Press, 1997), pp. 81–104. A more serious investigation of its cinematic and ontological foundations is required.

18 David Hancock, quoted by Colin Young in 'Observational cinema', p. 74.

19 'We end up by dropping whole scenes or sequences rather than trying to keep them all, but at shorter length. Each scene is made up of discrete pieces of information and behaviour and shortening it for dramatic effect would lose the resonances . . . and misrepresent the material', quoted by Young *ibid.*, p. 75. The moral commitment of observational film-makers echoes the stance of the Italian neorealist directors; and, as Young notes, taking up such a position involves an ethical decision concerning film subjects – that is, filming only those people with whom one has empathy, *ibid.* pp. 76–7.

20 David MacDougall 'Beyond observational cinema', reprinted in MacDougall, *Transcultural Cinema*.

21 Ironically Flaherty, who reconstructed scenes and presented them as 'natural', was often described as having an 'innocent eye'. See Frances Flaherty *The Odyssey of a Film-maker* (Urbana, Ill.: Beta Phi Mu, 1960); and Arthur Calder-Marshall *The Innocent Eye* (London: W.H. Allen, 1963).

22 'The ability of anthropologists to get us to take what they say seriously has less to do with either a factual look or an air of conceptual elegance than it has with their capacity to convince us that what they say is a result of their having actually penetrated (or, if you prefer, been penetrated by) another form of life, of having, one way or another, truly "been there"'. Geertz, *Works and Lives*. Within observational cinema, the role of the director resembles the one associated with an Italian neorealist approach, that is s/he acts as a 'filter' rather than as an animateur of the action. See Dudley Andrew's biography *André Bazin* (New York: Columbia University Press, 1990) p. 109; and chapter 5.

23 Andrew *André Bazin*, p. 123.

24 Bazin *What is Cinema?* Vol. I (Berkeley: University of California Press, 1967), p. 25.

25 Young 'Observational cinema', p. 70.

26 MacDougall *Transcultural Cinema*, pp. 127–8.

27 This feature is noted also by Lucien Taylor in his Introduction to David MacDougall's essays, *Transcultural Cinema*, p. 19. As the title of the collection reveals, the capacity of film to evoke the universal is an important idea in MacDougall's conception of anthropological cinema.

For me, the spirit of the MacDougalls' work, expressed perhaps most starkly in *To Live With Herds*, is evocative of the films made by Robert Bresson. It has many echoes with Sontag's interpretation of Bresson. In characterising the latter's cinema as 'reflective', Susan Sontag draws attention to the 'emphatic' presence of form in the work: 'the form of Bresson's films is designed (like Ozu's) to discipline the emotions at the same time as it arouses them: to induce a certain tranquillity in the spectator, a state of spiritual balance that is itself the subject of the film.' 'Spiritual style in the films of Robert Bresson' in *A Susan Sontag Reader* (Harmondsworth: Penguin Books, 1982), pp. 123–4.

28 Grimshaw and Papastergiadis (eds.) *Conversations*, p. 36. David MacDougall has always been aware of the inadequacy of these reflexive devices to express the complexity of social relationships embodied in the ethnographic encounter. Indeed he now considers the whole question of reflexivity as deeply problematic. See MacDougall, *Transcultural Cinema*.

29 Grimshaw and Papastergiadis (eds.) *Conversations*, pp. 36–7.

30 For the notion of 'crisis situation' in documentary film, see Stephen Mamber *Cinema Verite in America* (Cambridge, Mass.: MIT Press, 1974).

31 David MacDougall 'Unprivileged camera style', reprinted in MacDougall, *Transcultural Cinema*, p. 208.

32 Bill Nichols 'The voice of documentary', in (ed.) A. Rosenthal *New Challenges for Documentary* (Berkeley: University of California Press, 1988), pp. 60–2. As David MacDougall explained: 'I think we agree that We want to create the circumstances in which the spectator participates and arrives at certain meanings, and perhaps that leads to the development of a certain kind of language, film language. This is probably one of the great gulfs between conventional anthropology and the possibility of visual anthropology. The indeterminacy of film language and film expression requires a degree of participation on the part of the reader to arrive at conclusions' *Conversations*, p. 39.

33 See Colin Young 'MacDougall conversations' in *RAIN* 50 (June 1982), pp. 5–7; and David MacDougall's own essay 'Beyond observational cinema', reprinted in MacDougall, *Transcultural Cinema*.

34 David MacDougall 'Unprivileged camera style', reprinted in MacDougall, *Transcultural Cinema*.

35 *Ibid.*

36 Parallels found in literary anthropology include Vincent Crapanzano *Tuhami: Portrait of a Moroccan* (University of Chicago Press, 1980); and Kevin Dwyer *Moroccan Dialogues: Anthropology in Question* (Baltimore: Johns Hopkins University Press, 1982). For a recent discussion of anthropology as

conversation, see Nigel Rapport 'Edifying anthropology: culture as conversation, representation as conversation', 1995, ASAUK Conference Paper, University of Hull. See also James Clifford 'Partial truths', in J. Clifford and G. Marcus (eds.) *Writing Culture*, pp. 1–26.

37 James Agee *Agee on Film* (London: Peter Owen, 1963), p. 397.

38 See A.L. Epstein (ed) *The Craft of Social Anthropology* (Manchester University Press, 1963). For general discussions of the Manchester School see Lynette Schumaker 'A tent with a view', *OSIRIS* 1996, 11, pp. 237–58, and R.P. Werbner 'The Manchester School in South-Central Africa', *Annual Review of Anthropology*, 13 (1984), pp. 157–85.

39 David MacDougall, in his writings of the 1970s, refers to 'traditional' societies and the 'fragility' of certain ways of life. See, for example, his essay 'Beyond observational cinema'.

40 This is a version of what Rachel Moore has described with reference to the Yanomami films: 'The Asch/Chagnon films . . . used formal tropes for disorientation and unfixing authorial positions to gain a rhetorical advantage for science and explanation . . . What comes to us from the synch sound and apparently candid images of people is, always, strange and chaotic. The sound from the ethnographers by contrast . . . is full of reason and explanation', Rachel Moore 'Marketing alterity' in Lucien Taylor (ed.) *Visualizing Anthropology* (New York and London: Routledge, 1994) p. 129. Certainly the MacDougalls reject the kind of authorial devices used by Asch and Chagnon (narration, kinship charts, etc.), but they retain a similar rationalist orientation. Knowledge and evidence remain important principles for them. Their film-making is explicitly driven by an intellectual agenda, as the detailed accounts published by David MacDougall reveal.

41 David MacDougall 'Media Friend or Media Foe?', *Visual Anthropology* 1:1, 1987, pp. 54–8, p. 55.

42 Fred Myers 'From ethnography to metaphor: recent films from David and Judith MacDougall', *Cultural Anthropology* 3:2, 1988, p. 206.

43 David MacDougall 'Whose story is it?', reprinted in MacDougall, *Transcultural Cinema*, p. 163.

44 See also Myers, 'From ethnography to metaphor', p. 214.

45 The political battle, which became a stand-off between state and federal government, shares many similarities with *Crisis* (1963), one of the classic films of American direct cinema. An important difference, however, is Robert Drew's use of more than one camera, placing his film-makers at different key locations in order to capture a complex, interconnected world in which events are linked across time and space. By contrast David MacDougall has a single camera situated in Aurukun. The other world of 'big politics' lies outside and remains unseen.

46 David MacDougall, '*Photo Wallahs*'. His concern with authorship perhaps also reveals the difficulties inherent in his own working partnership with Judith MacDougall. See n. 1. above. But the problematic status of voice raises more general issues to do with anthropology's experimental moment. For the new commitment by contemporary ethnographers to 'giving voice' to subjects, to sharing authorship and devising multi-vocal texts, does not

necessarily solve the political burden of the discipline. Moreover, it raises deeper questions concerning the status of knowledge and reality as exposed in the MacDougalls' own work.

47 See J. Clifford and G. Marcus (eds.) *Writing Culture*; and G. Marcus and M. Fischer *Anthropology as Cultural Critique* (University of Chicago Press, 1986).

48 See MacDougall, *Transcultural Cinema*, pp. 48–70.

49 It is also articulated more fully within David MacDougall's writing. The most recent essays in *Transcultural Cinema* are an important statement of a new vision for anthropology. There remains, however, the recurrent problem of the films – namely a dissonance between what is self-consciously articulated and other resonances in the work. For, despite the striving for a new kind of ethnographic engagement, the writing itself remains contained within the rationalism and intellectualism of the MacDougalls' earlier work.

50 See Christopher Pinney: '"To know a man from his face': *Photo Wallahs* and the uses of visual anthropology', *Visual Anthropology Review* 9:2, Fall 1993, pp. 118–26. Also David MacDougall's own essay 'Photo hierarchus: signs and mirrors in Indian photography', *Visual Anthropology* 5, 1992, pp. 103–29; and Akos Ostor 'Filming photography with the MacDougalls in India', *Visual Anthropology Review*, 9:2, Fall 1993, pp. 126–31.

51 David MacDougall explains that the construction of the film was not consciously contrived; rather it resulted from the film-makers giving up control and allowing intuitive connections to emerge in the process of editing. The involvement of Dai Vaughan as the editor of the last two films is also an important indication of the changing nature of the project.

52 Pinney, 'To know a man from his face', p. 123.

53 See John Berger's contrast between still photography and moving film in 'The modernist moment and after', this volume.

54 See the discussion of Italian neorealist cinema in chapter 5, this volume.

55 It is a form of 'Sculpting in time', as the Russian film director Andrei Tarkovsky termed it. See his collected essays *Sculpting in Time* (London: Faber, 1989). See also Antonio Marazzi's review of the film, *Visual Anthropology Review*, 10:2, Fall 1994, pp. 86–90.

56 '[P]hotogenia evokes not just the beauty of certain film images or photographic effects, but the special resonance – the transcendence – that the act of film-making can bring to the phenomena under observation', Guynn, 'The art of national projection', p. 87.

8 THE ANTHROPOLOGICAL TELEVISION OF MELISSA LLEWELYN-DAVIES

This chapter is based upon an earlier publication 'Anthropology on television: the work of Melissa Llewelyn-Davies', *Journal of Museum Ethnography* 9, 1997, pp. 49–64.

1 Edmund Leach *A Runaway World?* (London: BBC Publications, 1967). See also Anna Grimshaw 'A runaway world? Anthropology as public debate'

Cambridge Anthropology, 13:3, 1989, pp. 75–9; and Marilyn Strathern 'Stopping the world: Elmdon and the Reith lectures', *Cambridge Anthropology*, 13:3, 1989, pp. 70–4.

2 Cris Shore 'Anthropology's identity crisis: the politics of public image', *Anthropology Today*, 12:2, 1996, pp. 1–2. See also Anna Grimshaw and Keith Hart *Anthropology and the Crisis of the Intellectuals* (Cambridge: Prickly Pear Press, 1993); J. Clifford and G. Marcus (eds.) *Writing Culture* (Berkeley: University of Calfornia Press, 1986); George Marcus and Michael Fischer *Anthropology as Cultural Critique* (Chicago University Press, 1986); R. Fox (ed.) *Recapturing Anthropology* (Santa Fe, New Mexico: School of American Research Press, 1992).

3 Notable exceptions include most prominently Faye Ginsburg. For a survey of the field, see her essay 'Institutionalizing the unruly: charting a future for visual anthropology' *Ethnos* 63:2, 1998, pp. 173–201; and 'Culture/media: a (mild) polemic', *Anthropology Today* 10:2, April 1994, pp. 5–15. See also George Marcus (ed.) *Connected: Engagements with Media* (Chicago University Press, 1996).

4 For useful surveys see, for example, Paul Henley 'The 1984 RAI film prize', *Royal Anthropological Institute Newsletter* 62, 1984, pp. 9–12; and 'British ethnographic film: recent developments', *Anthropology Today* 1:1, 1985, pp. 5–17; Peter Loizos 'Granada television's "Disappearing World" series: an appraisal' *American Anthropologist* 82 1980, pp. 573–94, and *Innovation in Ethnographic Film* (Manchester University Press, 1993). See also Liz Brown 'The two worlds of Marrakech', *Screen* 19:2, 1978, pp. 85–118; Faye Ginsburg 'Ethnographies on the airwaves: the presentation of anthropology on American, British, Belgian and Japanese television', in Paul Hockings (ed.) *Principles of Visual Anthropology*, second edn (Berlin and New York: Walter de Gruyter and Co, 1994), pp. 363–98; 'Television and the mediation of culture: issues in British ethnographic film', *Visual Anthropology Review*, 8:1, 1992, pp. 97–102; and Christopher Pinney 'Appearing Worlds', *Anthropology Today* 5:3, 1989, pp. 26–8.

5 'Anthropology on television: what next?' in P. I. Crawford and D. Turton (eds.) *Film as Ethnography* (Manchester University Press, 1992), p. 289.

6 Accounts of collaborative working by a number of anthropologists and television programme-makers are included in a special feature 'Notes on British tele-anthropology' edited by Faye Ginsburg in *Visual Anthropology Review*, 8:1, Spring 1992. See Ginsburg's own essay 'Television and the mediation of culture'. See also Jean Lydall's account 'Filming *The Women Who Smile*' in P.I. Crawford and J.K. Simonsen (eds.) *Ethnographic Film, Aesthetics and Narrative Traditions* (Aarhus, Denmark: Intervention Press, 1992), pp. 141–58.

A number of useful surveys of anthropology on television exist: For example David Turton 'Anthropology on television: what next?'. See also Marcus Banks 'Which films are the ethnographic films?' in Crawford and Turton (eds.), *Film as ethnography* pp. 116–29; and his essay 'Television and anthropology: an unhappy marriage?', *Visual Anthropology* 7:1, 1994, pp. 21–45.

Melissa Llewelyn-Davies is unusual in being both a trained anthropologist and television film-maker. Hence she is familiar with the approaches and conventions of each practice. This dual identity greatly assists her in creatively addressing the problem of 'translation' between two roles which are normally occupied by different people.

7 The two early Granada Television films share the same spelling, 'Masai'. It was altered in Llewelyn-Davies' later films to 'Maasai'.

It is important to acknowledge that many of Llewelyn-Davies' Maasai films involved the creative input of Chris Curling, with whom she worked closely for a decade. In describing the project as Llewelyn-Davies', however, I refer to its origins in her anthropological fieldwork; its reflection of her particular intellectual interests; and her distinctive directorial presence. The particular films are credited as follows:

> *Masai Women*: Producer/Director Chris Curling; Research Melissa Llewelyn-Davies.
>
> *Masai Manhood*: Producer/Director Curling; Research Llewelyn-Davies.
>
> *The Women's Olamal*: Director: Llewelyn-Davies; Co-producers: Curling and Llewelyn-Davies.
>
> *Diary of a Maasai Village*: Director: Llewelyn-Davies; Co-producers: Curling and Llewelyn-Davies.
>
> *Memories and Dreams*: Director: Llewelyn-Davies.

Llewelyn-Davies' ethnographic work, however, has not been confined by her engagement with the Maasai people. She has also directed a number of other important films, most notably, *Some Women of Marrakech* (1978). This film is particularly interesting as an early example of feminist anthropological film-making. It is about the lives of Muslim women. The exploration of the private world of secluded women involved an all-woman crew – not just as a means of getting access to tightly controlled gendered space but as part of an explicit attempt to use new, feminist inspired ways of working. See Liz Brown 'The Two Worlds of Marrakech'.

There are few serious assessments of Llewelyn-Davies' work. Peter Loizos is an important exception. There are many points of connection between his critical approach and my own appraisal, see *Innovation in Ethnographic Film* (Manchester University Press, 1993). See also Karen Vered 'Feminist ethnographic films: critical viewing required' in J.Rollwagen (ed.) *Anthropological Film and Video in the 1990s* (New York: The Institute Press, 1993), pp. 177–219.

Llewelyn-Davies, while never completing her doctoral thesis, published two academic articles from her research – 'Two contexts of solidarity among pastoral Maasai women', in P. Caplan and J. Burja (eds.) *Women United, Women Divided* (London: Tavistock, 1978), pp. 206–37, and 'Women, warriors and patriarchs', in S. Ortner and H. Whitehead (eds.) *Sexual Meanings: The Cultural Construction of Gender and Sexuality* (Cambridge University Press, 1981), pp. 330–58.

8 Lila Abu-Lughod 'Writing against culture', in R. Fox (ed.) *Recapturing Anthropology*, p. 157. For a discussion of Llewelyn-Davies' fieldwork methods see Anna Grimshaw (ed.) *Conversations with Anthropological Film-makers: Melissa Llewelyn-Davies* (Cambridge: Prickly Pear Press, 1995), pp. 24–5.

9 E. Ann Kaplan *Looking for the Other: Feminism, Film and the Imperial Gaze* (New York and London: Routledge, 1997), pp. 180–81.

10 Corner *The Art of Record* (Manchester University Press, 1996), p. 2. See also William Bluem *Documentary in American Television* (New York: Hastings House, 1965).

11 See Raymond Williams *Television: Technology and Cultural Form* (London: Fontana, 1974). Other important sources include John Ellis *Visible Fictions: Cinema, Television, Video* (London: Routledge, 1982); John Fiske *Television Culture* (London: Routledge, 1994); and E. Ann Kaplan (ed.) *Regarding Television* (Frederick, Md. American Film Institute, 1983).

The question of the reader/viewer and interpretive practice has now become a focus of attention for anthropologists studying media. See Wilton Martinez, 'Who constructs anthropological knowledge? Toward a theory of ethnographic film spectatorship', in Crawford and Turton (eds.) *Film as Ethnography*, pp. 131–61, was a landmark essay. It has been followed by the recently published P. I. Crawford and S. B. Hafsteinsson (eds.) *The Construction of the Viewer: Media Ethnography and the Anthropology of Audiences* (Aarhus, Denmark: Intervention Press, 1996).

12 See Fiske *Television Culture*.

13 Grimshaw (ed.) *Conversations*, p. 24.

14 *Masai Manhood* was transmitted in the year following *Masai Women*. It was not initially conceived as a film in its own right, but it was subsequently assembled from footage shot during the filming of *Masai Women*. Both of these *Disappearing World* films have remarkably similar features, hence I do not discuss *Masai Manhood* here.

15 Grimshaw (ed.) *Conversations*, pp. 33–4.

16 Henrietta Moore *Feminism and Anthropology* (Cambridge: Polity Press, 1988), p. 1. An important example of the early attempt to correct 'male bias' in anthropological representation is the volume edited by S. Ortner and M. Rosaldo *Women, Culture and Society* (California: Stanford University Press, 1974). Moore distinguishes this early gendered approach premised upon 'sameness' from the later feminist anthropology which recognises 'difference'. It is worth quoting her in full on the evolution of the relationship between anthropology and feminism: 'feminist anthropology began by criticizing male bias within the discipline, and the neglect and/or distortion of women and women's activities. This is the phase in the "relationship" which we can refer to as the "anthropology of women". The next phase was based on a critical reworking of the universal category "woman", which was accompanied by an equally critical look at the question of whether women were especially well-equipped to study other women. This led, quite naturally, to anxieties about ghettoization and marginalization within the discipline of social anthropology. However, as a result of this phase, feminist anthropology began to establish new approaches, new areas of theoretical enquiry, and to redefine itself not as the "study of women" but as the "study of gender"', *ibid.*, p. 11.

Women film-makers were engaged in many similar debates to their anthropological counterparts during the 1970s. 'Women's cinema', too, was about challenging male bias in every area of film-making activity. Film-makers were committed to discovering 'real women'. They sought to give voice to experiences and histories previously marginalised by a male discourse. Such a commitment was inseparable from a commitment to new working practices – sharing, co-operation and empathy between women. An important early essay was Eileen McGarry's 'Documentary, realism and women's cinema', *Women and Film* 2:7, 1975, pp. 50–9. See also P. Erens (ed.) *Issues in Feminist Film Criticism* (Bloomington: Indiana University Press, 1990).

17 Acknowledged by T.O. Beidelman in his sympathetic review of the film, *American Anthropologist* 78, 1976, pp. 958–59.

18 See Faye Ginsburg's essay 'Television and the mediation of culture' in *Principles of Visual Anthropology*, Paul Hockings (ed.) 2nd edn (Berlin and New York: Mouton de Gruyter, 1995).

19 See Corner, *The Art of Record*, p. 33. In the context of a debate, Drew declared: 'everything that has been referred to as a documentary here thus far [by his fellow discussants] is what I would call a "word-logic" show – that is, the logic of the film is contained in the narration or in the words', Bluem, *Documentary in American Television*, p. 258.

20 This was a criticism first made by Paul Spencer 'The Masai', *Royal Anthropological Newsletter* 6, 1975, p. 10–11. See Llewelyn-Davies 'Masai women' (reply to Spencer, 1975), letter in *Royal Anthropological Institute Newsletter* 8, p. 16. Also Roger Sandall 'Matters of fact', in P. Hockings (ed.) *Principles of Visual Anthropology* 2nd edn, pp. 457–77. See also Beidelman's 1976 film review and Loizos *Innovation*.

21 It is symbolised most starkly by the aerial shot which forms the opening scene of *Masai Women*. We approach Maasai-land from a place both outside and above. The initial perspective contrasts sharply then with the intimate place inside the Jie compound, and at cow level, where the MacDougalls' film *To Live With Herds* begins.

See Johannes Fabian *Time and the Other* (Columbia University Press, 1993); and Stephen Tyler's castigation of the 'failure of a whole visualist ideology of referential discourse, with its rhetoric of "describing", "comparing", "classifying" and "generalizing" and its assumption of representational significance. In ethnography there are no "things" there to be the objects of description, the original appearances that the language of description "represents" as indexical objects for comparison, classification, and generalization. Ethnographic discourse is itself neither an object to be represented nor a representation of an object.' 'Post-modern ethnography' in J. Clifford and G. Marcus *Writing Culture*, pp. 122–40.

22 The film opens with a Maasai woman singing about her lover. It is repeated later when this illicit practice is addressed by Llewelyn-Davies in conversation with a number of young women. Revealingly, by raising this issue, the film provoked more hostility than usual from another Maasai ethnographer, Paul Spencer. See Spencer, 'The Masai'.

23 My emphases, Fiske *Television Culture*, p. 22.

24 Adopting such a stance brings Llewelyn-Davies' work closer to approaches associated with the Manchester school of anthropologists, especially those of Max Gluckman and Victor Turner. It also, of course, establishes important

connections with the MacDougalls' Turkana film, *The Wedding Camels*. See chapter 7, 'The anthropological cinema of David and Judith MacDougall'.

25 See 'Cinema and anthropology in the postwar world', and my discussion of the MacDougalls *ibid*.

26 Corner *The Art of Record*, p. 44.

27 Grimshaw (ed.) *Conversations*, pp. 43–5.

28 *Ibid.*, p. 39.

29 See, for example, Charlotte Brunsdon '*Crossroads*: Notes on Soap Opera', *Screen* 22:4, 1981, pp. 32–7. Tania Modleski 'The rhythms of reception: daytime television and women's work' in E. Ann Kaplan (ed.) *Regarding Television* (Los Angeles: American Film Institute, 1983), pp. 67–75. Christine Geraghty *Women and Soap Opera* (Cambridge: Polity Press, 1991). See also C. Brunsdon and L. Spigel (eds.) *Feminist Television Criticism* (Oxford: Clarendon Press, 1997); and Fiske *Television Culture*.

30 Original emphases, Fiske *Television Culture*, p. 106. He lists the key characteristics of oral modes as including, dramatic, episodic, mosaic, dynamic, active, concrete, ephemeral, social, metaphorical, rhetorical, dialectical. By contrast, features associated with a literate mode include: narrative, sequential, linear, static, artifact, abstract, permanent, individual, metonymic, logical, univocal/'consistent'.

31 See n. 16 above. All of the early feminist paradigms, the anthropology of women and women's cinema, were subject to critique on the grounds of their failure to interrogate the process of representation itself. It was deemed not radical enough merely to introduce new content into older forms. In place of a realist project, certain feminist critics advocated formal experimentation as an integral part of a feminist politics. Claire Johnston's essay 'Women's cinema as counter-cinema' was a landmark in the articulation of a new agenda for feminist cinema: 'Any revolutionary strategy must challenge the depiction of reality; it is not enough to discuss the oppression of women within the text of the film; the language of the cinema/the depiction of reality must also be interrogated, so that a break between ideology and text is effected', in Bill Nichols (ed.) *Movies and Methods*, Vol. I (Berkeley: University of California Press, 1976), p. 215. See also Alexandra Juhasz '"They said we were trying to show reality – all I want to show is my video": the politics of the realist feminist documentary', *Screen* 35:2, Summer 1994, reprinted in J. Gaines and M. Revov (eds.) *Collecting Visible Evidence* (Minneapolis: University of Minnesota Press, 1999), pp. 190–215.

Debates about the politics of representational forms came later to anthropology and were largely associated with the publication of such texts as *Writing Culture*. The contribution of feminist anthropologists to these debates was, on the whole, unacknowledged (see Introduction to Clifford and Marcus *Writing Culture*), provoking a number of responses, for example Frances Mascia-Lees *et al.* 'The postmodernist turn in anthropology: cautions from a feminist perspective', *Signs* 15:1, 1991, pp. 7–33; and Lila Abu-Lughod 'Writing against culture' in Fox (ed.) *Recapturing Anthropology*, pp. 137–62.

Questions of difference are now also to the forefront of feminist debate in anthropology and cinema. See Moore *Feminism and Anthropology* and her collection of essays *A Passion For Difference* (Cambridge: Polity Press, 1994); Jane Gaines 'White privilege and looking relations: race and gender in feminist film theory', *Screen* 29:4, 1988, pp. 12–27; and Kaplan, *Looking for the Other*.

32 See p. 69, Tania Modleski 'The rhythms of reception: daytime television and women's work' in E. Ann Kaplan (ed.) *Regarding Television* (Los Angeles: American Film Institute, 1985), pp. 67–75.

33 Fiske, *Television Culture*, pp. 105–6.

34 Trinh T. Minh-ha 'Reassemblage', in *Framer, Framed* (New York and London: Routledge, 1992), p. 96. As Kaplan explains it: 'Trinh's ultimate philosophy in *Reassemblage* is to claim that all one can do is try not to "speak about" but to "speak nearby". The language tries to locate a position that does not end with possession or pretending knowledge *of*, as the phrase "speaking about" implies. But Trinh does not want to claim total impossibility of knowing the other . . . She seeks a position that functions in the gap, namely, "speaking nearby." The phrase conveys an idea of closeness but with a necessay distance because of difference; a concept of "approaching" rather than "knowing" an Other.' Kaplan *Looking for the Other*, p. 201. See also Trinh's *When the Moon Waxes Red* (New York and London).

35 Grimshaw (ed.) *Conversations*, pp. 37–8. Within the area of feminist filmmaking practice, debates have now moved beyond the older realist/formalist positions to focus upon what is called 'image ethics discourse' in which consideration of the relationships between subjects and film-makers is central, see D. Waldman and J. Walker (eds.) *Feminism and Documentary* (Minneapolis, Minn.: University of Minnesota Press, 1999).

36 For a fuller discussion of this question, see David MacDougall's essay 'Visual anthropology and ways of knowing', in *Transcultural Cinema* (Princeton, N.J.: Princeton University Press, 1998), pp. 61–92.

37 'It takes a bit of time to develop courage as a film-maker . . . When I showed the Marrakech film to a young Moroccan, he made an absolutely key remark that I try and remember whenever I make a film. He said: "you're showing too much sympathy and not enough solidarity"; and actually you have to learn the courage to let things hang out', in Anna Grimshaw ed. *Conversations*, pp. 36–7. See also Kaplan's discussion of the political debate provoked by *Warrior Marks*, a film critical of female circumcision practices made by Alice Walker and Pratibha Parmar, Kaplan, *Looking for the Other*.

38 Grimshaw (ed.) *Conversations*, p. 55.

39 Turton in Crawford and Turton (eds.) *Film as Ethnography*, p. 284.

40 The gendered dimensions of anthropological work pursued through the use of visual media has not been much discussed. Leslie Devereaux's essay, however, is an important starting point for any consideration of the issues, 'Experience, re-presentation and film' in L. Devereaux and R. Hillman (eds.) *Fields of Visions* (Berkeley: University of California Press, 1995), pp. 56–73. See also Abu-Lughod, 'Writing against culture'.

41 This echoes David MacDougall's discussion of the distinction between films about anthropology and anthropological film, *Transcultural Cinema*, p. 76.

EPILOGUE

1 Faye Ginsburg 'Institutionalizing the unruly: charting a future for visual anthropology', *Ethnos* 63:2, 1998; and David MacDougall 'The visual in anthropology' in M. Banks and H. Morphy (eds.) *Rethinking Visual Anthropology* (New Haven and London: Yale University Press, 1997) and *Transcultural Cinema* (Princeton, N.J.: Princeton University Press, 1998).
2 MacDougall *Transcultural Cinema*; Lucien Taylor 'Iconophobia: how anthropology lost it at the movies', *Transition* 69, 1996, p. 86.
3 MacDougall *Transcultural Cinema*, p. 63.
4 Moore *Feminism and Anthropology* (Cambridge: Polity Press, 1988), p. 4.

Index